THE People's RELIGION

THE People's RELIGION

AMERICAN FAITH IN THE 90'S

George Gallup, Jr.

AND

Jim Castelli

MACMILLAN PUBLISHING COMPANY

New York

COLLIER MACMILLAN PUBLISHERS

London

Macmillan Publishing Company
866 Third Avenue, New York, NY 10022
Collier Macmillan Canada, Inc.

Library of Congress Cataloging-in-Publication Data
Gallup, George, 1930–
The people's religion : American faith in the 90's / George
Gallup, Jr. and Jim Castelli.
p.   cm.
ISBN 0-02-542381-9
1. United States—Religion—Public opinion.   2. United States—
Religious life and customs—Public opinion.   3. Public opinion—
United States.   I. Castelli, Jim.   II. Title.
BL2525.G35   1989
291′.0973′09048—dc20   89-13116   CIP

Macmillan books are available at special discounts for bulk purchases for sales promotions, premiums, fund-raising, or educational use. For details, contact:

Special Sales Director
Macmillan Publishing Company
866 Third Avenue
New York, NY 10022

10 9 8 7 6 5 4 3 2 1

Designed by Jack Meserole

PRINTED IN THE UNITED STATES OF AMERICA

CONTENTS

PART

II

LIST OF TABLES

CHAPTER 6

CHAPTER 7

CHAPTER 8

INTRODUCTION

The People's Religion

PICK UP THE Religion Page of just about any newspaper, and look at
the headlines. There may be a story about the latest pronouncement
from the pope. There will probably be another article about a statement
on some important church or social issue from the leaders of a particular
denomination, or a report on the latest clash between rival factions within a
denomination. There could be a story about a speech by a prominent theologian.
Or there might be a profile of a local pastor.

But that typical Religion Page will not tell the whole story of American
religious life. What is often missing from media coverage of religion is the
people in the pews, the people whose lives are influenced by the actions of
church leaders and who, literally, make up the church's body. We don't mean
to single out the media for criticism; the "top-down" approach to religion
characterizes much of organized religious life itself.

When it comes to religion, Americans do not see their role, as it once was,
to "pay, pray and obey." They see their role as taking part fully in church life;
the church, they believe, serves them, not the other way around.

What's missing, then, is an understanding of what we call "the People's
Religion"—the contours of the faith that exists within the American people,
often irrespective of their institutional religious ties. The "People's Religion"
has three dimensions.

First, we need to understand the details of Americans' faith: what do
Americans believe? How do they act out their religious faith? What do they
want from their churches? How do they understand their own faith life and
its relationship to other people and institutions?

Second, we need to understand the "American Faith," the consensus of
religious beliefs that characterize our nation's religion. Every community has
its own ethic, and ours is often little appreciated.

Third, we need to understand both the differences and similarities that

XV

characterize Americans' religious beliefs and practices. The American religious "ethic," the American Faith, assumes and is built upon diversity. This diversity does not merely entail denominational differences between, say, Catholics and Baptists; it knows that there are also different kinds of Catholics and different kinds of Baptists. Demographic groups, as well as religious groups, often have dramatically different perspectives on religion.

Certainly, every good pastor, just like any other leader in society, has a sense of the nature and needs—of his people. But social science surveys—public opinion polls—can provide unique and vital information about the people. It's common in religious circles to talk dismissively about not wanting to "govern by the polls." Of course, religious leaders should no more "govern by the polls" than should any other leaders—if so doing means changing core beliefs to suit every change in fashion. But no one can truly lead without knowing what the people think and believe, and polls can provide that vital information.

We don't want to fall into the trap of talking only about church leaders. Polls are in many ways a populist device; they empower the people themselves by letting them know what their neighbors, what all other Americans believe. To use one obvious example: a Catholic woman who rejects her church's teaching on birth control may act very differently if she knows her views are widely shared than if she believes she is isolated in her opinion.

There are three basic reasons why public opinion polls on religion are important. The first is *sociological*: differences in religion are often a greater factor in forming public opinion than differences in gender, age, race or education. The second reason is *practical*: as we suggested, it is impossible to plan for successful leadership without knowing what people believe. Finally, the third reason is *religious*: believers, and those who would study believers, need to understand the way people view their relationship to God.

The Gallup Organization has understood the importance of religion in American lives since its inception more than a half century ago; one of the first areas studied by George Gallup, Sr., was churchgoing practice. Over the years, the organization has continued to focus on religion and has conducted many specialized studies for religious organizations. In addition, virtually every survey that goes out into the field contains questions about religious affiliation, producing a massive amount of information about the relationship between religion and public attitudes.

In 1986, we began tapping this reservoir of information to produce the weekly "Gallup Religion Poll," distributed by the *Los Angeles Times* Syndicate. *The People's Religion* is a direct outgrowth of those columns. But this book is not simply a collection of columns. Material has been expanded, updated and reorganized to present a clear, coherent picture of American religious life from the standpoint of the American people themselves.

The book is divided into two parts. Part I deals with the dimensions of faith. Chapter 1, "A Half Century of American Religion," provides a brisk overview of the major religious trends found in more than fifty years of public opinion surveys. This chapter contains both long-range trends and more detailed looks at specific questions that particularly reflected the religious tenor of their times.

Chapter 2, "Trends in Religion," describes trends in religious affiliation, religious practice and attitudes toward religion; it goes into detail about the beliefs and behaviors of key groups.

Chapter 3, "An American Faith," reports on Americans' beliefs about major issues of religious faith, offering a picture of both the responses of the American people as a whole and of key religious and demographic groups.

Chapter 4, "Religious Profiles," provides profiles of major religious groups. This includes major denominations; Evangelicals, who cut across denominations; and key demographic groups—blacks, Hispanics, teens and "Baby Boomers."

Chapter 5, "Case Studies," looks in depth at two major religious subjects. The first, "The Unchurched," looks at the differences between churched and unchurched Americans, profiles the unchurched and examines the reasons they have left the church and the factors which may bring them back. The second case study, "Religious Television," reports on a decade's worth of research on those who watch and contribute to television evangelists, and public attitudes toward the "televangelists."

Part II focuses on faith and public life. Chapter 6, "Religion and Public Issues," takes a detailed look at the relationship between religious affiliation and attitudes on the major social issues of the day, from abortion to government spending.

Chapter 7, "Religion and Politics," examines American attitudes toward the mixing of religion and politics, describes the way different religious groups approach politics and provides a detailed tracking of the attitudes of major religious groups during the 1988 presidential campaign, from before the primaries up through Election Day.

Chapter 8, "America's Faith in the 1990s," draws on material in the earlier chapters, as well as responses to questions commissioned especially for this book, to draw conclusions about the shape of American religious life between now and the turn of the century.

The People's Religion is organized so that it may be read in several ways. One, of course, is to simply begin at the beginning and read on straight through to the end. Some readers, however, may wish to first zero in on a few subjects of particular interest, and we have tried to make it easy for them to do so. First, we have used a detailed table of contents, listing the many subheadings within each large chapter. Second, we have, where it is necessary for clarity, repeated information. For example, when we write about Americans' attitudes toward the Bible, we include findings on attitudes among various groups. Then when we profile, say, the religious views of blacks, we will include information about their beliefs about the Bible.

Before turning to our findings, it is important to clarify some technical and definitional points which will make it easier to use the following material. One point involves the nature of public opinion surveys themselves. Polls, it has been said, provide a "snapshot" of people's attitudes; they are valid for the time they are taken, but they cannot be used to flatly predict future behavior. This is generally true, but it would be inaccurate to suggest that only polls conducted within the past twenty-four hours have any validity. That may well be the case with polls taken, for example, during a hotly contested political campaign, when opinions are subject to dramatic change. But many attitudes are not subject to such rapid change; in fact, religious belief is one of the most stable attitudes we have found.

Pollsters are also candid about the limits of their craft; they talk in terms of the "margin of error." This means, quite simply, that sampling techniques have been refined to the point where results from a scientifically selected sample can be said to be accurate 95 percent of the time within a margin of error appropriate to the size of the sample. For a typical poll with a sample size of 1,500, we can say that there is a 95 percent chance that the findings will be accurate within 3 points in either direction. For example, to stay with a political analogy, let's say that a sample has a margin of error of 4 points, and it finds Candidate A with 52 percent of the vote and Candidate B with 48 percent of the vote. This means that it is possible that Candidate A is actually ahead by 56 to 42 percent; it is also possible that Candidate B is actually ahead by 52 to 48 percent.

Other factors can also enter into consideration; differences in the wording of questions can produce differences in response. We have included the exact wording of questions in many instances, for clarity's sake. We have also provided the sample size and margin of error for each question cited; in order to preserve the narrative flow, we have used endnotes, which are placed at the end of the book.

The material in this book comes from a variety of surveys taken at different points in time. We want to avoid confusion on one point. The reader may notice, for example, that on one page, we may say that 54 percent of Americans say that religion is "very important" in their lives; on another page, we may say that 56 percent of Americans say it is "very important." These figues come from the surveys cited, but the margin of error and shifts in attitudes, such as in political affiliation, are responsible for minor differences between surveys.

Some other technical clarifications:

· In many cases, figures cited will not add up to 100 percent. This is because we have dropped figures for those who do not respond, who say they "don't know" or who say that a particular issue "makes no difference" to them.
· At the same time, in some cases, figures will add up to more than 100 percent. This is usually due to rounding. For example, if 50.5 percent choose response A and 49.5 percent choose response B, we must use the same rules of rounding in each case; thus, A becomes 51 percent and B becomes 50 percent, for a total of 101 percent. There is one other instance in which figures will add up to more than 100 percent—when we discuss race and ethnicity. Many surveys categorize responses by "white," "black"

and "Hispanic"; because some people are counted as both Hispanic and white, these figures together will total more than 100 percent.

· There is a difference between referring to an increase in terms of percent and percentage points. For example, if over the course of a year a figure changes from 40 to 50 percent, this represents an increase of 10 percentage points and of 25 percent, because 10 is 25 percent of 40.

· Some sections will refer to religious groups by specific denomination—Baptist, Lutheran, Methodist—and others will refer to broader groups, such as "white non-evangelical Protestants." This is because different surveys use different classifications, and we must work with the figures we have. At the same time, looking at larger groups produces a different perspective than looking only at denominations. Sometimes, we have figures for some denominations that are too small to be reliable, but which can be reliable when combined; on occasion, we combine findings for Methodists, Lutherans, Presbyterians and Episcopalians as "mainline Protestants."

· Unless otherwise specified, figures for denominations refer to those who identify with a particular denomination, without any other qualification about their degree of involvement. So, for example, "Catholics" refers to all of those who identify themselves as "Catholic," including approximately 20 percent who are not church members. (The chapter on the unchurched will show what percentage of each denomination is not church members.)

· The term "Evangelical" refers to those who describe themselves as "Born-Again" Christians.

· With the exception of one section on teenagers, survey results refer to adults, those over age 18.

· When we discuss educational levels, the term "some college" refers to those who have attended but not completed college, or who have attended technical school which lasts less than four years.

· The term "church," unless the context is quite specific, is used generically to refer to churches, synagogues, and, in an increasingly pluralistic America, mosques and temples.

Finally, a word about sources. Much of the material in this book comes from surveys conducted for the Gallup Poll. But important material comes from Gallup studies conducted for other organizations, and we would like to credit those:

· The Times Mirror Corporation's study, "The People, Press and Politics," is one of the most comprehensive public opinion surveys ever conducted. It produced untold amounts of information about "the press and politics," but in studying "the people," it also generated a remarkable body of information about American religious life.

· "The Unchurched American—1988," conducted for a coalition of twenty-two religious groups for Congress '88: A National Festival of Evangelism.

An earlier survey, "The Unchurched American," was conducted for a similar coalition in 1978.

· Much material on the 1988 presidential election came from Gallup surveys conducted for CONUS, a consortium of television stations.

· Several studies, including "The Spiritual Climate in America Today" and "24 Hours in the Religious and Spiritual Life of Americans," were conducted for the Christian Broadcasting Network.

· Several studies, including "Jesus Christ in the Lives of Americans Today" (1983) and "How Can Christian Liberals and Conservatives Be Brought Together?," were conducted for the Robert H. Schuller Ministries.

· "Religion and Television" was conducted for the Ad Hoc Committee on Electronic Church Research.

· We used several editions of the "Annual Survey of the Public's Attitudes Toward the Public Schools," conducted for Phi Delta Kappa, Inc.

· Some questions come from a 1988 survey conducted in part for the Society for the Scientific Study of Religion and the Religious Research Association.

PART

I

CHAPTER

1

A Half Century of American Religion

T HE SHAPE of America's faith in the 1990s will be influenced by the trends and developments that have shaped America's faith in the past. Some changes came about gradually. Others were more dramatic. The changes that have occurred in the United States over the past half century, and the speed with which they came about, are unprecedented, and have had a powerful impact on the religious life of Americans.

Consider the major events of this period that have conditioned religious thought and belief: the Great Depression of the 1930s, World War II, the postwar economic recovery, the invention of television, the Cold War and concern over the internal threat of communism, the Korean War, the Second Vatican Council, the civil rights movement, the Vietnam War, urban riots, campus unrest, Watergate and the resignation of Richard Nixon, stagflation, environmental and ecological problems, the nuclear threat, and, in the last few years, a period of growing national optimism followed by concern about the future.

There have been several significant long-range trends in religious beliefs and attitudes in America. One trend is volatility; certain of the Gallup indicators do show marked changes. For example, the proportion of Americans who say religion is "very important" in their lives dropped from 75 percent in 1952 to about 55 percent in the late 1970s and 1980s. In addition, the number of Biblical "literalists" declined sharply from the early 1960s to the late 1970s,

3

and in 1988 was half what it was in 1965. Church attendance has declined steadily since the 1950s. And attitudes about the influence of religion have jumped around dramatically; it seems that in times of social satisfaction, Americans believe the influence of religion has increased, while in times of turmoil, such as the 1960s, they believe the influence of religion has decreased.

Yet despite these changes, perhaps the most appropriate word to use to describe the religious character of the nation as a whole over the last half century is "stable." Basic religious beliefs, and even religious practice, today differ relatively little from the levels recorded fifty years ago. In fact, the nation in some respects has remained remarkably orthodox—even fundamentalist— in its beliefs. For example:

- Nine Americans in ten say they have never doubted the existence of God.
- Eight Americans in ten say they believe they will be called before God on Judgment Day to answer for their sins.
- Eight Americans in ten believe God still works miracles.
- Seven Americans in ten believe in life after death.

These patterns have held constant throughout a period that has seen several major swings in religious life. In broad terms, there was, first, a post–World War II surge of interest in religion, characterized by increased church membership and attendance, a growth in Bible-reading, increased giving to churches, and extensive church-building. Religious leaders such as Billy Graham, Norman Vincent Peale, and Bishop Fulton Sheen had wide followings during this period.

The surge lasted until the late 1950s or early 1960s, when it was replaced by a decline in religious interest and involvement in the 1960s and 1970s. Finally, the 1980s saw a "bottoming out" of certain indicators, if not a reversal of some of the declines. In addition, surveys indicate a new interest in religious and spiritual matters.

Pronounced changes have also occurred in the *focus* of religious interest and activity over the last half century: The 1950s were marked by a tendency to view religion as supportive of the American way of life. The 1960s, on the other hand, saw an antiestablishment mood coupled with an emphasis on social activism. The 1970s were characterized by a retreat from activism to individualism and a concentration on personal spirituality. The 1980s saw a renewed search for spiritual moorings, as well as evidence of a "new activism" on the part of church leaders, speaking out on issues such as the relationship between church and state, abortion, peace and economics.

In examining the trends of the last half century, it should be borne in mind that most of the changes have been relatively small and have been most pronounced among young adults. Shifts in religious practice have been generally in the same direction for churches of the three major faiths—Protestant, Catholic and Jewish—although some differences in growth patterns are noted between the moderate to liberal churches, as opposed to the conservative churches.

Writing about the period from 1950 to the late 1970s, Jackson W. Carroll,

Douglas W. Johnson and Martin Marty noted these additional characteristics of the trends since the fifties: "Evidence of a tendency to view religion as useful for some personal or social end rather than as an expression of devotion to God alone; an increase in the concern for adjustment to this life, in contrast to preparing for life after death." They further note that "growth seems to have occurred most frequently among two kinds of religious expressions—on the one hand, the conservative or Evangelical Protestant churches, and, on the other hand, in the various non-traditional, often non-Christian, religious movements, and in related quasi-religious movements that provide the technologies of the spirit."

Following is a decade-by-decade summary of Gallup data on religion in America.

1930s

Although scientific surveys on religion for the nation as a whole were virtually nonexistent prior to the 1930s, the observation of astute commentators on the American scene, including Alexis de Tocqueville, clearly pointed to a vigorous religious tradition stemming from colonial times. While the available data indicate that church attendance was far lower in the nineteenth century and in the first decades of the twentieth century than it is today, it is probably safe to assume that the vast majority of Americans were "believers."

At any rate, a high level of religious involvement was apparent in the late 1930s, when seven in ten were church members and about four in ten attended church or synagogue in a typical week—the same proportions we find today.

A 1938 Gallup survey found the Bible to be the most frequently encountered book on American bookshelves, slightly ahead of *Gone With the Wind*. The Bible was also the number-one book in many subsequent surveys, but then, as now, comparatively few read it. Age was an important factor in responses to the 1938 survey, with 37 percent of persons 50 and over naming the Bible as their top choice, compared to 17 percent among those 30–49 years old and only 6 percent among the youngest group, 21–29.

An interesting survey in 1936 sought the public's views on a proposed moratorium on preaching. The Rev. Dr. Frederick S. Fleming, rector of Trinity Church in New York City, in August of that year declared that the Christian Church "would once again bring salvation to the world and begin to save its own soul" if it had the "courage" to declare a temporary moratorium on preaching. But his views were strenuously opposed by Dr. John Haynes Holmes, pastor of New York City's Community Church, who said, "Dr. Fleming is wrong, terribly wrong . . . Christianity never had greater preachers than at this hour, as witness Dr. [Harry Emerson] Fosdick, Bishop McConnell . . . Dr. Henry Sloan Coffin . . . and the late beloved Dr. S. Parkes Cadman. A moratorium on such men would be moral bankruptcy."

When the Gallup Poll put the issue to the public, the vote was 8 to 2 against omitting sermons and lectures from Sunday worship for a period of one

or two years. Large majorities of both church members and nonmembers opposed a moratorium on sermons, although the latter were somewhat more
inclined to support such a move.

At the end of the decade, in 1939, a cross section of Americans was asked
if their parents went to church more or less often than they did. Half (50
percent) said more often, while 18 percent said less often and 32 percent said
the same. Asked whether interest in religion had increased in their own communities, 27 percent of survey respondents in farm areas, 29 percent in small
towns and 42 percent in the cities answered in the affirmative.

When asked what churches could do to increase the interest of the public
in religion, a majority said nothing, but those with views gave the following
responses:

1. Select ministers who are more intelligent.
2. Arrange more social activities around the churches.
3. Become more modern and liberal.
4. Eliminate hypocrisy.
5. Stop emphasizing money and contributions.
6. Let church people be more friendly.

1940s

The role of the church in wartime was a controversial issue in the early
1940s and stirred up heated debates among the clergy. A July 1942 Gallup Poll
showed six in ten among the clergy believing the church should support the
war and give full cooperation to the war effort, but four in ten were either
opposed or unsure.

In another 1942 survey, 10 percent of Americans reported reading the Bible
daily, but as many as 41 percent said they had not read the Bible within the
previous twelve months. Concern about the war, however, caused increasing
numbers of Americans—particularly young adults—to turn to the Bible, and
"occasional" Bible reading registered an upswing.

Four in ten adults (43 percent) reported to Gallup interviewers in 1947
that they said grace aloud at home before family meals.

Church membership, survey evidence showed, moved up slightly during
the 1940s. Upwards of four in ten Americans attended church or synagogue
weekly. And a 1947 survey showed more than eight in ten having attended
religious services during a twelve-month period.

Belief levels among Americans were very high in the 1940s. A 1947 Gallup
survey in eleven nations showed nine in ten Americans saying they believed
in God, the highest proportion recorded for any nation, in sharp contrast to
two out of three in France who said they believed. Seven in ten Americans
said they believed in an afterlife; the lowest proportion holding this belief was
found in Great Britain and Sweden, 49 percent in each nation.

Clearly, many Americans in this period felt the need to grow spiritually, with two in three Catholics favoring religious retreats and at least half the Protestants saying they liked the idea of going to a quiet place for a few days to meditate about their spiritual life.

One area of debate in the late forties was the question of whether Christianity and communism could mix—could a person be a good Christian and a communist at the same time? In the Catholic Church's battle against communism in Europe, Pope Pius XII had laid down the dictum that Christianity and communism were irreconcilable. Some communists, on the other hand, maintained that communist theory was very similar to the teaching of Jesus Christ. A Gallup survey, however, showed an overwhelming proportion of Americans agreeing with the pope's position on the matter.

In 1947, the *Ladies Home Journal* commissioned a nationwide Gallup survey to assess the intensity of religious faith in the United States and the degree to which it governed the ethics and behavior of the American people at that time. The survey followed three lines of inquiry: What did Americans believe? How fervent were their beliefs? Did they live according to their faith?

This survey, one of the first scientific efforts to explore the religious views of Americans in depth, drew the conclusion that, while the religious potential in the United States was very great, the quality of religion and its influence on American life were not so apparent.

Social observers would likely maintain that the findings of that survey shed light not only on the religious thinking of the 1940s, but on the situation today, as well. Lincoln Barrett, in a *Ladies Home Journal* article on the survey, wrote, "Although 95 percent of the Americans say they believe in God, it is by no means clear that they acknowledge the God of biblical revelation, who speaks to man from beyond himself and awakens in him a sense of dependency, moral unworthiness and obligation to obey his will."

Barrett further noted a "profound gulf" between America's avowed ethical standards and the observable realities of national life. "What may be more alarming," he wrote, "is the gap between what Americans think they do and what they do. The extent of this national schizophrenia is made perfectly clear by the paradox that (1) eight out of ten Americans think that most of America's problems would be solved by absolute adherence to the law of love, and (2) eight out of ten Americans think they themselves obey the law of love. Thus, someone else is at fault. Here indeed is a revelation of man's final sin, which Luther defined as the unwillingness to admit that he is a sinner."

Completing this rather bleak picture was another set of findings from the same survey that gave clear evidence that the average American's religious thinking had not advanced beyond the Sunday school level.

A 1948 survey asked Americans what churches could do to increase attendance. Table 1.1 shows what they said.

A Christmas Day 1949 release, part of a series on expectations for the next half century, found Americans predicting more rather than less churchgoing in the next fifty years. Their predictions proved to be on target for the next decade, if not beyond.

Table 1.1
WHAT CHURCHES CAN DO TO INCREASE ATTENDANCE

Better Services	17%
More Programs to Rouse Interest of Youth	9
More Social Functions	8
Better Leaders, Men of Higher Caliber	7
Make Religion More Practical, More Down-to-Earth	6
More Evangelism, Drive for Members	6
Be Less Secular, More Democratic	4
Less Hypocrisy	3
Other	5
Nothing Needed	4

1950s

The 1950s were ushered in by a wave of post–World War II recovery, with business and industry expanding and a tremendous growth in the cities and suburbs. It was also a decade of religious revival, with rapid growth in church membership, especially in the booming new suburbs. But some social observers have questioned the authenticity of the revival and the depth of religious commitment, charging that many Americans were attending church in greater numbers because it was "the thing to do."

Sociologists saw Americans' lives influenced by civil religion, a shared, public faith in the nation, a faith linked to people's everyday life through a set of beliefs, symbols and rituals that contain religious elements and overtones but that are not formally associated with any particular religion.

The state of religious knowledge in this period (as in later decades) was anything but impressive. Fewer than half the respondents in a 1950 survey could give the names of any of the first four books of the New Testament. And only one person in three could name all four books of the Gospels. This sad state of biblical knowledge was also apparent in a later, 1954, survey in which it was discovered that only 34 percent of Americans knew who, according to the Bible, delivered the Sermon on the Mount. Survey respondents did better on naming Jesus' birthplace—two-thirds were able to do so.

Despite the low level of religious knowledge, church attendance, which Gallup Polls had been charting since 1939, reached new heights in 1955 and 1958, when 49 percent of Americans said they had attended church or synagogue in the past week. In 1952, 75 percent of Americans said religion was "very important" in their lives. In the same year, the proportion of Americans who read the Bible daily inched up from 10 percent in the 1940s, to 12 percent. In 1957, seven in ten (69 percent) said religion was increasing its influence on American life, compared to only 14 percent who felt its influence was waning.

In a 1954 survey, Americans were asked to try to account for the rise in church-building in the fifties. The chief reason given—named by 30 percent —was fear, unrest and uncertainty about the future. Next were renewed faith in God as the Supreme Being (19 percent), the effect of religion on military personnel during the war (11 percent), and improvement in church programming and publicity (9 percent).

A remarkable 24 percent of American adults said that at some time in 1957 they had called on people, to ask them to attend or join their church. And as many as 60 percent said they had been called upon to attend or join a church. Most active in evangelization efforts were Baptists, a finding that helps explain why Baptist churches (particularly Southern Baptist churches) did not suffer the membership losses of other denominations during the 1960s and 1970s.

The upsurge of religious interest in the 1950s was, according to historians, the seventh in a series of "awakenings" that have swept the continent, starting with the Great Awakening of 1730, associated with Jonathan Edwards and George Whitefield. The last previous revival took place in the 1920s and is associated with Billy Sunday and his "old-time" religion.

Before we leave the fifties, we would do well to be aware of an important perspective on the decade's religious growth when we compare the fifties to later periods. William R. Hutchinson, Charles Warren Professor of the History of Religion at the Harvard Divinity School, notes that "for the oldline churches, it was the higher growth rates of the 1950s that was unusual, not the relatively lower ones that set in after the early 1960s. The immediate postwar period was, for the oldline establishment, a brief, shining moment that is not a particularly good benchmark for measuring subsequent 'decline.' "

1960s

The 1960s was a period of major change and upheaval: rapid technological advances, the full emergence of the civil rights movement—sit-ins, freedom rides, bombings, the March on Washington and the passage of the Civil Rights Act of 1964; urban riots and the assassinations of Martin Luther King, Jr., Malcolm X and Robert Kennedy; antiwar protests over Vietnam; the beginnings of the women's liberation movement; the rise of the counterculture; and strong antiestablishment feelings, particularly on the part of young people.

Marked change and upheaval were found in the church as well: the involvement of the clergy in civil rights and antiwar protests; radical theology; situation ethics and the "new morality"; stirrings of the charismatic and neo-Pentecostal movements within the Roman Catholic and mainline Protestant churches; widespread activity in social justice causes.

Churches in the 1960s were facing a crisis. The age of technology and urbanization was causing many people to question basic doctrines. There were efforts to "modernize" faith and encourage greater involvement in social issues. Among the most dramatic changes taking place were those in the Roman Catholic Church. The Second Vatican Council ushered in an age of reform in the church, but it also brought in considerable controversy. Many Catholics, particularly young adults, were dropping out and attending Mass less frequently, in considerable measure out of the belief that they could not oppose Pope Paul VI's encyclical on birth control and remain good Catholics. Priests were leaving, seminary enrollment was declining and parochial schools were closing.

Church membership, attendance and the importance people place on religion were declining, not just among Catholics, but also among Protestants (particularly in the mainline churches) and among Jews. Overall, attendance dropped from 49 percent in 1958 to 42 percent in 1969, with the decline most pronounced among those age 21–29 (down 15 points) and Catholics (down 11 points) in that period.

Even though the proportion of daily Bible readers had increased to 14 percent of the population, and 69 percent of Americans reported that they said grace before meals (up from 43 percent in 1947), overall survey evidence suggested that the much-heralded postwar religious revival in America had passed its peak. In 1962, 31 percent of Americans, as opposed to 14 percent in 1957, felt that religion was losing its influence. In the 1962 survey, younger adults were far more inclined than others to believe that religion was losing its influence—53 percent held this view.

The view that religion was on the wane was held to an even greater extent by those attending college. The key reasons given were that student life reflected the trend toward secularization in American life, with its emphasis on material rather than spiritual values; that religion was unable to meet the challenge of science and the intellect; that religion on the whole was failing to solve contemporary moral, social and economic problems; and that students associated religion with churchgoing and church participation, which they found unnecessary for fulfillment in their lives. Some observers at the time, noting these trends among young people, viewed them as a clear warning signal to churches that they were not getting through to the current student generation and needed to make a sweeping reappraisal of their presentations.

In the sixties, the view was advanced in some theological circles that orthodox religion was outmoded and that it was no longer possible to believe in a "Supreme Being"—that "God is dead." Certainly some of the harsh and brutal aspects of the society at the time, such as the growing crime rate, tended to support the view that God is dead and contributed to an uneasy feeling that basic religious beliefs were being eroded.

Yet for the American people as a whole, God appeared to be very much alive. Traditional religious beliefs generally held firm throughout this period. Large majorities, for example, continued to say that they "strongly" believed in God and received a great deal of comfort and support from their beliefs.

Most persisted in believing in a "personal" God who watches over humankind and can be reached by prayer, rather than in God as an impersonal force.

As the sixties wore on, however, an ever-increasing proportion of Americans believed religion to be losing its influence on American life. In 1968, 67 percent said religion was losing ground, five times the proportion who felt that way a decade earlier. Those who held that view generally cited one of four reasons:

1. Young people were losing interest in formal religion, finding it not "relevant."
2. The increase in crime, immorality and violence.
3. Materialistic distractions.
4. The church was not playing its proper role in society—equal numbers said the church was not keeping up with the times, and that it was too involved in current social and political issues.

1970s

The activism of the 1960s gave way to the disillusionment and cynicism of the 1970s. In fact, the early 1970s may have marked one of the lowest points of national morale in history. Americans were growing more pessimistic about the economy, the prospects for peace in the world, social institutions and the future facing themselves and their families.

The Vietnam War had a devastating effect on the public's regard for government, and with Watergate following closely on the end of the conflict in Southeast Asia, there was little wonder that surveys at the time showed respect for government at both the presidential and congressional levels at a low ebb. Vietnam indicated to many that government was unresponsive to the wishes of the people; Watergate suggested that people in high office had reached their positions by corrupt and illegal means.

At the same time, surveys showed that Americans had not lost faith in the American proposition or in the nation's future. The generally uneasy national mood, however, had a strong carryover into the churches. Sociologists William McCready and the Rev. Andrew Greeley, in viewing societal changes and a new challenge to the Catholic Church on the part of the rank-and-file, saw Catholic loyalty disappearing and worried about the church's future.

Pessimism also hit the Protestant churches, with mainline churches suffering serious membership losses, declines in church attendance, as well as losses in the proportions identifying with a particular denomination. Conservative churches, on the other hand, continued to experience growth, which was attributed, in part, to their having more clear-cut answers on religious issues as well as to greater efforts in evangelization on the part of members.

A Gallup survey conducted at the beginning of the seventies showed three-fourths (75 percent) of the American people saying religion was losing its impact on society while only 14 percent said it was gaining. Key reasons given by respondents for the decline in influence of religion were that the church was outdated and not relevant to the modern world, morals were breaking down and people were becoming materialistic. The loss of confidence in religion was, again, strongest among college students—58 percent said religion was not a relevant part of their lives.

It was not a good time for organized religion; in a 1971 survey, almost four in ten among Catholic and Protestant clergy under 40 said they had seriously considered leaving the ministry. The figure was even higher, six in ten, among rabbis. But the survey offered little evidence that a weakening of faith was implicated in the desire to leave the religious life. Many of the clergy blamed an inability to communicate with their parishioners, while others admitted they were confused about their role and what was expected of them. Still others thought religion was irrelevant, while still another group said they felt they were in a straightjacket of rules and regulations.

Protestants frequently cited financial reasons as a consideration in leaving the ministry, while a prominent reason cited by Catholic priests—roughly one in five—was the desire to get married. Two basic tenets of the Catholic church—priestly celibacy and strictures on birth control—were then being challenged by a large majority of young priests. In fact, two of three under age 40 expressed disapproval of their church's ban on the use of artificial means of birth control. Furthermore, more than half of young priests admitted having counseled persons to use such methods. But a generation gap was apparent, with two of three priests over 40 saying they agreed with the church ruling on birth control. And fewer in this older group had counseled people to use birth control.

The Catholic laity strongly opposed the church's position on birth control, with roughly six in ten of those over 40 and seven in ten of those under 40 expressing opposition.

Nearly eight in ten priests under 40 said they would like to see the church change its age-old ban on priests marrying, but a 56 percent majority of older clergy stood by their church's teaching. The laity agreed with the younger clergy.

Two other basic church teachings—the absolute authority of the pope in matters of faith and morals, and mandatory weekly attendance at Mass—were also being questioned by a sizable proportion of priests, with much of the opposition centered among the younger clergy.

Much survey evidence from the early 1970s could be cited to show that religion had fallen on difficult days, but it is important to note that discontent among the clergy and laity at the time stemmed not from a weakening of religious convictions, but from a reluctance to accept certain aspects of institutionalized religion.

In fact, Americans were found to have held to basic beliefs since the beginning of scientific polling in the 1930s, while rather sharp declines had occurred among Europeans since World War II. And while the mood of America during the 1970s was one of disillusionment, revealing a lack of confidence in American institutions, confidence in the church or organized religion was higher than confidence in seven other institutions listed in the surveys, including Congress, business, labor and the media.

Between 1958, when 49 percent attended church in a typical week, and the early seventies, churchgoing declined by 9 percentage points. The decline traced almost entirely to falling attendance among Catholics. In 1973, the attendance figure for Catholics was 55 percent; a decade earlier, the figure had been 71 percent.

The dramatic rise to political prominence in 1976 of Jimmy Carter, a Born-Again Christian, focused new attention on the Evangelical movement in America. A well-publicized Gallup Poll that year found that 34 percent of the respondents said they had had a "born-again" experience—that is, had had a turning point in their lives when they committed themselves to Christ. This percentage projected to nearly 50 million American adults. When the definition was narrowed to those who had been "born again," had a literal interpretation of the Bible (or believed the Bible to be without error in its teachings) and had tried to encourage others to accept Jesus Christ as savior, the percentage of Evangelicals was about one-fifth of the adult population.

Survey statistics in 1976 indicated that the decade-and-a-half slide in religious interest and involvement was leveling off. A marginal upturn (to 42 percent) was recorded in weekly churchgoing. The proportion of Americans who said religion was increasing its influence on life in this country was growing, and, in fact, was three times as high as in 1970. Furthermore, surveys showed that a surprising number of Americans were developing an interest in the inner, or spiritual, life. A projected six million persons were involved in Transcendental Meditation, five million in yoga, three million in the charismatic movement, three million in mysticism and two million in Eastern religions.

Many churches in the sixties and seventies became increasingly aware of their "youth problem." Traditionally, churches had counted on winning back large numbers of young defectors when they reach their thirties, settle down and raise families. Survey findings indicated that a very high proportion did indeed return to the fold, but there was some indication they were doing so at a decreasing rate. Many young people said religion was simply not "relevant" to the concerns of the day. But considerably larger proportions said they were losing interest in religion because they were not getting the answers they sought.

In the face of these warning signs, it was important for the clergy and religious educators to keep in mind three salient facts about youth:

1. The antiestablishment mood prevalent among students was directed at most other major institutions as well as at the church.
2. The levels of religious belief among young people continued to be extremely high, despite their disenchantment with the forms of religion; indeed, they were manifesting new interest in discovering the meaning of life (for example, through the Jesus Movement and interest in mysticism and meditation).

3. Young people were eager to serve others; a majority of college students reported that they had done at least some work among the poor and underprivileged.

A sixty-nation survey conducted in the midseventies by the Gallup International Research Institutes (GIRI) revealed that while belief levels had remained high in the United States since the end of World War II, they had declined in most European nations. In the United States, 56 percent of respondents said religion was "very important" to them. By contrast, only 27 percent in Western Europe said their religious beliefs were very important to them. The only major nation in which the importance of religion exceeded that in the United States was India, where 81 percent said their religion was "very important."

Regarding specific religious beliefs, sharp declines had occurred in most Western European nations since 1948, when an earlier survey studied many of the same beliefs. At that time, 61 percent of Scandinavians said they believed in life after death; by 1976, this figure had fallen to 35 percent. By contrast, 69 percent of Americans believed in life after death in 1976, compared to 68 percent in 1948. Belief in life after death dropped 34 points in Canada and 20 points in the Benelux Countries (Belgium, the Netherlands and Luxembourg) in the same period.

Similarly, in the case of belief in the existence of God or a universal spirit, 94 percent of Americans professed belief, compared to 89 percent in Canada, 88 percent in Italy, 78 percent in Western Europe and 38 percent in Japan. Among the developed nations, the Scandinavian countries ranked above only Japan in their level of religious belief.

Nearly all people in the nations surveyed, however, reported identifying with a church or faith, and throughout the non-Communist world there was (and continues to be) widespread belief in the existence of God or a universal spirit and majority belief in life after death.

The Jonestown tragedy in 1978—a mass murder-suicide of some 900 people led by People's Temple head Jim Jones—contributed to the debate over what was widely regarded as the "threat" of cults. A cult is generally defined as a religious group based on a substantially new revelation of insight, usually provided by a person believed to possess special knowledge. Cult members generally reject the rest of society, and the leader often has a personal magnetism that convinces followers that he or she has supernatural powers.

For weeks after the Jonestown tragedy, historians, religious leaders, psychiatrists and others asked, "How could this have happened? Could it happen again?" Amid this speculation, the Gallup Poll sought to find what Americans in all walks of life believed were the reasons that people were attracted to cults. The key reasons given were "the need for leadership and a father figure" and "unhappy lives and a feeling of hopelessness." Others cited the need for deeper meaning to life as well as the failure of the nation's churches to answer spiritual needs.

While public concern over cults was at times intense, there was little evidence that any great numbers of Americans were being drawn into the ranks of the cults. A "*Newsweek* on Campus" poll later found that 93 percent of college students felt there was "no chance" they might join such a group, while another 5 percent saw "very little chance." Eighty-five percent believed the cults to be dangerous to their members, but only one in ten believed the cults seriously threatened mainstream religion.

On a more positive note, the visit of Pope John Paul II to the United States in 1979 gave a spiritual lift to the American people. A Gallup survey showed an overwhelmingly favorable response, with people saying he brought new hope and faith to the populace.

In 1978, a major study, "The Unchurched American," was conducted by the Gallup Organization and the Princeton Religion Research Center for The Religious Coalition to Study the Backgrounds, Values and Interests of Unchurched Americans. The coalition, a group of thirty denominations and religious groups, was convened and coordinated through the National Council of Churches of Christ in the U.S.A. The study discovered that for many Americans, *believing* was becoming increasingly divorced from *belonging*. The survey, however, offered encouraging findings for organized religion: Most of the unchurched remained "believers," with at least half saying they could see a situation that could bring them back into the active community of worshipers. And many of the unchurched claimed that religion remained very important in their lives.

Why were the unchurched resisting joining the community of active believers? One basic reason was, simply, that they had not been invited to do so. Another important reason why people rejected organized religion stemmed from the view that the churches place too much emphasis on organizational rather than spiritual matters. Similarly, many Americans said they would consider returning to church if they could find a minister, priest or rabbi with whom they could discuss their spiritual needs and religious doubts. Other factors included lifestyle changes, the questioning of traditional values and an emphasis in society on self-fulfillment.

The straying away from organized religion, the questioning of religious authority, coupled with the obvious gap between high levels of religiosity and observable reality—the high crime rate, the growing divorce rate, and so on —prompted some social observers to conclude that the nation was entering a post-Christian period of growing secularism and to predict a further decline in the relevance of religion in American life. As the trends in the 1980s indicate, however, such predictions were premature.

1980s

The public mood of discouragement, noted during most of the 1970s, gave way in the eighties to a far more upbeat frame of mind, which accompanied economic optimism. Concern over the many problems confronting society—

crime, unemployment, the nuclear threat and others—remained, but Americans were far less apprehensive about the immediate future than they were in the previous decade. One of the key reasons was their conviction that, in the face of the sometimes sluggish response of government and institutions, they as individuals *could* make a difference. Indeed, voluntarism remained a strong force in America.

The victory of Ronald Reagan over Jimmy Carter in 1980 and his re-election against Walter Mondale in 1984 were widely attributed to a national shift to a conservative point of view. Yet surveys show that any movement to the "right" in America's political philosophy was only slight.

In many ways, the 1980s have been a decade of stability in American religious life, with many trends remaining flat. For example, church membership and attendance held steady throughout the decade, with seven in ten Americans claiming church membership and four in ten attending once a week. The percentage of Americans who said religion was "very important" in their lives also held steady, at about 55 percent.

Religious involvement has remained remarkably constant for at least a decade:

- 92 percent of Americans currently state a religious preference, statistically the same as has been recorded regularly since the late seventies.
- 68 percent say they are members of a church or synagogue—statistically unchanged since the midseventies.
- 40 percent of adults attend church or synagogue in a given week—unchanged since the midsixties.
- 56 percent say religion is "very important" in their lives, representing little change over the past decade.
- Better than six in ten have consistently expressed "a great deal" or "quite a lot" of confidence in organized religion since the 1970s.
- The percentage of unchurched Americans—including those who had not attended church or synagogue except for weddings, funerals or religious holidays for six months—edged up from 41 percent in 1978 to 44 percent in 1988.
- The decline in affiliation with mainline Protestant churches continued, particularly the decline in affiliation among those under 30.

A comparison of membership figures in 1973 and 1983, supplied by the denominations themselves, showed a gain in membership for the Evangelical churches, but a falloff among mainline churches, as seen in Table 1.2 (from the *Yearbook of American and Canadian Churches*).

But there were also signs of a moderate religious revival in the 1980s. At two points in the decade, almost half of all Americans said they were more interested in religion than they had been five years before. Perhaps most significant was the increase in the percentage of those who believed that Jesus was God or the Son of God and those saying they had made a personal commitment to Christ. In 1978, 78 percent of Americans believed Jesus was God or the Son of God; this rose to 84 percent in 1988. In 1978, 60 percent of

Table 1.2

MEMBERSHIP CHANGES IN EVANGELICAL AND MAINLINE CHURCHES, 1973–1983

EVANGELICAL CHURCHES

	1973	1983	Change
Southern Baptist Convention	12,295,400	14,185,454	Up 15%
Church of Jesus Christ of Latter-Day Saints (Mormons)	2,569,000	3,593,000	Up 40
Assemblies of God	1,099,606	1,879,000	Up 71
Seventh-Day Adventists	464,276	623,563	Up 34
Church of the Nazarene	417,732	507,574	Up 22

MAINLINE CHURCHES

	1973	1983	Change
United Methodist Church	10,192,265	9,405,083	Down 8%
Presbyterian Church U.S.A.	3,715,301	3,157,372	Down 15
Lutheran Church in America	3,017,778	2,925,655	Down 3
Episcopal Church	2,917,165	2,794,139	Down 4
Christian Church (Disciples of Christ)	1,330,747	1,156,458	Down 13

Americans said they had made a commitment to Christ; in 1988, 66 percent said they had made such a commitment.

There were other signs of revival:

- There was an upturn in participation in Bible study groups since 1978.
- There was new religious ferment on college campuses. Attendance at churches and synagogues on campus increased during the first half of the 1980s, as did the proportion of students who say religion is very important in their lives.
- More Americans say they want their faith to grow and religion to play a greater role in society.

The level of religious knowledge increased slightly in the 1980s, but that increase was not particularly impressive given the vast increase in the proportion of college-educated Americans between 1954 and 1982, and the fact that a majority of Americans had attended Sunday school. Table 1.3 shows this change.

Table 1.3

INCREASE IN BIBLICAL KNOWLEDGE, 1954–1982

	1954	1982
Knew Who Delivered the Sermon on the Mount	34%	42%
Could Name All Four Gospels	35	46
Knew Where Jesus Was Born	75	70

The eighties was a time of continued change for American Catholics. In the two decades since the end of the Second Vatican Council (1962–5), called by Pope John XXIII, upheavals in the Catholic world have been almost commonplace, and the church in the United States has been in a state of flux, due to a number of factors, including: the growth in the Hispanic population, political activism, the clergy shortage; new movements (an estimated six million Catholics are charismatics), healing, feminism and renewal. Survey researcher William McCready noted in *USA Today* that the Catholic Church in America is "headed for a new era of diversity. Rather than one sort of American Catholic model, there will be several."

Despite the upheavals in the church, the percentage of Americans who are Catholic increased from 20 percent in 1947 to 28 percent in the eighties. The influx of Hispanic immigrants helped swell the ranks of Catholics in that period. Not only has the proportion of Catholics in the population increased, so has the proportion of Catholics who are "upscale," that is, in higher socioeconomic groups. The percentage of upscale Catholics became as high as that of upscale Protestants for the first time in history.

Survey findings suggest that Catholics in the eighties, while disagreeing with certain of their church's teachings and practices, feel better about themselves as Catholics. In the 1960s, many Catholics left the church because they felt they could not agree on certain issues—most notably birth control—and still remain good Catholics. By the eighties, many felt they could disagree on issues like birth control and still be part of the church. In 1987, eight Catholics in ten (77 percent) said they relied on their consciences, rather than the church's teaching as expressed by the pope, in making moral decisions.

Furthermore, Catholics have gained greater credibility among the populace as a whole. There was a time not long ago when a Catholic had little chance of being elected president. This has changed, of course. And far fewer Americans today than in earlier years object to interfaith marriages. We also note a dramatic drop in the percentage of Americans who cite incidents that have caused them to dislike Catholics.

While attendance at Mass among Catholics has held fairly firm during the last few years, the current level is, of course, far below that of the period prior to the early 1960s. A 1985 survey conducted for the Paulist National Catholic Evangelization Association revealed that 60 percent of Catholics who have left the church say they do not expect to return. Reasons cited for not rejoining the church include an inability to accept some of the church's teachings, negative factors relating to priests, and finding the Catholic way of life too demanding.

One in ten Americans who were raised Catholic has left the church, but those who remain are fairly upbeat about their church. They remain members on their own terms, however.

The relationship between religion and politics was much in the news in the eighties. One of the unique aspects of the 1980 presidential race was that all three of the leading contenders—Reagan, Carter and Independent candidate John Anderson—considered themselves Born-Again Christians. On balance, being identified as an Evangelical seemed to be more a political asset than a liability. Although most voters said it made no difference to them whether a candidate was an Evangelical or a non-Evangelical, roughly twice as many voters said they would be more likely rather than less likely to vote for an Evangelical.

By 1987, however, this had reversed; while a majority of Americans still said a candidate's status as a Born-Again Christian made no difference to them, a solid majority of those who said it would make a difference now said they would be less likely to vote for such a candidate.

Interestingly, the views of Evangelicals and non-Evangelicals were similar on a number of key voter issues—Evangelicals were by no means monolithic in their views. However, on issues related to personal morality and religion— allowing homosexuals to teach in the public schools, abortion, and prayer in the schools—Evangelicals were considerably more conservative than non-Evangelicals.

Debate over the separation of church and state was a prominent issue in the 1984 presidential campaign. The position of voters was fairly clear on this issue—they believed it was wrong for religious groups to work actively for the defeat of candidates who did not agree with their position on certain issues, but at the same time felt it was important for religious leaders to speak out on the moral implications of political issues.

Two ministers—Jesse Jackson and Pat Robertson—ran in the presidential primaries in 1988, and surveys found considerable resistance to ministers running for the highest office in the land: 39 percent of Americans said it was a bad idea for a minister to run for president. Only 16 percent said it was a good idea; 41 percent said it would make no difference to them.

During the 1980 and 1984 presidential years, much attention was focused on the Moral Majority, the fundamentalist political movement founded by the Rev. Jerry Falwell. The Moral Majority, which claimed to have registered four million new fundamentalist voters in 1980, assigned candidates "morality ratings" depending on their votes on issues ranging from abortion to the second Strategic Arms Limitation Treaty (SALT II). Some political observers believed the Moral Majority to be largely responsible for the defeat of certain key members of Congress in the 1980 election.

In a 1980 survey, less than half (40 percent) had heard or read of the Moral Majority, while even fewer (26 percent) were familiar with its goals. Among the "informed" group, disapproval (13 percent) outweighed approval (8 percent), with 5 percent undecided.

A survey taken a year later found that public awareness of the Moral Majority had increased from 40 to 55 percent, but unfavorable attitudes continued to outweigh favorable views by a 2-to-1 margin.

By the end of the decade, Falwell, personally, had become one of the most unpopular figures in American life, with more Americans giving him an unfavorable rating than a favorable one. Americans also increasingly frowned upon political involvement by religious leaders, with a majority rejecting their involvement in day-to-day political affairs and their efforts to persuade members of Congress to adopt new laws.

The issue of school prayer made headlines during the 1980 elections and was an issue through the first part of the decade. Since the U.S. Supreme Court's 1962 and 1963 rulings that religious exercises and devotional Bible reading in the public schools were unconstitutional, the courts have consistently struck down efforts to restore those practices. Surveys show that Americans have just as consistently favored some form of school prayer. At the same time, however, the prevailing opinion among all groups and faiths in the United States was that the home was more important than either the school or church in the religious training of children.

Much was written in the seventies and eighties on the "Electronic Church," with mainline Protestant denominations concerned that religious TV and radio were drawing members and money from local churches. But a 1984 survey conducted by the Annenberg School of Communications and the Gallup Organization found that when levels of religiosity and other factors are held constant, religious television viewing does not seem to be associated with lower levels of church attendance, volunteer work or church contributions.

But confidence in the Electronic Church was rocked by scandals and controversies involving major evangelists—Oral Roberts, Jim Bakker and Jimmy Swaggart—in 1987 and 1988. The image of virtually every TV evangelist except Billy Graham declined, and public perceptions of those evangelists turned sharply negative.

THE RELIGIOUS CHARACTER OF AMERICA

Certain basic themes emerge from the mass of survey data collected over more than five decades—themes that probably apply not just to the period in which we have had scientific polling, but to the entire history of the nation. The first is the enduring popularity of religion. There have been several periods of heightened interest in religion, but the baseline of religious belief is remarkably high—certainly, the highest of any developed nation in the world.

At the same time, American religious life is characterized by a series of gaps. First, there is an "ethics gap" between Americans' expressed beliefs and the state of the society they shape. While religion is highly popular in America, it is to a large extent superficial; it does not change people's lives to the degree one would expect from their level of professed faith. Related to this is a "knowledge gap" between Americans' stated faith and the lack of the most basic knowledge about that faith. Finally, there is a gap between "believers" and "belongers," with millions of Americans who are nominal Christians or Jews failing to participate in the congregational lives of their denominations.

CHAPTER

2

Trends in Religion

ELIGIOUS TRENDS are primarily concerned with movement—Is church membership up? Is attendance down? Are people moving in and out of a particular denomination?

Different trends move in different ways and at different rates. It takes a long time, for example, for changes in religious affiliation to show up, because people are reluctant to change what is often a lifelong habit—affiliation with a particular church. Similarly, changes in membership and church attendance are fairly slow in coming because involvement—or lack of involvement—is a hard habit to break. It takes either long-range population shifts or dramatic events, such as the social turmoil of the 1960s, to bring about a more sudden change. Attitudes toward organized religion are the most subject to sudden change—views on the influence or relevance of religion or levels of confidence in religion are likely to be influenced by church scandals or other highly visible church activity.

In terms of long-range change, the past decade has seen the continued growth of pluralism in American religion. Church membership and attendance and the importance which Americans place on religion have remained stable. Attitudes toward religion have gone through a variety of changes that partly reflect the religious tenor of the 1980s.

22

U.S RELIGIOUS MAKEUP BECOMING MORE PLURALISTIC

The religious makeup of the American people has shifted in dramatic ways over the past four decades—and there is every indication that those trends will continue in the future. In general, the nation has become less distinctly Protestant and more pluralistic in character[1].

The most remarkable story is the change in the relative proportion of Protestants to Catholics in America. In 1947, Protestants outnumbered Catholics by a 3.5-to-1 margin (69 to 20 percent). In 1987, Protestants outnumbered Catholics by only a 2-to-1 margin (57 to 28 percent). The gap is even narrower among young people. Among those age 18–24, 49 percent state their religious preference as Protestant and 31 percent as Catholic; among those age 25–29, it is 50 to 32 percent.

If we were to extrapolate from this trend, it's possible to conclude that by some time in the early decades of the next century, Catholics could vie with Protestants as the dominant religious group in America. Whether or not this happens, it does seem likely that, with the percentage of Protestants hovering around 50 percent among young people, the time is not far off when—for the first time in U.S. history—nominal Protestants will no longer make up a majority of the American people.

Several factors account for the shifting proportion of Protestants and Catholics. The first is that Catholics have had a higher birth rate than Protestants, although the gap has narrowed considerably. A second factor is the heavy immigration of Hispanics in recent years—American Hispanics today are 70 percent Catholic, 18 percent Protestant.

But an increase among Catholics alone does not account for the shift in relative proportions: the percentage of Americans stating their preference as Protestant has fallen considerably, from a peak of 70 percent in 1962 to a low point of 56 percent in 1983, before a slight increase in 1984.

In *Understanding Church Growth and Decline: 1950–1978*, sociologists Dean Hoge and David Roozen argue that while conservative churches are growing, many young people from mainline Protestant churches are moving in a different direction, leaving the church altogether. Our findings support this view. The decline in those identifying themselves as Protestants has come at the same time as an increase in those stating no religious preference. In 1952, only 2 percent of Americans stated no religious preference; in 1987, it was 9 percent. The figure is even higher among young people: 12 percent of those 18–24 and 14 percent of those 25–29 state no religious preference.

The percentage of Americans identifying themselves as Jewish has also declined significantly over the past four decades. It has held steady at 2 percent since the early seventies, but this marks a decline from a peak of 5 percent in 1947, 4 percent in 1952 and 3 percent throughout the 1950s and 1960s. The percentage of Americans who are Orthodox—for example, Greek or Russian—has declined from 2 percent in 1947 to less than 1 percent today.

Table 2.1 shows the shifts in affiliation with key denominations over the years.

Table 2.2 shows shifts among Protestant denominations.

While the percentage of some religious groups in the population has declined, other groups have increased their share. Mormons, who made up only a handful of the population in 1947, now make up 2 percent of the population. Seven percent of those in the West—and 19 percent in the Rocky Mountain states—are Mormons.

This increase in the proportion of Americans whose religion is "other" is one of the most significant religious trends of the past 40 years[2]. In the 1950s, sociologist Will Herzberg wrote an influential book entitled *Protestant, Catholic, Jew,* which described the dominant American religious groups. But America is far more pluralistic today than it has ever been in the past, and patterns of religious affiliation among teenagers indicate that it is going to become even more pluralistic over the next generation.

For example, in 1947, only 6 percent of Americans identified themselves as anything other than Protestant, Catholic or Jewish. In 1987, that figure had grown to 13 percent among adults, 15 percent among teenagers and 19 percent among those age 18–24. This pattern is even more pronounced in some areas of the country: 21 percent of teenagers living in the suburbs and 31 percent of teens living in the West belong to religious traditions other than Protestant, Catholic or Jewish.

While there was no significant difference in the religious makeup of the

Table 2.1
RELIGIOUS AFFILIATION

	Protestant	Catholic	Jewish	Other	None
1987	57%	28%	2%	4%	9%
1984	57	28	2	4	9
1980	61	28	2	2	7
1976	61	27	2	4	6
1972	63	26	2	4	5
1967	67	25	3	3	2
1962	70	23	3	2	2
1957	66	26	3	1	3
1952	67	25	4	1	2
1947	69	20	5	1	6

Table 2.2

SHIFTS IN MEMBERSHIP IN PROTESTANT DENOMINATIONS

	Baptist	Methodist	Lutheran	Presbyterian	Episcopalian
1987	20%	9%	6%	3%	2%
1984	20	9	7	2	3
1980	19	10	6	4	2
1976	21	11	7	5	3
1974	21	14	7	6	3
1969	20	14	7	6	3
1967	21	14	7	6	3

adult population between 1986 and 1987, the difference in makeup of the adult and teen populations in 1987, though small, is indicative of increased religious pluralism.

In particular, Protestants continue to decline as the dominant religious group in the population; 52 percent of teens are Protestant. At the same time, Catholics continue to slightly increase their representation in the population; 30 percent of teens are Catholic. Jews made up 2 percent of the adult population in 1986 and 1987 and 3 percent of the teen population in 1987. Mormons accounted for 3 percent of teens in 1987. Two percent of adults in 1986 and 1987 were members of "other" religions, a group that includes Moslems, Buddhists, adherents to American Indian religions, Jehovah's Witnesses and others. Among teens, however, 5 percent in 1987 belonged to this group.

Key factors in the increasing religious pluralism among teens are, again, immigration and birth rate patterns. In recent years, there has been heavy immigration from Latin America and Asia, where the population is heavily Catholic and Buddhist. These groups also now have higher birth rates than others, so they make up a larger percentage of young people.

The percentage of adults claiming no religious affiliation was 7 percent in 1986 and 9 percent in 1987. Among teens, 7 percent cited no religious preference in 1987. It seems probable that teens are less likely to cite no religious preference because most are still living at home and are influenced by their parents' religious preferences. Once they leave home, however, some changes occur; among those 18–24, 13 percent cite no religious preference. Surveys of unchurched Americans show that a major reason for leaving the church is an emphasis on "making my own decisions"; this opportunity usually comes when young adults leave home.

Table 2.3 shows the religious makeup of adults and teens by region in 1987.

Table 2.3

RELIGIOUS MAKEUP OF ADULTS AND TEENS, BY REGION

	East		Midwest		South		West	
	Adult	Teen	Adult	Teen	Adult	Teen	Adult	Teen
Protestant	40%	41%	61%	49%	74%	72%	47%	41%
Catholic	42	43	28	34	17	17	26	28
Jewish	5	6	1	2	1	1	2	1
Mormon	–	–	–	1	1	1	7	14
Other	2	3	1	6	1	5	3	6
None	9	7	8	9	6	4	15	12

MAINLINE PROTESTANTS LOSING YOUNG ADULTS

The decline in the proportion of mainline Protestants in the population is due mainly to losses among young adults. A lower proportion of members of mainline Protestant denominations were under 30 in 1987 than in 1983, reflecting a continuation of a decades-long trend[3].

There has also been a decline in the percentage of American Jews who are under 30. In contrast, Catholics and Baptists are holding their own with those age 18–29.

Declining membership among those under 30 reflects two major factors— lower birth rates and a greater defection rate as young people drift away from church when they graduate from high school and leave home. Conversely, the groups maintaining their membership rate for under-30s have had higher birth rates and seem to be doing a better job of retaining their younger members.

In 1983, 24 percent of all Americans were adults 18–29. An identical percentage of Protestants were in that age group. In 1987, however, the percentage of adults 18–29 rose to 27 percent of the population, while only 23 percent of Protestants were under 30.

Among Catholics, 31 percent in 1983 and again in 1987 were under age 30. Twenty-five percent of Jews were under 29 in 1983, but only 19 percent were in 1987. Thirty-two percent of members of "other" religions were under 30 in both years. Among those who stated no religious preference, 41 percent in 1983 and 38 percent in 1987 were under 30.

Twenty-eight percent of Baptists were under 30 in both years. But six mainline Protestant denominations showed declines:

- Methodists: 18 percent were under 30 in 1983; 17 percent in 1987.
- Lutherans: 22 percent were under 30 in 1983; 20 percent in 1987.

- Episcopalians: 21 percent were under 30 in 1983; 17 percent in 1987.
- Presbyterians: 21 percent were under 30 in 1983; 17 percent in 1987.
- United Church of Christ: 17 percent were under 30 in 1983, 14 percent in 1987.
- Christian Church (Disciples of Christ): 32 percent were under 30 in 1983; 26 percent in 1987.
- Among "other Protestants," 24 percent were under 30 in 1987.

The declining membership of mainline Protestant denominations among those under 30 is reflected in a comparison of the denominational makeup of the general population and the makeup of those under 30. Table 2.4 shows the percentage of each group belonging to each denomination.

Overall, those under 30 are less interested and involved in religion than those over 30. For example, 58 percent of those over 30 and only 41 percent of those under 30 say that religion is "very important" in their lives. Twenty-nine percent of those over 30 and 40 percent of those under 30 say it is "fairly important." Twelve percent of those over 30 and 18 percent of those under 30 say religion is "not important."

Seventy-two percent of those over 30 and 62 percent of those under 30 are members of a church or synagogue. The difference is even greater when it comes to church attendance—while 50 percent of those over 30 say they attended church or synagogue in the past seven days, only 28 percent of those under 30 report doing so.

DENOMINATIONAL SWITCHING

Birth rates and immigration patterns are not the only influences on long-term trends in religious affiliation. Switching from one denomination to an-

Table 2.4

PERCENTAGE UNDER 30 BY DENOMINATION

	U.S.	Age 18–29		U.S.	age 18–29
Catholic	28%	31%	Protestant	56%	50%
Jewish	2	2	Baptist	20	21
			Methodist	9	6
Other	4	4	Lutheran	6	4
None	9	13	Episcopalian	2	1
			Presbyterian	4	2
			United Church	2	1
			Christian Church	2	2

other, or dropping out of church, also affect the pattern. Responses from a survey that asked Americans to name both the religion in which they were raised and their current affiliation revealed important shifts. The most dramatic findings were that one in three Americans who were raised Methodist and one in ten who were raised Catholic no longer identify with those churches[4]. These findings come from "Unchurched Americans—1988," a Gallup study conducted for Congress '88, a coalition of twenty-two religious groups.

The survey also found movement toward two smaller groups with almost opposite viewpoints—those who claim no religious affiliation, on the one hand, and smaller, fundamentalist and Pentecostal churches on the other. These groups make up the majority of those found in the "other Protestant" category, comprising churches whose memberships are too small to be recorded separately. Six percent of Americans were raised in "other Protestant" churches, while 8 percent now belong to those churches. Five percent of Americans say they were raised with no religious affiliation, while 8 percent now claim no affiliation.

The survey results give some sense of the level of "switching" between religious affiliations that takes place in America. By some estimates, one Protestant in three has switched denominations within the Protestant family. While the present sample is not large enough to show, for example, what percentage of those who were raised as Methodists now belong to the Episcopal Church, or vice versa, it does illustrate some significant broad patterns and provide some insight into which denominations are doing the best job of retaining their members.

Proportionately, the major loss came among Methodists. While 13 percent of Americans say they were raised in the Methodist church, only 9 percent identify with that church today. The proportion of decline was fairly constant across all demographic groups.

While the percentage decline among Catholics is not as great as among Methodists, millions of Americans have stopped identifying with the Catholic church: 31 percent of Americans say they were raised as Catholics, while 27 percent now identify with the church. The decline among Catholics was particularly pronounced among the young and college educated. For example, 36 percent of Americans under 30 say they were raised as Catholics, but only 31 percent now identify themselves as Catholics. Similarly, 35 percent of Americans 30–49 say they were raised as Catholics, while only 29 percent now identify with the church. There was no significant difference among those over 50—22 percent of Americans in that age group say they were raised as Catholics, and 21 percent still identify themselves as such.

Among college graduates, 31 percent say they were raised as Catholics, but only 21 percent say they are Catholics today. The findings were similar among those who had attended, but not completed, college: 29 percent say they were raised as Catholics, but only 24 percent say they are Catholics today. There was no significant change among those with lower levels of education.

There has been considerable attrition among Hispanic Catholics. Eighty-four percent of Hispanics say they were raised as Catholics, and only 10 percent say they were raised as Protestants. Today, however, the proportion of Hispanics who say they are Catholic has fallen to 74 percent, while the proportion of Hispanics who say they are Protestant has risen to 17 percent. The increase was greatest for the Christian Church (Disciples of Christ), a mainline denomination strongest in the West and Midwest. While 1 percent of Hispanics say they were raised in this denomination, 5 percent say they now belong. While 3 percent of Hispanics say they were raised in "other Protestant" churches, 6 percent now say they belong to those churches.

These findings partly reflect the fact that conservative, Evangelical churches have targeted members of minority groups for recruitment in recent years. They have also had some success attracting blacks: 5 percent of blacks say they were raised in "other Protestant" churches, but 9 percent now say they belong to those churches.

In addition, the proportion of blacks who cite no religious affiliation is 10 percent, up from the 6 percent who say they were raised with no affiliation. The movement to "no affiliation" and "other Protestant" among blacks seems related to a slippage among Baptists—62 percent of blacks say they were raised as Baptists, but 52 percent say they are Baptists today. The proportion of black Catholics has remained stable: 10 percent of blacks say they were raised as Catholics, and 11 percent say they are Catholics today.

MEMBERSHIP

The percentage of Americans who identified themselves as members of a church or synagogue in 1988—65 percent—was the lowest since the Gallup Poll began tracking such figures in 1937. Church membership and attendance figures for 1988 were also historic for American Catholics—for the first time, Catholics were no more likely than Protestants to be church members. Table 2.5 shows the long-range trend in U.S. church membership.

Church membership declined sharply among Catholics and remained fairly stable among Protestants, so that 72 percent of each group claimed church membership. Catholics have historically been more likely than Protestants to claim church membership. In 1987, for example, 79 percent of Catholics and 73 percent of Protestants were church members.

The previous low for overall church membership was 67 percent in 1982. As recently as 1985, 71 percent of Americans claimed membership in a church or synagogue. In 1987, 69 percent of Americans were church members.

The largest single decrease in church membership was among college graduates. While 74 percent were church members in 1987, membership fell by 10 percentage points to 64 percent in 1988. There was a similar nine-point decline at the other end of the educational scale. Among those with less than a high school degree, membership fell from 69 percent to 60 percent.

Membership remained more stable among those in the middle education

Table 2.5

CHURCH-SYNAGOGUE MEMBERSHIP

1988	65%	1975	71%
1987	69	1965	73
1984	68	1952	73
1983	69	1947	76
1982	67	1944	75
1981	68	1942	75
1980	69	1940	72
1979	68	1939	72
1978	68	1938	73
1977	70	1937	73
1976	71		

levels. Membership among high school graduates fell one point to 68 percent, while membership among those with some college fell one point to 66 percent.

There was no difference in membership decline by gender. Membership fell by four points to 58 percent among men and by four points to 71 percent among women.

The 1988 decline in church membership was strongest among young adults. Among those age 18 to 29, membership fell seven points to 55 percent. Among those 30 to 49, it fell by 3 points to 65 percent. Among those over 50, membership fell by 4 points to 73 percent.

The membership decline was stable across regions. Membership in the East fell by five points to 64 percent; it fell by 3 points in the Midwest to 68 percent; by 5 points in the South to 71 percent and by 5 points in the West to 53 percent.

Among Evangelicals, membership fell by only one point to 87 percent. Among Non-Evangelicals, membership fell by 3 points to 59 percent.

CHURCH ATTENDANCE

Church attendance in America has remained stable for the past generation, with four Americans in ten attending church or synagogue in a typical week since the early 1960s. The peak in church attendance was 49 percent in 1955 and again in 1958; the low point was 37 percent in 1940. Table 2.6 shows the long-range trremds.

Table 2.6

CHURCH ATTENDANCE BY YEAR

Year	Church Attendance	Year	Church Attendance
1988	42%		
1987	40	1969	42%
1984	40	1967	43
1983	40	1962	46
1982	41	1958	49
1981	41	1957	47
1980	40	1955	49
1979	40	1954	46
1978	41	1950	39
1977	41	1940	37
1972	40	1937	41

Most of the decline in church attendance since the 1950s stems from a dramatic decline in attendance among Catholics. In 1988, church attendance among Catholics reached an all-time low, with 48 percent saying they had attended church in the past seven days. The historic gap between Catholics and Protestants on church attendance all but disappeared. Catholics were only three percentage points more likely than Protestants to attend church weekly; the gap had never been below double figures before. Table 2.7 compares church attendance by Catholics and Protestants since 1958.

For the most part, the patterns that emerge on church membership also hold up on church attendance—women, southerners, those over 50 and college graduates are the most likely to attend church in a given week. Table 2.8 shows church attendance by group.

While church attendance in a typical week has remained stable, surveys show that Easter week is not typical—church attendance in the United States increases 17 percent on Easter Sunday, with denominational increases ranging from 5 percent for Baptists to 29 percent for Catholics[6].

Overall, a survey conducted in April 1986 found that 42 percent of Americans reported having attended church within the past seven days, while 49 percent said they had attended on Easter Sunday.

The greatest increase in church attendance came among Catholics: 52 percent said they had attended within the past week, while 67 percent said they had attended on Easter.

Table 2.7
CHURCH ATTENDANCE FOR PROTESTANTS AND CATHOLICS

Year	Protestants	Catholics	Year	Protestants	Catholics
1988	45%	48%	1980	39	53
1987	38	52	1979	40	52
1984	39	51	1978	40	52
1983	39	52	1968	68	65
1982	41	51	1958	44	74
1981	40	53			

Baptists were at the other extreme, with attendance increasing only from 38 to 40 percent.

Among all Protestants, attendance increased from 43 to 47 percent, a 9 percent increase. The increase was higher for members of mainline Protestant churches—defined here to include Methodists, Lutherans, Presbyterians and Episcopalians.

Table 2.8
CHURCH ATTENDANCE BY GROUP

Group	Attendance	Group	Attendance
Men	38%	White	41%
Women	46	Black	47
18–29	33	College Grad.	47
30–49	41	Some College	43
50+	48	High School Grad.	41
East	37	Less Than High School	39
Midwest	48	Protestant	48
South	45	Catholic	45
West	36		

Among this group, attendance increased from 40 to 48 percent, a 20 percent increase. The increase was somewhat smaller among Methodists and Lutherans. The increase in church attendance among Presbyterians and Episcopalians appears to be at least as high as among Catholics, but the sample size is too small to say so with certainty.

Other demographic groups showed interesting patterns. The largest increase—31 percent—came among those under 30; 46 percent said they attended church on Easter, up from 35 percent within the past week. The increase in attendance among those over 30 was lower, partly because attendance in this group is higher to start.

Regionally, the largest increase in church attendance on Easter—30 percent—came in the East, with attendance climbing from 40 percent in a typical week to 52 percent on Easter. This partly reflects the fact that the East is the most heavily Catholic region in the country.

The highest church attendance rate on Easter—55 percent of the population—came in the Midwest, a 20 percent increase over a normal Sunday. Attendance in the South increased by 10 percent, to 45 percent. In the West, 43 percent of the population attended church on Easter, up only 8 percent over a normal week.

While about 40 percent of Americans attend church in a given week, it is not the same 40 percent every week. Questions on frequency of church attendance reveal interesting patterns; in a given month, for example, more than half of all Americans attend church at least once. Overall, 26 percent of Americans say they attend church weekly, 14 percent say they attend almost weekly, 14 percent say they attend once or twice a month, 30 percent say they attend several times a year, 15 percent say they never attend and 1 percent say they don't know[7].

There was a dramatic decrease in the frequency with which American Catholics attended church between 1985 and 1987. In 1985, 78 percent reported attending church at least once a month; in 1987, that figure dropped to 64 percent. Even with this decrease, however, Catholics rank behind only Evangelicals—those who describe themselves as Born-Again Christians—among major religious groups in frequency of church attendance.

In a Gallup survey conducted for sociologist Dean Hoge at the Catholic University of America in 1985, 59 percent of Catholics said they went to church weekly, 12 percent said they went two or three times a month, 7 percent said they went at least once a month, 13 percent said they went several times a year and 9 percent said they never went to church.

In a 1987 Gallup survey—part of the Times Mirror Corporation's study "The People, Press and Politics"—33 percent of American Catholics said they attended church weekly, 16 percent said they attended almost weekly, 15 percent said they attended once or twice a month, 28 percent said they attended several times a year and 8 percent said they never attended.

Black Protestant Evangelicals reported the highest rates of church attendance in 1987, with 89 percent attending church at least once a month: 44

percent said they attended weekly, 22 percent almost weekly and 23 percent once or twice a month; only 11 percent said they attended several times a year.

White Protestant Evangelicals ranked closely behind, with 79 percent saying they attended church at least once a month; 45 percent said they attended weekly, 20 percent almost weekly and 14 percent once or twice a month; 17 percent said they attended church several times a year and 4 percent said they never went to church.

Among members of "other" religious groups—including Mormons and Orthodox Christians—57 percent reported attending church at least monthly: 34 percent said they went weekly, 8 percent almost weekly, 15 percent once or twice a month; 27 percent said they went several times a year and 15 percent said they never went to church.

Among black non-Evangelical Protestants, 56 percent report attending church at least once a month: 16 percent weekly, 12 percent almost weekly, 28 percent once or twice a month; 40 percent said they went several times a year and 6 percent, never.

Frequency of church attendance reported by white Protestant non-Evangelicals was low—only 38 percent reported attending at least monthly: 13 percent said they went to church weekly, 13 percent almost weekly and 12 percent once or twice a month; 41 percent said they went several times a year and 21 percent said they never went to church.

Only one-fourth of American Jews—24 percent—reported attending synagogue at least once a month: 8 percent said they attended weekly, 4 percent almost weekly, 12 percent once or twice a month; 52 percent said they attended several times a year and 25 percent said they never attend synagogue.

One-third of those who cited no religious affiliation—32 percent—said they attended church at least several times a year: 2 percent said they attended weekly, 2 percent almost weekly, 4 percent once or twice a month and 24 percent several times a year; 61 percent said they never attended church.

As Table 2.9 shows, among various demographic groups, women attend church more frequently than men, nonwhites more frequently than whites, the elderly more frequently than the young and those with less education more frequently than those with more education.

A special analysis of churchgoing on the basis of age, parenthood and marital status underscores earlier findings that show that one's having children of school age has a decided impact on one's rate of churchgoing. This analysis, from the 1987 Times Mirror Corporation's study, shows these major findings:

· Among young married couples (under 40) who do not have children, 15 percent attend church or synagogue every week. Among young marrieds with children, however, the figure is 27 percent.
· Among older married couples (40 and older), little difference in the rate of churchgoing is found between those couples who have children and those who do not. A total of 48 percent of the older couples without children attend every week or almost every week, matching the 48 percent among

Table 2.9
FREQUENCY OF CHURCH ATTENDANCE

	Weekly	Almost Weekly	1–2 Times a Month	Several Times/Year	Never
Men	22%	12%	14%	33%	19%
Women	30	16	15	27	12
Whites	26	14	13	30	17
Nonwhites	26	15	23	30	7
18–24	16	11	21	37	15
25–29	15	14	16	35	19
30–39	23	15	13	30	17
40–49	26	14	13	31	16
50–59	32	14	15	26	12
60 +	38	15	11	24	12
College Grad.	29	15	11	28	16
Some College	25	15	15	28	17
High School Grad.	24	15	15	32	14
Less than High School	29	11	15	30	15

those who have children. (It is important to bear in mind, of course, that a significantly high proportion of these children would be adults.)

· Among young singles (under 30) relatively few attend church or synagogue, whether or not they have children—23 percent in the case of those who do not have children and 21 percent in the case of those who do. However, in the next age group (30–49), singles without children are less likely to attend than singles who have children. Table 2.10 shows these findings in more detail.

IMPORTANCE OF RELIGION

The degree of importance Americans attach to religion is another area that has shown remarkable stability for more than a decade. The 1987 responses were typical—54 percent of Americans said religion was "very important" in

Table 2.10

FREQUENCY OF CHURCH ATTENDANCE BY COUPLES

	Weekly	Almost Weekly	1–2 Times a Month	Several Times/Year	Never
Single/18–29	13%	10%	15%	38%	23%
W/Children	10	11	12	38	28
Single/30–49	12	14	20	36	18
W/Children	19	13	19	39	8
Married/18–40	15	12	18	37	15
W/Children	27	16	13	27	16
Married/40+	34	14	14	26	12
W/Children	32	16	11	28	12
Single/40–59	22	11	17	31	18
Single/60+	39	15	11	21	13

their lives, 32 percent said it was "fairly important" and 14 percent said it was "not very important"[8].

Table 2.11 shows trends for Protestants and Catholics and Americans as a whole who said that religion was "very important" in their lives.

Americans indicate that religion is more important to them as adults than

Table 2.11

IMPORTANCE OF RELIGION

Year	U.S.	Protestant	Catholic
1987	54%	60%	54%
1984	56	62	53
1983	56	62	56
1980	55	61	56
1978	52	60	51
1965	70	74	76
1952	75	76	83

it was when they were growing up[9]. There is, however, one glaring exception—American Catholics indicate that religion is considerably less important to them as adults than it was as children. These findings come from "Unchurched Americans—1988," a Gallup study conducted for Congress '88, a coalition of twenty-two religious groups.

The 1987 survey found that 54 percent of adults said religion is "very important" in their lives today; 31 percent said it was "fairly important" and 14 percent said it was "not very important." The same survey asked, "When you were growing up, how important was religion to you?" In response, 47 percent said it was "very important," 34 percent said it was "fairly important" and 18 percent said it was "not very important."

The 7 point increase, from 47 percent who said religion was "very important" while they were growing up to 54 percent who said it was "very important" today, represents a 15 percent increase in Americans reporting religion as "very important," as they become adults.

American Catholics, however, showed the opposite trend. Fifty-eight percent said religion was "very important" while they were growing up, 32 percent said it was "fairly important," and 11 percent said it was "not very important." As adults, the proportion saying religion was "very important" in their lives fell to 49 percent, while the proportion saying it was "fairly important" rose to 40 percent. Eleven percent said religion was "not very important." This shift marks a 16 percent decrease in the number of Catholics reporting that religion was "very important," as they become adults.

In contrast, American Protestants are considerably more likely to view religion as "very important" as adults than as children. Forty-eight percent said religion was "very important" when they were growing up, 35 percent said it was "fairly important" and 16 percent said it was "not very important."

However, 63 percent of Protestants said that, as adults, religion is "very important" to them; 28 percent said it is "fairly important" and only 8 percent said it is "not very important."

This represents a 31 percent increase in Protestants reporting religion as "very important," as they move into adulthood.

Patterns in several other demographic groups are particularly interesting:

- Blacks were among the most likely to say that religion was "very important" while they were growing up (52 percent), but they were also the most likely to report an increase in the importance of religion in their lives—69 percent say religion is "very important" today, a 33 percent increase.
- While college graduates are one of the least likely groups to say that religion is "very important" in their lives, they show a dramatic increase in reporting that religion is important as they become adults: 37 percent said religion was "very important" while they were growing up, while 47 percent say it is "very important" today, a 27 percent increase.

Table 2.12 shows the shift for other groups.

Table 2.12
IMPORTANCE OF RELIGION WHILE GROWING UP

	Religion Very Important While Growing Up	Religion Very Important Today	Change
Men	40%	47%	+18%
Women	54	61	+13
18–29	41	45	+10
30–49	45	50	+11
50+	55	65	+18
White	46	52	+14
Hispanic	52	57	+10
East	47	47	–
Midwest	45	52	+16
South	54	65	+20
West	41	49	+20
Less Than High School	52	60	+16
High School Grad.	49	56	+14
Some College	47	51	+9
College Grad.	37	47	+27
Married	49	57	+16
Single	38	42	+11
Divorced/Separated/ Widowed	51	59	+16

RELIGION—INFLUENCE/RELEVANCE

There has been a dramatic decline since 1986 in the percentage of Americans who believe that religion as a whole is increasing its influence in society. In 1986, 48 percent of Americans said religion's influence was increasing, while 36 percent said it was decreasing. Today, the figures have almost reversed—36 percent of Americans say religion's influence is increasing, while 49 percent say it is decreasing.

During the same two-year period, however, the percentage of Americans who said they believe that religion can answer all or most of today's problems held steady—it was 58 percent in 1986 and 57 percent this year. Twenty percent of Americans said in 1988 that religion is "largely old-fashioned and out-of-date," down slightly from 23 percent who made that claim in 1986[10].

The basic stability since 1986 in the belief in the relevance of religion suggests that the belief that the influence of religion is decreasing is due to external factors. For example, this year's survey was conducted in March, shortly after widely publicized revelations about evangelist Jimmy Swaggart's relationship with a prostitute. A series of scandals involving television evangelists, and the presidential campaigns of two ministers, the Rev. Jesse Jackson and Pat Robertson, have been the dominant religion stories over the past two years.

Among religious groups, the biggest shift in opinion occurred among Evangelicals, those who identify themselves as Born-Again Christians, and all Protestants. Both groups saw a 17-point decline in the percentage saying religion was increasing in influence.

In 1986, Evangelicals by a margin of 56 to 34 percent saw the influence of religion increasing. Today, 39 percent of Evangelicals believe religion is increasing in influence, while 48 percent say it is losing influence. The shift among all Protestants was from 51 to 34 percent saying religion was increasing in influence and from 37 to 49 percent saying it was losing influence.

The shift was far smaller among non-Evangelicals and Catholics. In 1986, 43 percent said religion was increasing in influence, while 41 percent said it was losing influence. Today, non-Evangelicals by a margin of 49 to 35 percent believe religion is losing influence. Among Catholics, 41 percent in 1986 and 39 percent in 1988 said religion was gaining in influence; 45 and 50 percent, respectively, said it was losing influence.

Table 2.13 shows the shift in views among other demographic groups.

Table 2.14 shows the long-range trend in national opinions on religious influence.

There has been considerably more stability in attitudes on the relevance of religion. Since 1974, the percentage saying that religion can answer all or most of life's problems has fluctuated in a fairly narrow range between 57 and 65 percent. These figures represent a significant decline since 1957, however, when 81 percent of Americans said religion could answer all or most of life's problems.

On this question, the greatest gap comes between Evangelicals and non-Evangelicals: 82 percent of Evangelicals and 45 percent of non-Evangelicals say religion can answer all or most problems. Sixty-four percent of Protestants and 53 percent of Catholics say religion can provide answers.

There are also significant gaps by gender and race: 51 percent of men, 63

Table 2.13
INFLUENCE OF RELIGION

	1986		1988	
	Increasing	Losing	Increasing	Losing
Men	50%	35%	37%	45%
Women	47	42	34	52
18–29	53	38	40	51
30–49	48	41	38	49
50+	45	36	30	47
College Grad.	52	33	38	48
Some College	55	36	38	50
High School Grad.	45	42	34	53
Less Than High School	42	42	33	42
White	43	38	35	48
Black	48	44	36	55
East	45	40	38	48
Midwest	43	43	39	45
South	52	39	31	53
West	54	31	36	48

percent of women, 55 percent of whites and 75 percent of blacks say religion can answer life's problems.

INTEREST IN RELIGION

While attitudes about the influence of religion fluctuated in the eighties, interest in religion grew throughout the decade. In 1987, four Americans in ten (41 percent) said they were more interested in religion today than they were five years ago, while 14 percent said they were less interested and 43 percent said their interest has remained about the same[11].

This represents a decline in the percentage citing an increased interest in religion and suggests that a stabilization of religious interest may be in progress.

Table 2.14
LONG-RANGE TREND IN INFLUENCE OF RELIGION

	Increasing	Losing		Increasing	Losing
1988	36%	48%	1974	31%	56%
1986	48	39	1970	14	75
1984	42	39	1968	18	67
1980	35	46	1965	33	45
1978	37	48	1962	45	31
1976	44	45	1957	69	14

The 43 percent of Americans who said they were neither more nor less interested in religion than they were five years ago marks a sharp increase over the 29 percent in 1985 and 25 percent in 1983 who made that statement.

In 1985, 51 percent of Americans said they were more interested in religion than they were five years before and 19 percent said they were less interested. In 1983, 57 percent of Americans said they were more interested in religion and 17 percent said they were less interested.

The largest shifts between 1985 and 1987 occurred among Catholics, blacks, Hispanics and those who live in the East.

The percentage of blacks saying they were more interested in religion than they were in the past dropped from 68 percent in 1985 to 53 percent in 1987. Sixteen percent in 1985 and 10 percent in 1987 said they were less interested; 15 percent in 1985 and 34 percent in 1987 said there was no change in their level of interest.

In 1985, 58 percent of Hispanics said they were more interested in religion than they were five years before. This figure dropped to 40 percent in 1987. The percentage saying they were less interested in religion rose from 19 to 29 percent. Twenty percent in 1985 and 28 percent in 1987 said they were neither more nor less interested.

Americans over 50 were more likely than younger Americans to report no change in their level of interest in religion over the past five years. In 1987, half (54 percent) said their level of interest in religion had stayed about the same; 37 percent said they were more interested and only 8 percent said they were less interested. In 1985, 47 percent of those over 50 said they were more interested in religion, 15 percent said they were less interested and 38 percent reported no change in interest level.

Among those 18–29, 43 percent said they were more interested in religion, down from 54 percent in 1985; 21 percent said they were less interested, down from 27 percent in 1985; 34 percent said they were neither more nor less interested, up from 18 percent in 1985.

Among those 30–49, 44 percent said they were more interested in religion, down from 53 percent in 1985; 15 percent said they were less interested, about the same as the 16 percent who said this in 1985, and 39 percent said their interest level was unchanged, up from 30 percent in 1985.

The gap between Catholics and Protestants has increased. In 1985, 50 percent of American Catholics said they were more interested in religion than they were five years before, but in 1987, that figure fell to 33 percent. The percentage of those saying they were less interested in religion remained steady—21 percent in 1985 and 19 percent in 1987. Twenty-nine percent in 1985 and 46 percent in 1987 said their interest in religion had not changed over the previous five years.

Among American Protestants, 56 percent reported higher interest in religion in 1985 and 48 percent did so in 1987. The percentage reporting less interest in religion dropped from 15 to 11 percent, while the percentage reporting stability rose from 28 to 40 percent.

There was a huge gap between Evangelicals and non-Evangelicals in response to the 1987 survey. Sixty-five percent of Evangelicals said they were more interested in religion than they were five years ago and only 4 percent said they were less interested; 30 percent reported no change in interest. The pattern for non-Evangelicals was almost identical to that for Catholics—33 percent reported more interested, 18 percent reported less and 48 percent reported no change.

In 1985, 77 percent of Evangelicals and 46 percent of non-Evangelicals reported more interest in religion; 6 percent and 21 percent, respectively, reported less interest and 17 and 32 percent, respectively, reported no change.

CONFIDENCE IN RELIGION

Americans continue to express more confidence in the church and organized religion than in other major social institutions, but that confidence has waned in recent years. It may well be that confidence in organized religion is becoming increasingly sensitive to transient social developments. For example, there was a big drop in confidence in organized religion in 1987 at about the same time that the media were providing in-depth coverage of the scandal surrounding Jim Bakker and the PTL Club[12].

Table 2.15 shows trends in Americans' confidence in organized religion compared to other institutions; figures are for those expressing a "great deal" or "quite a lot" of confidence in the institution.

Some groups are more likely than others to express high levels of confidence in organized religion. It's no surprise, for example, that Evangelical Christians have the highest level of confidence; in 1988, 73 percent of Evangelicals expressed a "great deal" or "quite a lot" of confidence in the church. Even so,

Table 2.15

CONFIDENCE IN ORGANIZED RELIGION

	1988	1987	1986	1985	1983	1979
Church	59%	61%	57%	66%	62%	65%
Military	58	61	63	61	53	54
U.S. Supreme Court	56	52	53	56	42	45
Banks	48	51	49	51	51	60
Public Schools	49	50	49	48	39	53
Newspapers	36	31	37	35	38	51
Television	27	28	27	29	25	38
Organized Labor	26	26	29	28	26	36

this represented a significant decline from the 82 percent of Evangelicals expressing high levels of confidence in the church only one year earlier. Again, this seems to reflect the impact, particularly on Evangelicals, of church scandals, in this case, the 1988 problems of Jimmy Swaggart. The decline in high levels of confidence among non-Evangelicals was only 3 points, from 55 percent in 1987 to 52 percent in 1988.

A cluster of groups express high levels of confidence: those over 50 (70 percent), Catholics and Baptists (68 percent each), blacks, southerners and those with less than a high school degree (67 percent each), mainline Protestants (66 percent) and women (64 percent).

The lowest level of confidence in organized religion is found among westerners (48 percent), non-Evangelicals (52 percent), Hispanics and those under 30 (53 percent each).

CONFIDENCE IN CLERGY ETHICS

Just as church scandals apparently hurt confidence in organized religion in 1988, they also apparently hurt confidence in the level of ethics among the clergy. In 1985, 67 percent of Americans rated the clergy "very high" or "high" on ethics, but in 1988, this figure dropped to 60 percent[13]. Sixty-two percent of Evangelicals expressed high levels of confidence in clergy ethics, only 2 points above the national average. We do not have 1985 figures for Evangelicals, but it seems likely that confidence decreased among this group. The greatest decreases in confidence came among Hispanics (22 percent), blacks (20 percent), those with less than a high school degree (15 percent), westerners (12 percent) and those under 30 (11 percent).

CONCLUSIONS

At the opening of this chapter, we said that trends focus on "movement." The movement we have described supports the notion of the growth of a "people's religion." First, the continued and growing pluralism in America reflects a movement away from a monolithic religious view; not only is America becoming a less white Anglo-Saxon Protestant nation, it is starting to become a somewhat less Judeo-Christian nation. The most interesting trends to watch in the nineties may not be changes in the size of particular denominations as much as movement in two different directions—toward smaller, more conservative, fundamentalist churches, and out of organized religion altogether. There's no monolithic view there, either.

A second "movement" is a clear increase in the level of interest in religion, despite the increase in unchurched Americans and those professing no religious affiliation.

A third "movement" we saw is, ironically, stability. Trends in religious membership, church attendance, the importance attached to religion and beliefs about the relevance of religion have held steady for more than a decade. In the context of this stability, however, is an interesting countertrend—volatility in attitudes toward the relevance of religion in society and in confidence in organized religion.

These trends, taken together, suggest that Americans are increasingly divorcing their personal religious behavior from their attitudes toward organized religion. They view their religion as a relationship between themselves and God; organized religion is an important part of that relationship. But if organized religion fails to live up to their expectations, Americans will hold it in less esteem—but they won't let that lowered esteem affect their own behavior.

CHAPTER

3

An American Faith

AMERICAN LIFE in general is famous for its diversity and the American people for their independent nature. The same is true when it comes to religion. American history has created a type of religious culture that is unique: it is marked by assigning great importance to religion, maintaining the focus of religion in the individual and respecting religious diversity.

It is easy to illustrate the importance of religion to Americans:

- 94 percent believe in God.
- 90 percent pray.
- 88 percent of Americans believe that God loves them, and only 3 percent believe this is not the case.
- More than three-quarters say their religious involvement has been a positive experience over their lifetimes, with 38 percent saying it has been "very positive."
- 78 percent say they have given "a lot" or "a fair amount" of thought to their relationship with God over the past two years.

But while Americans attach great importance to religion, they do not equate religion with church membership or attendance. For example, a 1985 survey on faith development asked respondents to agree or disagree with the statement, "You have to go to church or practice religious ritual if you expect God to do anything for you." On a scale of 1 to 5, with 1 representing strong disagreement and 5 representing strong agreement, six Americans in ten (59 percent) strongly

45

disagreed with that statement, while another 12 percent disagreed. Only 16 percent of Americans agreed (including 11 percent who agreed strongly).

These findings are consistent with a pattern of responses to similar questions going back thirty years. In 1957, 78 percent of Americans replied yes to the question, "Do you think a person can be a good Christian if he doesn't go to church?" In 1978, the identical percentage answered yes to the question, "Can a person be a good Christian or Jew without going to church or synagogue?"; 76 percent answered yes to the same question in 1988.

Americans also believe in the ideas that faith should not be static and that it is is strengthened by questioning. In a 1985 survey, 75 percent of respondents said faith is "strengthened by questioning early beliefs," while only 19 percent said it is weakened by such questioning. In the same survey, 65 percent of Americans said a person's faith "should change throughout life just as one's body and mind change"; 32 percent said faith should not change throughout life "because it is the foundation of change."

Another feature of American religious culture is respect for diversity. Religious diversity is an established fact in America—there are literally hundreds of denominations in the country, and, according to the U.S. Statistical Abstract, eighty-seven have more than 50,000 members. Ten denominations represent at least 2 percent of the population—Catholics, Baptists, Methodists, Lutherans, Presbyterians, Episcopalians, Jews, Mormons and members of the United Church of Christ and Disciples of Christ (Christian Church).

The 1985 faith development survey found that 62 percent of Americans agreed that "God reveals himself through a variety of religious beliefs and traditions," while only 22 percent disagreed. By a 5 to 3 margin, Americans also said that "People should just believe in God and not argue about religion." In a 1984 survey, 68 percent of Americans said greater understanding between liberal and conservative Christians was desirable, while only 8 percent said it was undesirable.

American religious pluralism has practical implications. For example, more than 90 percent of Catholics and 90 percent of Protestants say they would vote for a qualified presidential candidate from their own party who was Jewish. At the same time, 81 percent of American Protestants give Pope John Paul II a favorable rating, while 58 percent of Catholics give Billy Graham a favorable rating and 10 percent identify themselves as Born-Again Christians.

Religious tolerance works both ways in America. Three-quarters of unchurched Americans—those who say they are not church members and have not attended church in the past week—want school children to learn about the Bible and the major world religions[1].

The importance that Americans place on religion stands in stark contrast to the way their Western European allies view religion. Scandinavian countries have traditionally had low levels of church attendance and attachment to religion, but what is most surprising is the gap between the United States and Great Britain, West Germany and France[2].

Gallup International surveys in 1981 and subsequent years measured a number of religious beliefs and practices in the United States and Europe. Some of the findings have been reinforced by more recent data, but this type of deeply held belief is not subject to radical change in a short period of time. We have data for the United States and major European countries on six questions concerning religion: weekly church attendance, belief in a personal God, importance of God in daily life, belief in life after death, obtaining comfort from religion and whether the church in each country answers people's spiritual needs. By combining the percentages answering these questions affirmatively and dividing by 100 percent for each question, we obtain each country's "Religion Index"; Table 3.1 shows this index for each country.

Americans ranked at the top in rating the importance of God in their lives. On a scale of 1 to 10, with 10 the highest, Americans averaged a rating of 8.21, behind only tiny Malta (9.58). The U.S. figure was slightly higher than the rating in Ireland and Northern Ireland and higher than that in Italy (6.96) and Spain (6.39). Great Britain (5.72), West Germany (5.67) and France (4.72) ranked near the bottom.

The findings on the importance of God in daily life are directly related to findings about belief in God. On this issue, Americans are at the top, with more than 90 percent believing in either a personal God or God as "some sort of spirit or life force." Only Ireland ranked ahead of the 66 percent of Americans who believe in a personal God.

But there is a considerable drop in belief in God in other European countries. In Spain, 55 percent believe in a personal God, followed by Norway (40 percent), Belgium (39 percent), the Netherlands (34 percent), Great Britain (31 percent), Italy and France (26 percent each), Finland (25 percent), West Germany (24 percent), Denmark and Sweden (19 percent each).

Large percentages of Europeans believe in God as a spirit or life force, so that, for example, the percentage of all Swedes and Danes who believe in God rises to 58 percent. It is here that France stands out. While similar percentages

Table 3.1

RELIGION INDEX FOR U.S. AND EUROPEAN NATIONS

Republic of Ireland	73.	West Germany	37.
United States	67.	Norway	36.
Northern Ireland	65.	Netherlands	36.
Spain	51.	Great Britain	36.
Italy	43.	France	32.
Belgium	39.	Denmark	21.

of people in France, Italy and Finland believe in a personal God, Italians and Finns are far more likely to believe in God as a universal spirit. Only half of the French (52 percent) believe in any form of God, while 76 percent of Italians and 70 percent of Finns believe in God.

The French also rank low in saying they receive comfort and strength from religion. Only 37 percent say they do, while 57 percent say they do not. Only 46 percent of the English and 44 percent of West Germans say they receive comfort and strength from their religion, compared to 79 percent of Americans.

Americans are far more satisfied than Western Europeans with their religious leaders: 73 percent of Americans say the church in their country answers their spiritual needs. The Irish again rank high, with 64 percent of those in the Republic and 60 percent of those in the North rating their churches positively. Only 42 percent of those in Great Britain, 43 percent in Italy, 45 percent in Spain, 47 percent in West Germany and 48 percent in France say their church answers their spiritual needs.

About 40 percent of Americans attend church or synagogue each week. This ranks behind church attendance in Ireland (72 percent) and Northern Ireland (52 percent), is on a par with Spain (41 percent) and Italy (36 percent) and ranks well ahead of the Scandinavian countries. Church attendance in the United States is at least double that in West Germany (21 percent), Great Britain (14 percent) and France (12 percent).

The gap between the United States and Western Europe continues to grow. For example, a 1986 survey found that the percentage of Britons believing in God had dropped 5 points since 1981.

AMERICANS EXPERIENCE "PASSAGES" IN FAITH LIFE

For centuries it was assumed that faith was something given, constant, unchanging. Now, however, it is clear that people go through "passages" in their spiritual lives just as they do in other dimensions of their lives[3]. A Gallup study conducted for the Religious Education Association of the United States and Canada—"Faith Development and Your Ministry"—found that most Americans (71 percent) have experienced a change in their faith life, including 5 percent who say they have experienced more than one such change. Specific life experiences such as childbirth, divorce or the death of a loved one often, but not always, trigger a change in faith.

In order to understand these changes, it is necessary to know how Americans define faith. For half of all Americans (51 percent), faith means "a relationship with God." A fifth of Americans (20 percent) define faith as "finding meaning in life" and another fifth (19 percent) define it as "a set of beliefs." Only 4 percent of Americans equate faith with membership in a church or synagogue and only 1 percent say faith is not meaningful to them.

Americans are quite concerned about faith—70 percent say it is very important to them, while 25 percent say it is fairly important. Americans say they give "a lot" of thought to living a worthwhile life (67 percent), their relationship to God (59 percent), the basic meaning and value of their life (58 percent) and developing their faith (47 percent).

Adult Americans report an increase in faith during their lifetimes: 29 percent say they have "a great deal" of faith today, while only 17 percent say they had "a great deal" of faith at age 16. On a scale of 1 to 5, with 5 representing a great deal of faith, Americans on average score themselves 3.2 today, compared to 2.7 at age 16.

Most Americans who experience a change in faith have a positive experience—82 percent say that as a result of change, their faith is stronger. Only 15 percent say that as a result of change, their faith is weaker.

Americans believe that one's faith should change over his or her lifetime by a 2-to-1 margin. Some four in five Americans also believe that faith is strengthened rather than weakened by questioning their early religious beliefs.

Not all faith changes are substantial, however. Those who have experienced a change in faith are about equally divided between those who say that as a result of change their faith is "totally different" (45 percent) and those who say that as a result of change their faith is "a little different." Still, by multiplying the percentage of Americans who have experienced a change in faith by the percentage who say that change made their faith "totally different," we find that about one American in three—a dramatic proportion—has experienced a major change in faith life.

Changes in faith are usually associated with dramatic events such as a born-again experience. But those who have experienced a change in their faith are again equally divided, this time between those who say they arrived at a change through "a lot of thought and discussion" (46 percent) and those who say their faith changed because of "a strong emotional experience" (49 percent). Similarly, 59 percent say a change in faith came during a stable time of their life, while 40 percent said it came during a turbulent time.

Some interesting patterns emerge concerning the age at which Americans report having undergone a change in faith. The average age reported was 28. On the surface, it would appear that a change in faith is likely to occur under the age of 30. A majority of those under 30 report a significant change in their lives within the past five years and more than 40 percent of those in their 30s report a change before their thirtieth birthday.

But the ability to experience a change in faith at a certain age depends upon having reached that age. While everyone interviewed had passed his or her eighteenth birthday, only 36 percent had passed his or her forty-ninth birthday. When we control for the age of survey respondents, it becomes clear that we cannot assume that change in faith is most likely to occur before age 30. For example, of those over 50, half reported a change in faith after the age of 40. There is no reason to believe, then, that the under-30 respondent who reported a change of faith at 18 is not likely to experience another change at 40.

The study found that significant life events are associated with changes in faith. Positive experiences such as having a baby or a born-again experience seem to reinforce faith. Negative experiences such as divorce, considering an abortion or deciding to leave a church are associated with decreasing levels of faith.

GENDER, MARRIAGE AND RELIGION

Over the past decade, there has been a great deal of discussion of the "gender gap" in politics—a pattern in which a majority of women favor one candidate or party and a majority of men favor the other. The political "gender gap" does not appear in every election. But there is one "gender gap" in America that has a long history—the gap between men and women in matters related to religious belief and practice. Simply put, women continue to place a higher value on religious involvement and to be more active in religious activities than do men[4].

A number of surveys show that women give more importance to religion than do men. For example, while 45 percent of men say religion is "very important" to them, the figure jumps to 62 percent for women. Similarly, 41 percent of men and 52 percent of women say it is "very important" for Americans to become more interested in religion. This pattern repeats itself on other questions:

- 51 percent of men and 63 percent of women say that religion is not outdated and can answer all or most of today's problems.
- 58 percent of men and 69 percent of women say they have a "great deal" or "quite a lot" of confidence in the church as an institution.
- 51 percent of men and 69 percent of women say prayer is "very important" to them.
- 33 percent of men and 45 percent of women say reading the Bible is "very important."
- 30 percent of men and 46 percent of women say attending church is "very important."
- 38 percent of men and 55 percent of women say they receive a "great deal" of comfort and support from their religious beliefs.
- 47 percent of men said in 1985 that they were more interested in religion than they were five years before, while 20 percent said they were less interested. Among women, 54 percent said they were more interested and 17 percent said they were less interested.
- In a 1985 survey, 47 percent of men said they were more reliant on God than they were five years before and 15 percent said they were less reliant. Among women, 59 percent said they were more reliant on God and only 11 percent said they were less reliant.

Differences between men and women on the degree of importance placed on religion are reflected in differences in religious practice. One clear difference comes in the area of religious affiliation. Among the total U.S. adult population,

9 percent cite no religious affiliation. But when we look at responses by gender, we see that only 7 percent of women claim no religious affiliation, the figure rises to 12 percent among men. While the number of those citing no affiliation has increased in the past decade, the "gender gap" has held up consistently over the years.

Women are also more likely than men to be church members. For example, 63 percent of men and 75 percent of women said they belonged to a church or synagogue. These differences are also reflected in church attendance: 45 percent of women, but only 34 percent of men, said they had attended church in the past seven days.

The "religious gender gap" persists in other religious practices as well. Women read the Bible and pray more often than do men. For example, a 1984 survey found that 34 percent of men and 50 percent of women said they had prayed within the past twenty-four hours. Ten percent of men and 17 percent of women said they had read the Bible during the same time period.

There is a considerable difference between men and women when it comes to interpreting the Bible: 27 percent of men and 34 percent of women believe the Bible is the literal word of God; 21 percent of men and only 13 percent of women believe the Bible was not even inspired by God.

While survey results make an irrefutable case that a "religious gender gap" exists, they do not explain why. The existence of such a gap does not necessarily mean that American men are not religious, because in many respects, they are. But the "religious gender gap" is reflected in a daily reality—religious leaders across virtually all denominations point to women as the backbone of the local congregation.

Marital status has a dramatic influence on religious attitudes and behavior[5]. In general, interest and involvement in religion increase with marriage. When marriage ends in widowhood, ties to religion intensify. When marriage ends in separation or divorce, however, religious involvement decreases, often sharply. Differences are less clear on questions of religious belief. Here, belief increases with marriage, but generally does not change substantially after widowhood, separation or divorce.

These findings are consistent with the anecdotal experience of pastors and churchgoers. Single people, usually young, are less interested in religion because they are busy establishing their own lives and often experiment with breaking away, at least temporarily, from the religious tradition within which they were raised.

When people marry, particularly when they have children, they frequently turn to the church as a family resource and because of a desire for religious education for their children. When a spouse dies, the survivor often turns to his or her church or synagogue for solace and companionship. Also, widows and widowers are generally older than the rest of the population, and religious activity increases with age. But those who are separated or divorced often feel alienated from their church, complaining that the churches focus on the needs of intact families and often reject the divorced.

This pattern is reflected clearly in church membership. Sixty percent of single adults say they belong to a church or synagogue. This figure increases to 71 percent among married adults. Membership increases for the widowed: 78 percent are church members. But membership for the divorced and separated drops to 54 percent, even lower than the figure for singles.

A similar pattern is found in church attendance. Twenty-eight percent of single adults say they attended church or synagogue in the past seven days. This figure jumps to 42 percent for married adults, but drops back to 27 percent for the separated and divorced. In contrast, 49 percent of the widowed say they went to church in the past seven days.

Similarly, 15 percent of single adults say they attend church every week. Twice as many married adults—29 percent—say they attend weekly. Among the widowed, 43 percent say they attend church weekly. But among the separated and divorced, only 15 percent—the same as the figure for singles—say they attend church every week. Fifty-six percent of singles, 42 percent of those who are married, 53 percent of the separated and divorced and 32 percent of the widowed say they attend church just a few times a year or never attend.

The same pattern—more interest by married or widowed adults, less interest by singles and the separated and divorced—shows up on the question of the importance of religion. Forty-one percent of singles say that religion is "very important" in their lives. This figure increases to 57 percent for married adults, but slides back down to 51 percent for the separated and divorced. In contrast, 72 percent of the widowed say religion is "very important" in their lives.

On several key questions concerning religious belief, married adults show higher levels of belief than do singles, but those whose marriages have ended, regardless of how, often show increased levels of faith. This pattern reinforces the belief that separated and divorced persons feel alienated from their church community.

- 64 percent of singles, 79 percent of married adults, 73 percent of the separated and divorced and 89 percent of the widowed say that "prayer is an important part of my daily life."
- 72 percent of singles, 83 percent of the married, 84 percent of the separated and divorced and 89 percent of the widowed believe that "we all will be called before God at the Judgment Day to answer for our sins."
- 74 percent of singles, 83 percent of the married, 84 percent of the separated and divorced and 89 percent of the widowed believe that "even today, miracles are performed by the power of God."
- 71 percent of singles, 81 percent of the married, 86 percent of the separated and divorced and 87 percent of the widowed say, "I am sometimes very conscious of the presence of God."
- 81 percent of singles, 89 percent of the married, 92 percent of the separated and divorced and 95 percent of the widowed say, "I never doubt the existence of God."

Marital status is also related to religious belief and practice in another important way. One in five (18 percent) of Americans who are married have a spouse with a different religious affiliation than their own. Those in religiously mixed marriages are less active in church life and less orthodox in their beliefs than those in same-faith marriages[6].

Of those in religiously mixed marriages, 36 percent are Protestant, 26 percent are Catholic, 3 percent are Jewish, 13 percent belong to other denominations and 22 percent have no religious affiliation.

Those most likely to be in mixed marriages are those who belong to "other" religions, small denominations and religious groups; three in four (75 percent) in this group are married to persons from a different religious background. One surprising finding is that half of the married people with no religious affiliation (47 percent) have a spouse who also claims no affiliation.

Sixty-two percent of all Americans are currently married. Table 3.2 shows the percentage of various denominations in same-faith and in mixed marriages.

Those in religiously mixed marriages view religion as less important than those in same-faith marriages; 61 percent of those in same-faith marriages say religion is "very important" in their lives, but only 42 percent of those in mixed marriages make that claim. This gap opened up in adulthood, because the difference in attitudes between the two groups when they were growing up was small—50 percent of those in same-faith marriages and 45 percent of those

Table 3.2

DENOMINATIONS IN MIXED MARRIAGES

	Same-Faith	Mixed
Catholic	82%	18%
Protestant	89	11
Baptist	94	6
Methodist	90	10
Lutheran	79	21
Presbyterian	86	14
Episcopalian	73	27
United Church of Christ	96	4
Christian Church (Disciples of Christ)	93	7
Other Protestant	97	13
Unspecified Protestant	82	18
Jewish	78	22
Mormon	93	7

in mixed marriages say religion was "very important" when they were growing up.

This pattern is reflected in church membership. While 75 percent of those in same-faith marriages are church members, only 47 percent of those in mixed marriages are church members. While 37 percent of those in same-faith marriages say there was a period in their lives of two years or more when they were not active in church, 54 percent of those in mixed marriages say they were inactive for two years or more.

Not surprisingly, those in mixed marriages are less likely to believe that involvement with organized religion is necessary: 73 percent of those in same-faith marriages and 84 percent of those in mixed marriages believe that a person can be a good Christian or Jew without going to church or synagogue. Similarly, 46 percent of those in same-faith marriages and 54 percent of those in mixed marriages believe that people should arrive at their religious beliefs independent of any church or synagogue.

At the same time, 39 percent of those in same-faith marriages and 51 percent of those in mixed marriages agree with the statement that "I don't have to belong to an organized religion because I lead a good life."

Those in mixed marriages are also less likely to want or provide religious training for their children: 89 percent of those in same-faith marriages and 81 percent of those in mixed marriages say they want religious training for their children; 75 percent of those in same-faith marriages and 62 percent of those in mixed marriages who currently have children are now providing religious training. Table 3.3 shows other differences in views between those in same-faith and mixed marriages.

A RELIGIOUS PERSON

The "gender gap" increases dramatically with age when Americans are asked how well the description "a religious person" applies to them. There is no significant difference in the responses of men and women under 30, but the differences grow with age—women over 50 are substantially more likely than men over 50 to say that "a religious person" describes them[7].

A Gallup survey conducted for the Times Mirror Corporation asked Americans how well the phrase "a religious person" described them, with 10 being a "perfect" description, and 1 being "totally wrong." One American in five said the description applied perfectly. Table 3.4 shows these responses.

For convenience's sake, we have grouped the responses into three main categories: low (1–3), moderate (4–7) and high (8–10). Using this grouping, 11 percent of Americans rank themselves low, 39 percent moderate and 49 percent high in describing themselves as "a religious person."

Among those under 30, 36 percent of men and 39 percent of women rank themselves high, a 3-point gender gap. But among those 30–49, this gap increases to 12 points, with 40 percent of men and 52 percent of women ranking themselves high. The gap increases to 22 points among those over 50—48

Table 3.3
RELIGIOUS ATTITUDES IN MIXED MARRIAGES

	Same-Faith	Mixed
Churches Have a Clear Sense of the Spiritual	52%	39%
The Morality Taught by the Churches Is Too Restrictive	29	39
Churches Are Too Concerned With Organizational Issues	59	68
Churches Are Warm and Accepting	66	58
Believe Jesus Is God or Son of God	88	78
Made a Commitment to Jesus Christ	73	62
Believe Bible Is the Literal Word of God	33	19
Believe in Life After Death	76	64
Pray to God	91	85

percent of men and 70 percent of women rank high in describing themselves as "a religious person."

While interest in religion generally increases with age, the responses show it increases more sharply among women. The difference in a high ranking between men under 30 and over 50 is only 12 percentage points (from 36 to 48 percent), while the difference for women is 31 percentage points (from 39 to 70 percent).

Though there are significant differences in responses among other demographic groups, none is as surprising as the finding on differences by age and gender.

Table 3.4
SELF-DESCRIPTION AS "A RELIGIOUS PERSON"

1 (Totally Wrong)	4%	6	9%
2	3	7	13
3	4	8	20
4	4	9	11
5	13	10 (Perfect)	18

- 49 percent of whites, 54 percent of blacks and 46 percent of Hispanics score high.
- Differences by educational level are small: 49 percent of college graduates, 50 percent of those with some college, 46 percent of high school graduates and 52 percent of those who did not graduate from high school score high.
- Overall religious interest increases directly with age: 36 percent of those 18–24, 39 percent of those 25–29, 43 percent of those 30–39, 50 percent of those 40–49, 57 percent of those 50–59 and 62 percent of those over 60 score high.
- There is no significant difference between Catholics (50 percent) and Protestants (52 percent) in scoring high, but there are sharp differences between Evangelical and non-Evangelical Protestants: 75 percent of white and black Evangelicals score high, while only 36 percent of white non-Evangelicals and 38 percent of black non-Evangelicals do so.
- Only 27 percent of Jews ranked themselves high in describing themselves as "a religious person."

Table 3.5 shows the percentage of various groups saying "a religious person" is a "perfect" description.

GOD, JUDGMENT AND MIRACLES

Nine in ten Americans say they have never doubted the existence of God and eight in ten believe they will face God at Judgment Day. Eight in ten also believe that God works miracles today and say that they are "sometimes very conscious of the presence of God"[8].

In general, those most likely to agree with these statements were women, nonwhites, those over 50, those with less education, Catholics and Evangelicals. Those most likely to disagree were men, those with at least some college education and Jews.

Overall, 88 percent of Americans said they never doubted the existence of God. Eighty-six percent of men and 90 percent of women made that statement, as did 87 percent of whites, 93 percent of nonwhites and 91 percent of Hispanics. The percentage of those saying they never doubted God's existence rose with age—84 percent of those 18–24, 88 percent of those 25–29, 84 percent of those 30–39, 90 percent of those 40–49 and those 50–59 and 93 percent of those over 60.

There were significant differences in response according to education—94 percent of those with less than a high school education, 90 percent of high school graduates, 86 percent of those with some college and 78 percent of college graduates said they never doubted God's existence.

In terms of religious affiliation, 92 percent of Protestants, 90 percent of Catholics and 72 percent of Jews said they never doubted God's existence. Among Protestants, 96 percent of Evangelicals and 88 percent of non-Evangelicals said they never doubted God's existence. Among Evangelical Protestants, this

Table 3.5

PERCENTAGE CALLING "A RELIGIOUS PERSON" A "PERFECT DESCRIPTION"

Men	14%	18–24	9%
Women	22	25–29	12
Whites	17	30–39	14
Blacks	26	40–49	19
Hispanics	13	50–59	23
College Grad.	17	60+	27
Some College	18	Catholic	15
High School Grad.	15	Jewish	13
Less Than High School	23	All Protestant	21
18–29	10	White Protestant	
Men	10	Evangelical	35
Women	11	Non-Evangelical	8
30–49	16	Black Protestant	
Men	13	Evangelical	44
Women	19	Non-Evangelical	13
50+	25		
Men	17		
Women	32		

included 97 percent of whites and 95 percent of blacks. Among non-Evangelicals, this included 87 percent of whites and 93 percent of blacks.

Eighty-one percent of those surveyed agreed that "we will all be called before God at the Judgment Day to answer for our sins." The sharpest differences in response came along denominational lines: 87 percent of Protestants and 85 percent of Catholics, but only 37 percent of Jews said they believed in Judgment Day.

Among Protestants, 96 percent of Evangelicals and 80 percent of non-Evangelicals said they believed in Judgment Day. Black and white Evangelicals (96 percent) held identical views, with 96 percent of each believing in Judgment Day. But among non-Evangelical Protestants, 90 percent of blacks and 79 percent of whites believed in Judgment Day.

Seventy-nine percent of men and 83 percent of women believed in Judgment Day, as did 80 percent of whites, 90 percent of nonwhites and 84 percent of

Hispanics. The same age and education patterns found in response to the question about doubting God's existence held up in regard to the question of Judgment Day: 79 percent of those 18–29, 76 percent of those 30–39, 82 percent of those 40–49 and 86 percent of those over 50 answered positively.

Belief in Judgment Day decreases with education. Ninety-one percent of those who had not graduated from high school, 86 percent of high school graduates, 74 percent of those with some college and 66 percent of college graduates said they would face God on Judgment Day.

Eighty-two percent of those surveyed agreed that "even today, miracles are performed by the power of God." Table 3.6 shows responses by groups.

Seventy-nine percent of those surveyed said they were sometimes very conscious of God's presence. Table 3.7 shows responses by groups.

Table 3.6
PERCENTAGE SAYING "EVEN TODAY MIRACLES ARE PERFORMED BY GOD"

Men	77%	Protestant	86%
Women	86	Evangelical	96
		White	96
White	80	Black	97
Nonwhite	89	Non-Evan.	79
		White	78
Hispanic	83	Black	84
18–24	76	Catholic	84
25–29	81	Jewish	46
30–39	77		
40–49	82		
50–59	87		
60 +	86		

LIFE AFTER DEATH

Few facts dispute the notion of widespread secularization among Americans as much as the fact that seven Americans in ten believe in life after death— the identical proportion that has held that view for almost half a century. Overall, 71 percent believe in life after death, while 16 percent do not[9].

Belief in life after death is high even among the least religiously active groups. For example, while 81 percent of religiously active Americans hold that belief, so do 58 percent of the unchurched (defined as those who have not

Table 3.7

PERCENTAGE "SOMETIMES VERY CONSCIOUS OF GOD'S PRESENCE"

Men	76%	Protestant	83%
Women	83	Evangelical	95
		White	95
White	78	Black	93
Nonwhite	86	Non-Evan.	74
		White	72
Hispanic	83	Black	82
18–24	71	Catholic	81
25–29	77	Jewish	61
30–39	76		
40–49	81		
50–59	86		
60 +	84		

attended church in the previous six months except for special holidays and occasions like baptisms, weddings and funerals).

While many religious beliefs decline as educational level rises, this is not the case when it comes to belief in life after death: 67 percent of those with less than a high school degree, 73 percent of high school graduates, 75 percent of those with some college and 69 percent of college graduates hold this very traditional belief.

Protestants believe in life after death by a 78 to 12 percent margin, Catholics by 71 to 15 percent. Among all other Americans, however, 50 percent believe in life after death and 32 percent do not.

There are other demographic differences:

- 66 percent of men and 76 percent of women believe in life after death.
- 68 percent of those under 30, 73 percent of those 30–49 and 72 percent of those over 50 believe in life after death.
- Blacks, who normally hold the most traditional beliefs, are the least likely to believe in life after death—65 percent hold this view, compared to 67 percent of Hispanics and 72 percent of whites.
- Southerners (77 percent) are most likely to believe in life after death, followed by midwesterners (71 percent), westerners (69 percent) and easterners (65 percent).
- 74 percent of those who are married, 70 percent of those who have been married and 64 percent of singles believe in life after death.

AMERICANS AND THE BIBLE

Americans revere the Bible—but, by and large, they don't read it. And because they don't read it, they have become a nation of biblical illiterates[10]. Virtually every home in America has at least one Bible. Four Americans in five believe the Bible is the literal or inspired word of God, and many of those who do not, still regard it as the basis for moral values and the rule of law.

In addition, four in ten Americans say they would turn to the Bible first to test their own religious beliefs, while a solid one-third believe that "holding the Bible to be God's truth is absolutely essential for someone to truly know God."

But despite the large percentage of Americans who believe the Bible is the word of God, only one-third of Americans read it at least once a week—15 percent read it daily and only another 18 percent read it one or more times a week. Another 12 percent read the Bible less than weekly, but at least once a month. More than half of all Americans read the Bible less than once a month, including 24 percent who say they never read it and 6 percent who can't recall the last time they read the Bible.

This lack of Bible-reading explains why Americans know so little about the Bible that is the basis of the faith of most of them. For example, eight in ten Americans say they are Christians, but only four in ten know that Jesus, according to the Bible, delivered the Sermon on the Mount.

Fewer than half of all adults can name Matthew, Mark, Luke and John as the four Gospels of the New Testament, while many do not know that Jesus had twelve disciples or that he was born in Bethlehem. In addition, a large majority of Americans believe that the Ten Commandments are still valid rules for living today, but they have a tough time recalling exactly what those rules are.

Particularly shocking is the lack of knowledge of the Bible among college graduates. Only four in ten, for example, know that Jesus delivered the Sermon on the Mount. Sociologist Miriam Murphy notes that there are many people in America today with "a Ph.D. in aerodynamics, but only a third-grade knowledge of religion."

The cycle of biblical illiteracy seems likely to continue—today's teenagers know even less about the Bible than do adults. The celebration of Easter, which Christians believe marks the resurrection of Christ, is central to the faith, yet three in ten teenagers—and 20 percent of those teenagers who attend religious services regularly—do not know why Easter is celebrated.

The decline in Bible-reading is due to many factors: the feeling that the Bible is inaccessible; the belief that it has little to say to today's world; a decline in reading in general and less emphasis on religious training.

Despite the publicity given to fundamentalist ministers and televangelists in recent years, the proportion of Americans who are fundamentalists—that is, who believe that every word in the Bible is literally true—continues to decline. Only 31 percent of Americans believe the Bible is "the actual word of God and is to be taken literally, word for word," down from 34 percent in 1985.

There has also been an increase in the proportion of Americans who do not believe that the Bible was inspired by God, from 11 percent in 1985 to 17 percent in 1988.

Belief that the Bible is literally true is greatest among blacks, Hispanics, Protestants, southerners, the separated, divorced and widowed, those over 50 and those with less than a high school education. Education is the major variable, with belief in the literal truth of the Bible decreasing according to educational background. Literal belief in the Bible is 45 percent among those with less than a high school degree, 34 percent among high school graduates, 26 percent among those with some college and 11 percent among college graduates. One in three college graduates do not believe the Bible was inspired by God.

The biggest decline in literal belief in the Bible occurred in the late 1960s and early 1970s. The proportion of Americans who believe the Bible is literally true fell by half in a quarter of a century. In 1963, 65 percent of Americans believed the Bible was literally true. This figure fell to 38 percent by 1978. The proportion of fundamentalists hovered between 37 and 39 percent between 1978 and 1984, but has begun to inch down again since then.

While literal belief in the Bible is decreasing, the vast majority of Americans respect the Bible's religious authority. In addition to those who believe the Bible is literally true, 25 percent believe that "the Bible is the inspired word of God. It contains no errors, but some verses are to be taken symbolically rather than literally." Another 22 percent agree that "the Bible is the inspired word of God, but it may contain historical and scientific errors." The total of 47 percent who believe the Bible is inspired by God is about the same as the 49 percent who said it was inspired in 1985.

Ten percent of Americans believe that "the Bible is an ancient book of fables, legends, history and moral precepts." Finally, 7 percent believe "the Bible was not inspired by God, but it represents humankind's best understanding of God's nature." This last option was not offered in past surveys.

Table 3.8 shows some beliefs about the Bible according to educational level. In other demographic breakdowns:

- 44 percent of blacks, 40 percent of Hispanics and 29 percent of whites believe the Bible is literally true.
- 38 percent of those in the South, compared to 26 percent in the West and 28 percent each in the East and Midwest, believe the Bible is literally true.
- 24 percent of those in the West, 21 percent in the East, 16 percent in the Midwest and 11 percent in the South do not believe the Bible is inspired by God.
- 37 percent of Protestants and 26 percent of Catholics believe the Bible is literally true; 10 and 15 percent, respectively, believe it is not inspired by God.

Table 3.8

VIEWS ON AUTHORITY OF BIBLE, BY EDUCATION

	Less Than H.S.	H.S. Grad.	Some College	College Grad.
Inspired, No Errors	23%	24%	28%	24%
Inspired, Errors	13	23	25	28
Best Understanding of God	5	6	5	14
Book of Fables, etc.	6	7	10	20

The boom in small-group Bible study that has marked the 1980s appears to have slowed or even reversed. In 1978, 19 percent of Americans said they were involved in Bible study groups. In 1983, this grew to 26 percent of all Americans, a figure that held steady through most of the rest of the decade. But a 1988 study shows that only 22 percent of Americans say they have participated in either a Bible study or prayer group in the past two years.

It is impossible to make an exact comparison because of differences in question wording. For example, it is impossible to know how many of the 22 percent who say they took part in Bible study or prayer groups took part in each, and how many took part in both. In 1985, 26 percent of Americans said they took part in Bible study and 18 percent said they took part in prayer groups; again, it is impossible to tell how many took part in both. The figures clearly suggest a decline, however.

Half of those who said they took part in Bible study or prayer groups (49 percent) said they participate regularly. Another 45 percent said they participate occasionally; only 1 percent said they took part only once.

There was no significant difference in involvement with Bible and prayer groups by age, but other demographic differences emerged. Protestants (27 percent) were twice as likely as Catholics (14 percent) to take part in these groups; this appears to be due largely to the greater emphasis that Protestants place on Bible study.

The pattern for education is particularly interesting. While frequency of Bible-reading and belief in the literal or inspired nature of the Bible decreases with education, involvement in Bible and prayer groups tends to increase with education: 19 percent of those with less than a high school degree, 21 percent of high school graduates, 29 percent of those with some college and 22 percent of college graduates say they took part in Bible study or prayer groups.

Those who live in the East (17 percent) are the least likely to take part in Bible study and prayer groups, while those in the South and West (25 percent each) are most likely to take part; 21 percent of midwesterners have been involved in these groups in the past two years.

Hispanics (29 percent) are more likely than whites (22 percent) or blacks (20 percent) to take part. Those who are married (23 percent) or have been married (24 percent) are more likely than singles (18 percent) to be involved with prayer and Bible study groups.

Those most likely to take part in prayer and Bible study groups regularly are college graduates (57 percent); women and midwesterners (55 percent each); westerners (53 percent); those who are married and those with some college (52 percent each); Protestants, those over 30 and those who have been married (51 percent each).

Least likely to take part regularly are singles (36 percent), blacks (41 percent) and easterners (42 percent).

How helpful is National Bible Week in raising awareness of the Bible? In 1983, a special Gallup survey conducted for the Layman's National Bible Committee found that 29 percent of Americans had heard about Bible Week, and half of those said the observance had increased their interest in the Bible. When compared with figures for similar events, these findings are not unimpressive.

WHAT AMERICANS BELIEVE ABOUT JESUS

Christmas has become a secular as well as a religious holiday for many Americans, but it is, along with Easter, one of the two most important religious holidays of the year for Christians because it marks the birth of Jesus Christ, whom they believe to be the Son of God[11]. Both personal commitment to Jesus and belief that he is God or the Son of God increased during the eighties.

In 1978, 78 percent of Americans said Jesus was God or the Son of God; this increased to 84 percent in 1988. Thirteen percent in 1978 and 9 percent in 1988 said Jesus was another religious leader, like Muhammad or Buddha. One percent in each survey believe Jesus never lived and 2 percent in each survey had other beliefs. In 1978, 60 percent of Americans said they had made a personal commitment to Jesus; this rose to 66 percent in 1988. These increases are highly significant because basic beliefs of this kind are generally very slow to change.

The increased commitment and belief came across the board, with those under 30 registering the greatest increase in belief that Jesus is God or the Son of God; in 1978, 75 percent held this view, while in 1988, 84 percent did so. The increase among those 30–49 was from 79 to 83 percent; among those over 50, it was from 81 to 85 percent.

Among men, the percentage believing Jesus is God or the Son of God rose from 75 to 79 percent; among women, it rose from 82 to 88 percent. This belief increased from 84 to 92 percent among Protestants and from 85 to 91 percent among Catholics.

The sharpest differences in belief in 1988 were related to educational background. Ninety percent of those with a high school degree or less and 83 percent of those with some college believed Jesus is God or the Son of God. But only 66 percent of college graduates held that view; one in four (23 percent) viewed Jesus as another religious leader, like Muhammad or Buddha.

Blacks (94 percent) and Hispanics (89 percent) were more likely than whites (83 percent) to view Jesus as God or the Son of God. Marital status was also a factor; 86 percent of those who are not married and 84 percent of those who have been married believe Jesus is God or the Son of God, but this figure drops to 78 percent for singles.

The increase in those expressing a personal commitment to Jesus also came across the board. Table 3.9 shows changes for key groups from 1978 to 1988.

The difference in views between Protestants and Catholics is partly explained by the fact that Protestants are more used to talking in terms of a "personal relationship" with Jesus; for example, almost half of all Protestants describe themselves as Born-Again Christians. This also helps explain why Hispanics, who are predominantly Catholic, are somewhat less likely than blacks and whites to say they have made a commitment to Christ; 67 percent of whites, 67 percent of blacks and 58 percent of Hispanics make this claim.

Education is also a factor here, but not to the same extent as on beliefs about Jesus: 66 percent of those with less than a high school degree, 69 percent of high school graduates, 71 percent of those with some college and 57 percent of college graduates say they have made a commitment to Christ.

Marital status is again an important factor: 71 percent of those who are married and 70 percent of those who have been married, but only 50 percent of singles, have made a commitment to Christ.

For many American Christians, Christ is not just the object of theological belief—they feel that they have a personal relationship with Jesus, they try to follow his example, they feel he has an impact on their day-to-day lives. "Jesus Christ in the Lives of Americans Today," a 1983 survey conducted for the

Table 3.9
PERCENTAGE EXPRESSING COMMITMENT TO CHRIST

	1978	1988		1978	1988
Men	53%	60%	50+	68%	73%
Women	67	72	Protestant	70	77
18–29	51	57	Catholic	61	67
30–49	59	66			

Robert H. Schuller Ministries, offers a number of insights into Americans' beliefs about Jesus.

In response to one question, 70 percent said that Jesus was God. Asked to pick from four descriptions of Jesus' divinity, 42 percent said "Jesus was divine in the sense that he was in fact God living among men." Some 27 percent said "Jesus was divine in the sense that while he was only a man, he was uniquely called by God to reveal God's purpose to the world." Another 9 percent said "Jesus was divine in the sense that he embodied the best that is in all men," while 6 percent said "Jesus was a great man and teacher, but I could not call him divine."

Yet 58 percent said the belief that Jesus was "fully God and fully human" is "very important" and 23 percent said it was "fairly important" to them.

Six in ten Americans (61 percent) said that as a moral and ethical teacher, Jesus had had a great impact on their lives. Another 26 percent said Jesus had had some influence as a teacher, and only 7 percent said he had had very little or no impact.

A similar proportion of Americans—six in ten—were also able to cite ways in which they said Jesus had entered their lives. No one way was cited by more than 10 percent, although several separate responses reflected similar themes, crediting Jesus with providing moral leadership and providing personal blessings:

- 10 percent said Jesus "helped or guided me."
- 9 percent said he "set an example for me to follow."
- 8 percent said he "gave me health."
- 8 percent said he "helped me have compassion."
- 7 percent said he "helped my outlook and thinking."
- 6 percent said he "helped me have peace" or "calmed me."
- 6 percent said "his teachings have helped me to be a better person."
- 5 percent said Jesus "blessed me with a good life/family."

Three-quarters of Americans said they make at least some effort to follow Jesus' example: 12 percent said they make the "greatest possible" effort; 27 percent said they make a "considerable" effort and 34 percent said they make "some" effort. Only 17 percent said they make no or hardly any effort to follow Jesus' example.

Americans see a variety of ways in which people can follow Jesus' example. About half (48 percent) cite following the Ten Commandments, followed closely by 44 percent who believe that to follow Jesus' example means to be forgiving. About one-third of Americans (34 percent) said "putting others' needs above your own" was a way to follow Jesus, while 31 percent cited "living in such a way as to draw others to Jesus." Other activities cited included person-to-person charitable activities (23 percent), consoling those sick or in sorrow (23 percent), telling people about Jesus (22 percent), being active in a local church (20 percent), reading the Bible daily (19 percent) and having a regular prayer time (19 percent).

Only 10 percent of Americans, however, believe they themselves come very close to following Jesus' example. About half (47 percent) said they come fairly close, while 26 percent said they don't come very close and 8 percent say they don't come close at all.

About three-quarters of Americans said they have at some time or other sensed Jesus' presence in their lives. More than 40 percent said they had sensed his presence often in nature, in church services or in times of personal crisis.

Finally, 51 percent of Americans said that at some time in their lives they had encouraged others to believe in Jesus or accept him as their savior.

Christ promised to return to Earth someday, and 62 percent of Americans have no doubts that this will happen; 16 percent have some doubts and 10 percent have serious doubts. There are sharp differences among denominations and religious groups on this issue:

- 93 percent of Evangelicals have no doubts about Christ's return, 2 percent have some doubts and 3 percent have serious doubts.
- 74 percent of Protestants have no doubts, 11 percent have some doubts and 6 percent have serious doubts.
- 80 percent of Baptists have no doubts, 8 percent have some doubts and 3 percent have serious doubts.
- 66 percent of mainline Protestants (Methodists, Lutherans, Presbyterians and Episcopalians) have no doubts, 18 percent have some doubts and 7 percent have serious doubts.
- 59 percent of Catholics say they have no doubts, 24 percent have some doubts and 7 percent have serious doubts.

Belief in Christ's return increases with age—59 percent of those 18–29 and those 30–49, 65 percent of those 50–64 and 68 percent of those over 65 have no doubt Christ will return to Earth.

Belief in Christ's return decreases with education: 70 percent of those with a grade school education, 63 percent of those with a high school education, 64 percent of those with some college and 50 percent of college graduates say they have no doubts about the second coming. Among college graduates, 16 percent have some doubts about Christ's return and 22 percent have serious doubts.

RELIGIOUS TRAINING

There is a large gap between the number of Americans who say they want religious training for their children and the number of those with children who are actually providing such training. While eight in ten of today's adults had some form of religious training as children, only seven in ten of those with children age 4–18 are now providing such education. This represents an increase since 1978, however; in that year, only 60 percent of parents said they were providing religious education for their children[12].

Eighty-six percent of all Americans, including 90 percent of those with children age 4–18, say they want religious training for their children. But only

69 percent of those with children age 4–18 say they are currently providing such training.

The age of the children involved does not seem to be a factor in that the percentage of those saying their children are receiving religious training does not fall off significantly as the children's ages increase; 72 percent of those with children age 4–9, 73 percent of those with children 10–14 and 69 percent of those with children 15–18 say they are now providing religious training.

The groups showing the greatest gap between the percentage saying they want to provide religious training for their children and those actually providing training are single parents—both those who have never been married and those who are separated, divorced or widowed. Seventy-eight percent of single parents say they want religious training for their children, the lowest figure for any group responding. Only 54 percent of single parents are providing religious training for their children, a 24-point gap.

The gap is even higher—30 points—for parents who are separated, divorced or widowed; 89 percent want religious training, but only 59 percent are providing it. These figures suggest that the many demands made on single parents make arranging religious instruction for their children difficult. In contrast, 88 percent of those who are married want religious training for their children, and 72 percent of those with children 4–18 are providing it.

There are some interesting patterns by other demographic groups:

· While 69 percent of whites with children 4–18, the national average, are providing religious training for their children, blacks (75 percent) are more likely to provide such training, while Hispanics (61 percent) are less likely.
· College graduates (75 percent) are more likely than those with less education to provide religious education for their children.
· Not surprisingly, those who identify themselves as Protestants (90 percent) or Catholics (91 percent) are more likely than the average to provide religious instruction.

Eighty-two percent of adults had some religious education as children. This includes 81 percent who attended Sunday school; 22 percent who attended parochial school; 28 percent who had religious education at home; and 11 percent who had courses in religion in either public or private school. Obviously, many received more than one form of religious education.

Those under 30 (78 percent) were less likely than those over 30 to have received any form of religious education as children, suggesting a drop in interest in religious education among parents a generation ago. Even so, the 78 percent of those adults under 30 who received religious education is higher than the 69 percent of today's children who are receiving such training.

Blacks (78 percent) and Hispanics (76 percent) are somewhat less likely than whites (83 percent) to report having had religious training. Those with the least amount of secular education also had the least religious instruction —73 percent of those who had not graduated from high school had religious instruction, compared to 89 percent of college graduates.

Catholics (90 percent) are somewhat more likely than Protestants (82 percent) to say they had religious training as children. But the two groups had different types of religious education. Of those who had religious instruction as children, Protestants (93 percent) were far more likely than Catholics (61 percent) to have attended Sunday school. On the other hand, half of all Catholics (49 percent) reported having attended parochial school, compared to only 8 percent of Protestants. Protestants (33 percent) were more likely than Catholics (19 percent) to have received religious education at home.

RELIGIOUS EXPERIENCE

One American in three—33 percent—claims to have had a religious experience, a particularly powerful religious insight or awakening. This is approximately the same proportion who have responded in the affirmative to similar questions since 1976[13]. The most recent findings come from a Gallup survey, "The Unchurched American—1988," conducted for a coalition of twenty-two religious groups. The survey asked, "Would you say that you have ever had a religious or mystical experience, that is, a moment of sudden religious insight or awakening?"

The "religious experience," sometimes described as an otherworldly feeling of unity with God or a universal spirit, is one of the least explored, yet one of the most fascinating, aspects of religious life in America. Many who have a religious experience are able to recall details, even the exact date of the occurrence. Such an experience often appears to have a profound impact on a person's outlook and the direction of his or her life. Many recount experiences at a time of crises, others in answer to prayers. Survey evidence also reveals that these experiences are often gradual rather than sudden.

One of the most interesting aspects of these experiences is that they happen to the unchurched and nonreligious as well as to persons who attend church regularly or who say religion is "very important" in their lives. For example, in the 1988 survey, 25 percent of unchurched Americans reported having had a religious experience. The survey defined the unchurched as those who had not attended church or synagogue within the past six months except for occasions like weddings and funerals. Forty percent of "churched" Americans reported having a religious experience.

Past surveys show that religious experiences tend to fall into six general categories:

- An "otherworldly" feeling of union with a divine being, carrying with it the conviction of the forgiveness of sins and of salvation.
- A dramatic spiritual awakening related to nature.
- Experiences related to healing.
- Experiences involving visions, voices and dreams.
- A sudden insight and turning to God in moments of crisis (near-death experience, death of loved one, war, automobile accident, and so on).
- Experiences that cannot be described.

One particularly interesting finding in the 1988 survey is that parents are most likely to report having had a religious experience. Among those with children age 15–18, 48 percent say they have had such an experience; among those with children 10–14, 43 percent have had a religious experience; among those with children 4–9, it is 37 percent. Overall, 39 percent of those with children 4–18 have had a religious experience, compared to 30 percent of those with no children.

Among other groups, those most likely to have had a religious experience are Protestants (41 percent); blacks (40 percent); southerners (39 percent); those 30–49 (38 percent); westerners (37 percent); women (36 percent); the divorced, separated and widowed (36 percent); and those with some college education (36 percent).

Among those least likely to have had a religious experience are Catholics (24 percent), easterners (24 percent), singles (25 percent), Hispanics (27 percent) and those 18–29 (27 percent).

Following are questions from past surveys and the positive responses related to religious experiences:

- 1985: "Have you ever been aware of, or influenced by, a presence or a power—whether you call it God or not—which is different from your everyday self?"; 43 percent.
- 1985: "Have you ever had what you consider to be an important religious experience or revelation that reinforced your faith?"; 38 percent.
- 1983: Same as 1988 question; 37 percent.
- 1982: "Have you ever had a religious experience—that is, a particularly powerful insight or awakening, that changed the direction of your life, or not?"; 34 percent.
- 1981: Same as 1982 question; 34 percent.
- 1980: Same as 1982 question; 30 percent.
- 1978: Same as 1988 question; 35 percent.
- 1978: Same as 1982 question; 34 percent. Of those who had such an experience, 40 percent said it was sudden, 59 percent said it was more gradual and 1 percent did not know.
- 1976: Same as 1988 question; 31 percent.
- 1962: Same as 1988 question; 20 percent.

AMERICANS RELY ON SELVES TO SOLVE PROBLEMS

Americans are more likely to rely on themselves, rather than an outside power such as God, to solve life's problems. They are also more likely to believe that man's reason and intellect, based on his learning and experience, rather than traditional religious values, are responsible for the advancement of mankind, according to a survey conducted for the Christian Broadcasting Network. Americans are evenly divided, however, on the question of whether morality should be based on traditional religious values or man's experience over the centuries[14].

Overall, 45 percent of Americans say they rely more on themselves to solve life's problems, 36 percent say they rely more on an outside power and 17 percent say they rely on both. But there were sharp differences in response by sex, age, education and religion: Men, those under 50, those with some college education, Catholics and non-Evangelicals said they relied more on themselves. Those over 50, those with less than a high school education and Evangelicals said they relied more on an outside power such as God.

Men said they relied on themselves by a wide margin (52 to 33 percent), while women were evenly divided, with 40 percent saying "self" and 39 percent saying "outside power."

Americans 18–29 picked "self" by a 2-to-1 margin (55 to 27 percent) and those 30–49 chose "self" by 48 to 35 percent. Among those over 50, however, 44 percent said they relied more on an outside power and 35 percent said they relied more on themselves.

Those with less than a high school education said they were more likely to rely on an outside power (by 50 to 30 percent); high school graduates were evenly divided (41 percent said "self," 38 percent said "outside power"); those with some college picked "self" by 48 to 35 percent; and college graduates chose "self" by 62 to 22 percent.

Fifty-six percent of Evangelicals said they were more likely to rely on an outside power, while only 23 percent said they were more likely to rely on themselves. Among non-Evangelicals, however, 59 percent said they relied more on themselves, while only 24 percent said they relied more on an outside power.

Catholics said they were more likely to rely on themselves by 51 to 32 percent; Protestants were evenly divided, with 42 percent saying they relied more on an outside power and 39 percent saying they relied more on themselves. When we consider the views of Evangelicals, these figures suggest that non-Evangelical Protestants hold views similar to those of Catholics.

Half of all Americans (49 percent) believe man's reason and intellect are responsible for the advancement of mankind, while 40 percent credit traditional religious values and 7 percent cite both.

Men (50 to 38 percent) were slightly more likely than women (48 to 43 percent) to credit reason and intellect. Those over 50 were more likely to credit religious values (by 48 to 38 percent); those 30–49 picked reason and intellect (by 51 to 38 percent); and those 18–29 did so by a larger margin (58 to 32 percent.

College graduates chose reason and intellect by 61 to 31 percent; those with some college were evenly divided, with 47 percent picking religious values and 44 percent picking reason and intellect. High school graduates chose reason and intellect by 49 to 38 percent, while those with less than a high school education chose religious values by 48 to 38 percent.

Again, there was a sharp difference between Evangelicals and non-Evangelicals: 56 percent of Evangelicals credited traditional religious values with the advancement of mankind, while 36 percent credited reason and intellect; non-Evangelicals chose reason and intellect by 56 to 31 percent.

Catholics picked reason and intellect by 50 to 37 percent, while all Protestants were evenly divided, with 47 percent picking reason and intellect and 44 percent picking religious values.

Forty-four percent of all Americans said morality and ethics should be based on man's experience over the centuries, while 43 percent said they should be based on traditional religious values and 9 percent cited both. Table 3.10 provides the breakdown by groups.

GODTALK

About seven Americans in ten (69 percent) believe that God has "led or guided" them in making a decision at some point in their lives. One in three (36 percent) believe God has spoken to them directly, although only 11 percent believe that God actually speaks out loud to people today. Three Americans in

Table 3.10
FACTOR MAINLY RESPONSIBLE FOR PROGRESS

	Religious Values	Man's Experience
Men	41%	47%
Women	45	41
18–29	39	49
30–49	45	44
50+	45	40
College Grad.	42	48
Some College	43	45
High School Grad.	46	40
Less Than High School	39	46
Protestant	48	39
Catholic	41	47
Evangelical	57	36
Non-Evangelical	34	49

four (74 percent) believe that God has a specific plan for their lives, even if they do not know what it is[15].

The percentages of those holding these beliefs are higher among the 84 percent of Americans who say they believe in "a Heavenly Father who watches over us and can be reached by our prayers" and higher still among Evangelicals. Ninety-four percent of Americans believe in God or a universal spirit. Of that group of believers, 5 percent believe God is "an idea but not a being," 2 percent believe God is "an impersonal Creator who cannot be reached by our prayers" and 3 percent say they do not know the nature of God.

Only 7 percent of Americans offer no opinion on the way in which God spoke to people during the time of the Bible. Those surveyed and offering multiple responses were about evenly divided in their views: 39 percent said that God spoke out loud to people, 39 percent said God spoke through other people and 37 said God spoke "through an internal feeling or impression."

But Americans believe that God speaks to people differently today than in biblical times. They believe God is less likely to speak out loud (11 percent) or through other people (24 percent) and more likely to speak through internal feelings and impressions (48 percent) and through the Bible (49 percent).

Of the total sample, 36 percent said God had spoken directly to them "through some means," 44 percent said that had not occurred. The remainder did not believe in a God who answers prayers. Thirty-three percent of Americans say they have known someone to whom God has spoken, while 49 percent say they have not.

Among those who believe in a God who answers prayers, 43 percent believe God has spoken to them directly and 39 percent believe God has spoken to someone they know.

While 69 percent of Americans say that God has guided them in their decision-making, 12 percent said that has not happened. Among those who believe in a God who answers prayers, 81 percent say God has guided them in making decisions in their lives and 87 percent believe God has a specific plan for their lives.

The percentage of Americans who believe that God has spoken to them directly is considerably smaller than the percentage who say God has guided them in their decision-making. One likely explanation for this gap is that those who say God has guided their decision-making but has not spoken to them directly believe they have been guided by God through the Bible, through church teachings or through other people.

There are significant differences between Evangelicals and other Americans in their beliefs about the way God talks to people: 64 percent of Evangelicals believe that God has spoken to them directly, while 30 percent believe this has not happened; 55 percent of Evangelicals say they know someone to whom God has spoken, while 42 percent say they do not.

About one Evangelical in five (18 percent) believes that God speaks to people out loud today; 36 percent believe God speaks through other people, 56 percent believe God speaks through internal feelings or impressions and 71 percent believe God speaks through the Bible.

Among Evangelicals, 96 percent believe that God has a plan for their lives, while only 1 percent does not. Similarly, 93 percent of Born-Again Christians believe God has guided their decision-making.

STANDARDS FOR GOOD AND EVIL

An overwhelming majority of Americans—eight in ten—believe that "there are clear guidelines about what's good and evil that apply to everyone regardless of the situation." Seventy-nine percent agree with that statement, while only 17 percent disagree[16].

Despite the strong belief that clear ethical standards exist, the survey reveals a considerable amount of ambiguity. Thirty-eight percent of Americans say they "completely agree" with the statement, while 41 percent "mostly agree." This difference is significant. It means that those who "mostly agree" with the statement believe that there can be rare exceptions to clear ethical guidelines, while those who "completely agree" believe there can be no exceptions.

The same kind of ambiguity exists among those who take a more situational approach to ethics: 12 percent say they "mostly disagree" with the statement, while only 6 percent say they "completely disagree."

In general, those most likely to "completely agree" that there are clear ethical guidelines for everyone include white Evangelical Protestants, those over 50, those with less than a high school education, those in low-income groups, those living in rural areas and the divorced, separated and widowed.

Those least likely to "completely agree" that clear ethical guidelines exist include college graduates, those living in large cities, those in upper income groups, single people and those with no religious affiliation.

Among religious groups, white Evangelical Protestants are considerably more likely than others to believe in a universal ethical standard. Table 3.11 shows this pattern.

Some of the sharpest differences in attitude are found among those with different levels of education. Forty-five percent of those with less than a high school education, but only 23 percent of college graduates, completely agree that clear ethical guidelines exist. Table 3.12 shows this pattern.

The survey revealed surprising differences in attitudes toward ethics in several categories:

- Marital Status. Singles (22 percent) are the least likely to accept universal ethical standards, while those who are married (40 percent) and those who are divorced, separated or widowed (45 percent) are considerably more likely to accept such standards.
- Residence. While 45 percent of those who live in rural areas believe in universal ethical guidelines, this decreases to 38 percent for those living

Table 3.11

BELIEF IN CLEAR STANDARDS OF GOOD AND EVIL

	Completely Agree	Mostly Agree	Mostly Disagree	Completely Disagree
White Protestant	42%	42%	9%	4%
Evan.	54	36	6	2
Non-Evan.	35	46	11	5
Black Protestant	40	42	10	6
Catholic	33	42	13	7
No Affiliation	23	37	18	14

in the suburbs, 36 percent for those living in cities with a population of less than one million, and 27 percent of those living in cities with a population of more than one million.

- Income. Belief in universal ethical guidelines decreases from 45 percent among those with family incomes below $10,000 a year to 28 percent for those with family incomes above $50,000 a year.
- Age. The percentage of those who "completely agree" that there are clear ethical guidelines which do not change increases sharply at age 50: 33 percent of those 18–29 and 34 percent of those 30–49 completely agree with the statement, but this jumps to 45 percent for those over 50.
- Region. Thirty-three percent of those in the East, 36 percent of those in the West, 37 percent in the Midwest and 42 percent in the South "com-

Table 3.12

BELIEF IN CLEAR STANDARDS OF GOOD AND EVIL, BY EDUCATION

	Completely Agree	Mostly Agree	Mostly Disagree	Completely Disagree
College Grad.	23%	39%	20%	13%
Some College	34	42	14	7
High School Grad.	42	42	9	4
Less Than High School	45	41	7	2

pletely agree" with the statement. In the West, however, one resident in four (23 percent) disagrees with the statement.

ANGELS, DEVILS AND GHOSTS

Millions of Americans continue to believe in a wide range of paranormal phenomena. While two of these phenomena—angels and devils—are associated with traditional religious teaching, most others are not; for example, one American in ten believes that ghosts and witches really do exist[17].

Groups that generally rank low on scales of traditional religious belief—such as young people and westerners—rank high on a scale of "superstitious" beliefs, while groups that generally rank high on scales of traditional religious belief—those over 50 and southerners—rank low on a scale of superstitious beliefs. One exception, however, is belief in astrology, which is fairly consistent across most groups surveyed. Table 3.13 shows the percentage of Americans who say they believe in specific paranormal phenomena:

Table 3.14 shows the average scores for key demographic groups for two clusters of beliefs—religious (angels and devils) and nonreligious (the others).

Education is also a factor in belief about paranormal phenomena. Those who have not had any college education are more likely than those with at least some college to believe in angels, devils, ghosts, Big Foot, and less likely to believe in witches and the Loch Ness Monster. But those with less education are less likely to believe in unusual experiences. Table 3.15 shows these patterns.

The regional differences may be the most fascinating because of the high levels of belief in both religious and nonreligious phenomena in the West. Table 3.16 shows this pattern.

While only 15 percent of Americans say they believe in astrology, 25 percent

Table 3.13

BELIEF IN PARANORMAL PHENOMENA

Phenomenon	Believers	Phenomenon	Believers
Angels	50%	Big Foot	16%
ESP	46	Astrology	15
Devils	37	Ghosts	15
Déjà Vu	31	Witches	13
Precognition	24	Loch Ness Monster	10
Clairvoyance	18		

Table 3.14

BELIEF IN ANGELS AND DEVILS VS. OTHER PHENOMENA

	Angels/Devils	Others
U.S.	44%	21%
Men	41	20
Women	46	22
18–29	49	27
30–49	50	26
50 +	36	13
College Grad.	35	25
Some College	40	22
No College	51	19
East	29	21
Midwest	48	20
South	57	18
West	36	27

say they read newspaper astrology columns and 85 percent say they know their zodiac sign.

RELIGION AND PREMARITAL SEX

Only one American in three (33 percent) believes that premarital sex is always wrong. This figure drops by more than half, to 15 percent, in a group to whom the issue is particularly relevant—those who have never been married[18].

Twelve percent of all Americans believe that premarital sex is "almost always wrong." Twenty-six percent believe that it is wrong sometimes and another 26 percent believe that it is not wrong at all.

The findings come from "The Unchurched American—1988." The survey also found that Americans say they would not welcome more acceptance of sexual freedom in the future, by a 68 to 22 percent margin, with singles and those under 25 more likely to say they would welcome such a change.

The question asked in this survey gave respondents four choices and differs from past polls, which have simply asked whether premarital sex was wrong

Table 3.15
BELIEF IN PARANORMAL PHENOMENA, BY EDUCATION

Phenomenon	College Grad.	Some College	No College
Angels	42%	44%	58%
Devils	28	35	43
Ghosts	16	8	18
Witches	15	13	12
ESP	53	53	40
Déjà Vu	40	42	21
Precognition	31	24	21
Clairvoyance	27	18	15
Big Foot	14	14	18
Loch Ness Monster	18	13	6
Astrology	13	15	16

Table 3.16
BELIEF IN PARANORMAL PHENOMENA, BY REGION

Phenomenon	East	Midwest	South	West
Angels	35%	55%	64%	41%
Devils	23	41	49	31
Ghosts	15	15	10	21
Witches	8	13	13	18
ESP	49	44	42	52
Déjà Vu	33	30	25	40
Precognition	26	23	19	32
Clairvoyance	21	16	12	28
Big Foot	15	13	15	20
Loch Ness Monster	10	11	7	17
Astrology	15	14	15	15

or not wrong. If the responses are grouped together, however, a more consistent pattern emerges. Combining the responses from those who say that premarital sex is always wrong with the responses of those who say it is almost always wrong, we get a total of 45 percent saying it is wrong. If we combine the responses from those saying premarital sex is wrong only sometimes with the responses of those who say it is not wrong at all, we get a total of 52 percent.

Looking at the figures in this way suggests that moral opposition to premarital sex is declining after a temporary upsurge at the height of the AIDS scare.

There has been a dramatic change in attitudes toward premarital sex in the past generation. In 1969, 68 percent of Americans said it was wrong, and only 21 percent said it was not. By 1985, for the first time, more Americans said that premarital sex was not wrong (52 percent) than that it was (39 percent).

The trend reversed in 1987, however. In that year, 46 percent of all Americans said premarital sex was wrong, and 48 percent said it was not. It seems likely that this shift was due to concern about the spread of AIDS through casual sexual encounters. The 1988 figures—45 percent wrong, 52 percent not wrong—suggest that Americans are separating their concern about AIDS from their attitudes toward premarital sex.

The 1987 survey found that four in five of those who say that premarital sex is wrong do so for religious or moral reasons. There are significant religious differences in attitudes toward premarital sex. The 1988 survey found that unchurched Americans are far less likely to believe that premarital sex is wrong. The survey defined the unchurched as those who had not attended church or synagogue in the past six months except for major religious holidays or occasions like weddings or funerals.

The 1988 survey found that 43 percent of churched Americans said premarital sex was always wrong and that 13 percent said it was almost always wrong; 23 percent said it was sometimes wrong and 15 percent said it was not wrong at all. Among the unchurched, 19 percent said premarital sex was always wrong and 10 percent said it was almost always wrong; 30 percent said it was wrong sometimes and 34 percent said it was not wrong at all.

Those least likely to say that premarital sex is always wrong were singles (15 percent), those 18–29 (18 percent), the unchurched (19 percent), college graduates (22 percent) and those 30–44 (24 percent).

Those most likely to say that premarital sex is always wrong are those over 50 (52 percent); those with less than a high school degree (48 percent); the churched (43 percent); southerners (43 percent); the divorced, separated and widowed (38 percent); the married (37 percent); and women (36 percent).

There were also significant differences in attitudes between Catholics and Protestants. Among Protestants, 40 percent said premarital sex was always wrong and 14 percent said it was almost always wrong; 23 percent said it was wrong only sometimes and 18 percent said it was not wrong at all.

Among Catholics, 26 percent said it was always wrong and 12 percent said it was almost always wrong; 31 percent said it was sometimes wrong and 25 percent said it was not wrong at all. This difference reveals a major shift since 1969, when there was no difference in attitudes between Protestants and Catholics; in that year, 70 percent of Protestants and 72 percent of Catholics said premarital sex was wrong.

The differences in attitudes toward premarital sex are even more pronounced at the denominational level. A 1985 study found that among the major denominations, which all teach that premarital sex is immoral, only rank-and-file Southern Baptists agree with this tenet. Rank-and-file Catholics and mainline Protestants believe that premarital sex is morally acceptable.

Apart from denominational differences, we find that those who say religion is "very important" in their lives believe premarital sex is wrong by a 54 to 36 percent margin. On the other hand, large majorities of those who say religion is "fairly important" in their lives (66 to 25 percent) and those who say it is "not very important" (80 to 13 percent) believe premarital sex is not wrong.

The biggest gap in denominational attitudes today was between Southern Baptists, who believe premarital sex is wrong by 53 to 41 percent, and Catholics, who believe that it is not wrong by 58 to 33 percent.

The strength of opposition to premarital sex among Southern Baptists, who make up the largest Protestant denomination, is responsible for the fact that Protestants are evenly divided on the issue, with a 48 to 46 percent plurality saying premarital sex is wrong. This narrow margin reflects a decrease of 24 percent from the 70 percent of Protestants who said premarital sex was wrong in 1969.

Similarly, all Baptists are evenly divided, with a 48 to 45 percent plurality saying it is wrong. But, when we allow for the Southern Baptist showing, it seems that a plurality of other Baptists—primarily American Baptists and members of a variety of black Baptist denominations—approve of premarital sex. These Baptist groups are probably close to the Methodist view; 46 percent of Methodists believe premarital sex is not wrong, and 41 percent believe it is.

Our survey samples for Presbyterians and Episcopalians are too small to be definitive, but our findings fit the pattern, with a plurality in the 40 percent range approving of premarital sex.

Lutheran approval of premarital sex—by 55 to 38 percent—is almost as strong as that found among Catholics.

The shift in attitude among Catholics since 1969 was even more dramatic than that among the rest of the population. In 1969, a slightly larger percentage of Catholics (72 percent) than Protestants disapproved of premarital sex—that means there was a 39-point drop in sixteen years.

One reason the Catholic shift has been so great may be because of reaction to Pope Paul VI's 1968 encyclical, *Humanae Vitae*, which upheld the church's traditional ban on artificial means of birth control. Most Catholics had expected a change, and church observers like the Rev. Andrew Greeley, a sociologist, argue that the church lost its credibility on sex-related issues because of the encyclical.

RELIGIOUS COLLEGES

Graduates of religious colleges appear to be happier and more satisfied with their personal relationships and jobs than are graduates of secular institutions. The survey also shows that graduates of religious colleges are more involved in church life and more politically and socially conservative than their secular counterparts[19].

The survey compared responses from 1979, 1980 and 1981 graduates of five colleges affiliated with the Church of Christ and four secular colleges, all in the Southwest. The Church of Christ is a conservative, Evangelical denomination with more than one million members. The secular colleges surveyed were considerably more Protestant than the national average and had a large percentage of Church of Christ members. The study was conducted by the Gallup Organization for Oklahoma Christian College, one of the Church of Christ schools surveyed.

The survey found that while there was no significant difference between religious- and secular-college graduates in overall level of happiness, religious-college graduates were more likely to consider themselves "very happy": 53 percent said they were "very happy," compared to 39 percent of secular-college graduates. An additional 43 percent of religious-college graduates and 54 percent of secular-college graduates said they were "fairly happy."

This sense of greater happiness among religious-college graduates carried over into their feelings about their personal relationships:

- 78 percent of religious-college graduates, compared to 61 percent of secular-college graduates, said they were "very happy" in their marriages.
- 70 percent of religious-college graduates, compared with 61 percent of secular-college graduates, said they were "very satisfied" with their family lives.
- 50 percent of religious-college graduates, compared with 43 percent of secular-college graduates, said they were "very satisfied" with their friendships.

Religious-college graduates also showed higher levels of job satisfaction. They scored an average of 80 percent satisfaction on eight job-related issues, compared to 74 percent satisfaction among secular-college graduates. Table 3.17 shows the percentage expressing satisfaction with specific aspects of their jobs.

There were no significant differences in the level of employment of graduates of the two sets of schools, with more than 80 percent in each group employed full time. However, graduates of secular schools were more likely to be professionals—69 percent of secular-school graduates and 58 percent of

Table 3.17

ATTITUDES OF RELIGIOUS- AND SECULAR-COLLEGE
GRADUATES

	Religious College	Secular College
Chance to Do Something That Makes Use of Abilities	91%	86%
Freedom to Use Own Judgment	91	88
Feeling of Accomplishment	86	81
Amount of Work You Do	84	76
Working Conditions	83	78
Your Salary	71	61
Way Boss Handles Workers	69	63
Chance for Advancement	64	60

religious-school graduates described themselves as professionals. This was apparently related to the fact that 64 percent of secular-school graduates, compared to 51 percent of religious-school graduates, had gone on to postgraduate study.

The level of involvement in church and civic activities was high among both groups of graduates. The religious-college graduates were more likely to contribute to their church and do volunteer work for it, while secular-college graduates were more likely to give to and volunteer for more secular activities.

Religious-college graduates were slightly more conservative politically. Only 4 percent described themselves as liberals, 59 percent described themselves as middle-of-the-road and 37 percent described themselves as conservatives. Among the secular-school graduates, 8 percent described themselves as liberals, 66 percent said they were middle-of-the-road and 25 percent said they were conservatives.

On social issues, the largest difference came on abortion. Sixty-three percent of the religious-college graduates agreed with the statement "abortion should be banned," while only 29 percent of the secular-college graduates held that view.

Religious-college graduates were considerably more likely to believe that "the Bible is God's word, and all it says is true," that "sexual relations outside marriage are wrong," that "marriage is a permanent contract, broken only by death," that the "origin of man is explained by the Bible, not evolution," and were less likely to believe that "homosexuality is a private matter."

RELIGION AND DEPRESSION

Half of the 81 percent of Americans who at least occasionally feel depressed turn to prayer, meditation or reading the Bible for relief. Those who do so report a higher level of effectiveness—94 percent—than do those who turn to a dozen other activities when they feel depressed[20].

One fourth (27 percent) of those who occasionally feel depressed seek out a pastor or religious leader for help, and this, too, has a high rate of effectiveness—87 percent. These figures come from a Gallup study, "Depression—Frequency, Causes and How It Is Overcome," conducted for the Christian Broadcasting Network.

The survey found that 10 percent of all Americans say they feel depressed "most of the time" or "quite often," 45 percent say they "occasionally" feel depressed, 26 percent say they are "almost never" depressed and 19 percent say they are "never" depressed.

Of the 81 percent who report feeling depressed, 11 percent say their depression lasts a very long or fairly long time, while 87 percent say it does not last long at all, and 2 percent had no opinion.

The cause of depression most often cited was money problems and bills, mentioned by 27 percent of those reporting depression. This was closely fol-

---

Table 3.18

WAYS USED TO RELIEVE DEPRESSION

Spend More Time Alone With a Hobby, TV, Reading or Listening to Music	77%
Seek Out Friends to Talk With	68
Seek Out Family Members to Talk With	66
Eat More or Eat Less	64
Spend More Time in Prayer, Meditation or Reading the Bible	48
Spend More Time Exercising	40
Shop More, Spend More	31
Spend More Hours at Work	29
Seek Out Pastor, Religious Leader	27
Spend More Time Sleeping	26
Seek Help From a Doctor or Professional Counselor	14
Drink More Alcohol	10
Rely More Heavily on Medication	6

lowed by problems at work, cited by 22 percent. Other causes of depression cited included worry about health problems (11 percent), family problems (11 percent), life in general and frustration (7 percent), problems with children (7 percent), the state of the economy (5 percent) and world affairs (5 percent).

Table 3.18 shows what activities Americans engage in to relieve depression and the percentage of those who frequently or occasionally engage in them.

Those most likely to turn to prayer, meditation or Bible-reading are blacks (81 percent), southerners (64 percent) and women (54 percent). The same groups are most likely to turn to a pastor or religious leader: 45 percent of blacks, 40 percent of southerners and 32 percent of women do so.

Table 3.19 shows the percentage reporting that each of the thirteen methods mentioned is very or somewhat effective at relieving depression.

Overall, 37 percent of Americans said they are "very happy"; 53 percent said they are "quite happy"; 9 percent said they are "not very happy" or "not at all happy." This marked a slight increase since 1981, when 32 percent said they were "very happy" and 60 percent said they were "quite happy." There was no change in the number of respondents saying they were "not very happy" or "not happy at all."

In response to a slightly different question about general satisfaction with their life situation, 32 percent of all those in the new survey said they were

Table 3.19

EFFECTIVENESS IN RELIEVING DEPRESSION

Prayer, Meditation, Bible Reading	94%
Exercising	92
Talk With Friends	90
Talk With Family Members	88
Talk With Pastor, Religious Leader	87
Time Alone With Hobby, TV, etc.	84
More Time at Work	77
Doctor or Professional Counselor	71
Sleeping	59
More Medication	58
Shop, Spend Money	47
Alcohol	37
Eat More or Less	31

"very satisfied" with their lives, 53 percent said they were "quite satisfied" and 14 percent said they were "not very satisfied" or "not at all satisfied."

Those over 50 (37 percent) and those in the Midwest (36 percent) were more likely to report the highest level of satisfaction, while blacks (26 percent), those with less than a high school education (20 percent), women (17 percent) and easterners (17 percent) were more likely to report the lowest levels of satisfaction.

REGIONAL RELIGIOUS PROFILES

There are great differences among the religious profiles of the eight major geographical regions of the United States, with each region having its own unique profile[21].

The Midwest most closely parallels the nation as a whole in terms of religious affiliation, the South has the most homogeneous profile, and the West the most unusual. The East is the most Catholic region in the country, the South the most Protestant. Nationally, 58 percent of Americans are Protestant, 27 percent Catholic, 2 percent Jewish and 2 percent Mormon; 2 percent belong to other denominations, and 9 percent belong to none.

In terms of Protestant denominations, 20 percent of all Americans are Baptists, 9 percent Methodists, 5 percent Lutheran and 2 percent each are Episcopalian, Presbyterian, United Church of Christ or Christian Church (Disciples of Christ). The rest belong to denominations too small to register in surveys or describe themselves as Protestant without citing a denomination.

The East is the only region in the country in which Catholics outnumber Protestants. Catholics make up 45 percent of the population in the East and Protestants make up 39 percent. Jews make up 5 percent of the population, their highest representation nationally.

This pattern is more pronounced in the New England states, where 52 percent of the population is Catholic and only 32 percent is Protestant. In fact, in New England, the single "denomination" ranking behind Catholics is made up of those with no religious affiliation—11 percent of the population. The largest Protestant denominations in New England are Methodists and Episcopalians, each making up 6 percent of the population.

In the South, in contrast, 77 percent of the population is Protestant and only 15 percent is Catholic. The South is the strongest region for Baptists, who make up 42 percent of the population in the entire region, 45 percent in the Southeast and 36 percent in the Southwest.

In the Southeast, Protestants outnumber Catholics by 82 to 9 percent. This is the only region in which Catholics are not at least the second largest denomination; 12 percent of those in the Southeast are Methodist. In the Southwest, 25 percent of the population is Catholic and 66 percent is Protestant.

In the Midwest, 61 percent of the population is Protestant and 27 percent Catholic. Baptists are somewhat underrepresented and Lutherans somewhat overrepresented in this region, with each accounting for 12 percent of the population. In the West Central states, Lutherans are the second largest denomination, with 20 percent of the population, ranking behind Catholics with 28 percent.

The West is 51 percent Protestant and 24 percent Catholic. Here, as in New England, those with no religious affiliation make up the second largest "denomination," with 14 percent of the population. Those with no affiliation make up one in six (16 percent) of those living in the Pacific states. Five percent of those living in the Pacific states belong to "other" religions. Because these states, particularly California and Hawaii, include many Asian Americans, it is likely that many of those in the "other" category belong to Oriental religions.

The West is also the strongest region in the country for Mormons, who make up 6 percent of the population. In the Rocky Mountain states, however, the figure for Mormons jumps to 16 percent.

The regions do not differ only in their denominational makeup; they also differ considerably in religious belief and practice. One measure of those differences can be found in answers to a series of questions asking respondents to rank themselves on faith beliefs. A factor analysis used responses to create a 4-point scale, with 1 representing low interest and 4 representing high interest. This scale revealed that religion is least important to New Englanders and most important to those in the Southeast; 40 percent of New Englanders, and only 17 percent of those in the Southeast, scored a 1. Table 3.20 shows the responses.

Table 3.20
SCALE OF RELIGIOSITY, BY REGION

	1	2	3	4
U.S.	25%	26%	25%	24%
New England	40	29	16	15
Middle Atlantic	29	26	22	23
East Central	26	30	25	19
West Central	23	29	25	23
Southeast	17	24	29	30
Southwest	18	21	29	32
Mountain	24	27	29	20
Pacific	36	22	20	22

Following are key differences in religious belief and practice by region:

- Southerners (65 percent) are most likely to say religion is "very important" in their lives, followed by those in the Midwest (52 percent), West (48 percent) and East (45 percent).
- Church membership is highest in the South (76 percent) and lowest in the West (58 percent); it is 71 percent in the Midwest and 69 percent in the East.
- The same pattern holds for church attendance, highest in the South (44 percent attending in a typical week) and lowest in the West (33 percent); 40 percent attend weekly in the East and Midwest.
- Those in the South (74 percent) and Midwest (70 percent) are most likely to say they have made a personal commitment to Christ; 60 percent in the West and 58 percent in the East make this claim.
- 38 percent of those in the South believe the Bible is the literal word of God, compared to 28 percent in the East and Midwest and 26 percent in the West.
- Southerners (68 percent) are the least likely to believe it's possible to be a good Christian or Jew without attending church or synagogue, westerners (83 percent) the most likely; 81 percent of midwesterners and 77 percent of easterners hold this view.
- Only one-third of southerners (33 percent) say there has been a period of two years or more when they stayed away from church, compared to a majority of westerners (55 percent) who say this has happened to them; 41 percent in the East and 43 percent in the Midwest say they were away from church for two years or more at some point.

RELIGION AND EDUCATION

The United States is unique because it combines a high degree of education with a high level of religious faith. On many measures of religious belief, commitment decreases as the education level increases. Nevertheless, the level of faith among college-educated Americans remains quite high, and in some key areas—including belief in God and church membership and attendance—there are no significant differences among Americans on the basis of educational background[22].

Overall, 19 percent of Americans are college graduates and another 25 percent have either attended college or a technical school; 33 percent have graduated from high school but not gone on for further education, while 23 percent of Americans have not graduated from high school.

There are a number of areas in which increased education correlates with decreased religious activity or belief:

- The importance of religion declines with education. Table 3.21 shows the importance Americans place on religion in their lives, by educational level.
- While 40 percent of those with less than a high school education read the

Table 3.21

IMPORTANCE OF RELIGION, BY EDUCATION

	College Graduate	Some College/ Technical School	High School Graduate	Less Than H.S. Grad.
Very Important	50%	50%	52%	63%
Fairly Important	29	32	36	27
Not at All Important	19	18	11	9

Bible at least once a week, only 28 percent of those with education beyond high school do so.

- While 45 percent of those with less than a high school education believe the Bible is the literal word of God, only 11 percent of college graduates hold this view; only 11 percent of those with less than a high school degree believe the Bible is not even inspired by God, while 33 percent of college graduates hold that view.
- 90 percent of those with a high school degree or less and 83 percent of those with some college, but only 66 percent of college graduates, believe Jesus is God or the Son of God.
- 68 percent of those with less than a high school degree, but 84 percent of college graduates, believe it is possible to be a good Christian or Jew without going to church or synagogue; 77 percent of those with educational levels in between hold this view.
- 40 percent of those with less than a high school education, 35 percent of high school graduates, 31 percent of those with some college or technical school and 22 percent of college graduates describe themselves as Born-Again Christians.

Despite these differences, there are important religious issues on which there is no significant difference by educational level, and some on which college graduates are more active:

- 91 percent of college graduates, 93 percent of those with some college, 96 percent of high school graduates and 93 percent of those with less than a high school education believe in God. College graduates, however, are more likely to believe in an impersonal God.
- College graduates (74 percent) are more likely than those with less education to be church members; 67 percent of those with some college and 69 percent of those with high school degrees or less are members.
- Similarly, 46 percent of college graduates attend church in a given week, while 38 percent of those with some college, 39 percent of high school

graduates and 37 percent of those who did not graduate from high school attend weekly.

· College graduates are as likely as other Americans to regard themselves as "a religious person."

· College graduates are no less likely than other groups to believe in an afterlife.

· College graduates are no less likely than others to say they want religious training for their children, and are more likely to actually provide such training.

· Those with at least some college education are more likely than others to take part in Bible study or prayer groups outside of church.

AMERICANS' ATTITUDES TOWARD THEIR CHURCHES

Americans have become more critical of their churches and synagogues over the past decade. A large majority believes the churches are too concerned with internal organizational issues and not sufficiently concerned with spiritual matters. A plurality believes the churches are not concerned enough about social justice. And a growing minority—one American in three—believes that the morality being taught by the churches is too restrictive[23].

At the same time, Americans give churches high marks for being warm and accepting places and for being effective in helping people find meaning in their lives. They give them lower marks for having a clear sense of the spiritual.

In general, Catholics are less critical of the churches than are Protestants. Since church members are more likely to express their attitudes toward their own denominations than toward churches in general, this suggests that American Catholics are more satisfied than American Protestants with their churches. These findings come from "Unchurched Americans—1988," a Gallup study conducted for Congress '88, a coalition of twenty-two religious groups.

In 1978, 51 percent of Americans said the churches were too concerned with organizational issues, while 27 percent disagreed; the rest were uncertain. Ten years later, however, 59 percent said the churches were too concerned with organizational issues, while only 16 percent disagreed. This may partly reflect the widespread publicity over the past decade of developments such as the struggle between fundamentalists and moderates for control of the Southern Baptist Convention and tensions between American Catholics and the Vatican.

Protestants criticized the churches' concern with organizational matters by 62 to 16 percent, while Catholics were less critical, with 54 percent saying the churches were too concerned with organizational matters and 22 percent saying they were not.

A decade ago, Americans were evenly divided, with 35 percent agreeing that the churches were not concerned enough about social justice and another 35 percent disagreeing with that statement. In 1988, however, 41 percent said the churches were not concerned enough about social justice, while 29 percent said they were.

Catholics, again, were slightly less critical than Protestants. Among Protestants, 42 percent said the churches were not concerned enough about social justice, while 27 percent disagreed. Among Catholics, the margin was 37 to 35 percent. This may reflect the fact that Catholic leaders have been highly visible on peace and justice issues over the past decade; the U.S. Catholic bishops have issued lengthy, well-publicized pastoral letters on peace and economic justice.

Blacks were considerably more critical of the churches on social justice issues than were whites or Hispanics: 51 percent of blacks and 40 percent each of whites and Hispanics said the churches were not concerned enough about social justice; 23 percent of blacks, 28 percent of Hispanics and 30 percent of whites disagreed.

In 1978, Americans rejected by 52 to 27 percent the statement that "the rules about morality preached by the churches and synagogues today are too restrictive." In 1988, that margin fell to 46 to 32 percent.

A larger number of Catholics than Protestants were uncertain in their responses. Catholics (28 percent) were as likely as Protestants (26 percent) to say the morality was too restrictive, but they were less likely—by 41 percent to 55 percent—to disagree.

Those under 50 were more likely than those over 50 to view the churches' morality as too restrictive: 34 percent of those under 30, 36 percent of those 30–49 and 25 percent of those over 50 held this view.

In only two groups did a plurality say the churches' morality was too restrictive: Hispanics (by 39 to 33 percent) and single people (by 37 to 34 percent).

In other findings:

- 64 percent of Americans agree that "most churches and synagogues today are warm and accepting of outsiders"; only 17 percent disagreed.
- 67 percent of Americans agreed that "most churches and synagogues today are effective in helping people find meaning in life"; 15 percent disagreed.
- 48 percent of Americans agreed that "most churches and synagogues today have a clear sense of the real spiritual nature of religion"; 31 percent disagreed.

CONCLUSIONS

This survey of Americans' beliefs about important religious issues paints a picture of the faith of both the "typical" American and individual groups of Americans. It certainly shows that Americans are unique for the way they combine high levels of religious belief with high levels of education. Their education may change that faith, but it doesn't necessarily weaken it. As Americans become more educated, their faith tends to become more intellectual—or at least they look for more intellectual ways to confront it—and their religious practices may change; but their faith does not disappear.

Americans do, however, take a very independent approach to religion. Their faith must make sense to them, and it must reflect the values of freedom that they assume in their daily social and political lives. The pattern is clear:

- While Americans value church membership and religious activity, they do not believe that formal institutional ties are necessary for faith.
- They welcome changes in their own faith lives and feel strengthened by the challenges of questioning their faith—and, in so doing, show a great deal of confidence in their faith.
- While they believe in God, and most believe in a personal God, they look to themselves to make the critical moral decisions in their lives; they see ambiguity in moral questions, particularly regarding sex, and want to make up their own minds.
- They have a clear sense of what they want from their churches—and, in fact, they tend to view their churches less as sources of faith than as resources for their personal and family religious and spiritual needs. Earlier, we saw that Americans' religious practice does not fall off when they lose confidence, even temporarily, in their religious institutions. Now, we see that their faith itself does not weaken when they become increasingly critical of their churches' activities.

Given this strong, typically American independent streak, the degree of religious orthodoxy found among Americans is simply amazing. A country in which such large proportions of the population believe in a personal God who will call them to Judgment Day to determine how they spend the afterlife; in which so many believe that God has a plan for their lives and communicates with them; in which one-third report intense, life-changing religious experiences; in which so many worship Jesus Christ—such a nation cannot by any stretch of the imagination be described as secular in its core beliefs.

Not all Americans, however, match up to this "typical" profile. It would be inaccurate, and unfair, to categorize groups of people as more or less "religious" on the basis of their religious practices and beliefs; we would need to know both their behavior and what we mean by "religious." But, in terms of attitudes toward basic religious beliefs, we can draw conclusions about group behavior because some patterns recur too often to be meaningless.

For example, we have seen the religious "gender gap" again and again, with women considerably more likely than men to hold traditional religious beliefs. Similarly, belief in traditional religious views consistently increases with age; those over 50 are the most traditional in their views, those under 30 the least traditional. By most measures, blacks are more "religious" than whites. Those with less education are far more traditional in their beliefs than those with more education, although, as we have seen, college graduates have their own brand of religion. Protestants and Catholics hold similar views of basic beliefs; Protestants rely more on the Bible and emotional experience, while Catholics are more independent in their approach to religion. Evangelicals consistently score the highest on levels of traditional belief.

One of the most fascinating insights survey data provide is the relationship between significant changes in life situations and faith. We saw that young adults, forming their own identities as they break away from their families and begin their careers, have the least interest in religion and the least traditional beliefs. But religious interest and belief increase with age, more so for women. When a person marries, interest in religion increases; divorce leads to decreased religious activity, though not necessarily decreased religious belief, while widowhood intensifies both. Traumatic events like abortion weaken faith. Understanding this deceptively simple pattern is crucial to understanding the present and future status of religious life in America.

CHAPTER

4

Religious Profiles

AMERICA is a land of rich religious diversity. So far, we have looked at American religion from the angle of particular questions, trends and issues. But the attitudes revealed by those questions form unique patterns along denominational lines—proving, certainly, that denominational affiliation does make a difference in the way Americans view religion and the world. At the same time, other groups—Evangelicals, blacks, Hispanics, teens and "Baby Boomers"—have distinct religious profiles that we need to understand. This chapter will profile the major denominations and religious groups in America today.

EVANGELICALS

Perhaps no religious group has had more publicity in the past decade and a half than Evangelical or Born-Again Christians. Much of that publicity stems from the attention that Jimmy Carter drew in 1976 when, in running for president, he openly discussed his Evangelical Southern Baptist faith. But Evangelicals have also become more visible through increased presence on radio and television, in print and through their involvement in social movements against abortion and for school prayer. In some ways, Evangelicals emerged in the midseventies, because the media had largely ignored them before that time.

Evangelicals are not a denomination per se; they can be found to some degree in virtually every denomination, yet their distinctive worldview clearly sets them apart from other religious groupings. Public opinion polls have tried several ways to define Evangelicals. In the past, the Gallup Organization has used several different definitions of Evangelicals. One question asked Americans if they had had a "born-again" experience, or "a turning point in your life when you committed yourself to Jesus Christ?" Those saying yes ranged from 34 percent of the population in 1976 to 40 percent in 1984. But because of the way the wording of this question defined born again, it provoked affirmative answers from many people who would not normally consider themselves Born-Again Christians.

A separate effort defined "Evangelicals" as those who had had a born-again experience and also held a literal view of the Bible and had attempted to lead someone else to Christ. Using this definition, Evangelicals accounted for 18 percent of the population in 1976 and 22 percent in 1984. But because this approach was so strict, it left out many Americans who normally consider themselves Born-Again Christians.

Since 1986, the Gallup Organization has defined Evangelicals with the question, "Would you describe yourself as a Born-Again Christian, or not?" This question is most likely to get an accurate response; it also follows Gallup practice of accepting religious self-identification—for example, listing respondents as "Catholics" or "Baptists" solely on the basis of their self-description —without trying to refine the definition. Comparing findings resulting from different definitions, it seems safe to say that the percentage of Americans who are Born-Again Christians has remained fairly stable since 1976. Three in ten Americans (31 percent) are Evangelicals, or Born-Again Christians[1].

The born-again language has traditionally been used by American Protestants, but the phrase has entered the national vocabulary and is used by members of denominations that have not used it in the past. For example, 13 percent of Catholics and 20 percent of Mormons identify themselves as Born-Again Christians.

Among Protestants, 44 percent say they are Born-Again Christians. But Protestant denominations differ considerably in the percentage of members who are Born Agains: 57 percent of Baptists, 32 percent of Methodists, 29 percent of Lutherans, 27 percent of Presbyterians and 14 percent of Episcopalians say they are Born Agains. In addition, 25 percent of Protestants in other, smaller denominations (or who identify themselves as Protestants without citing a denomination) say they are Born Agains.

The makeup of Evangelicals differs sharply from that of the general population. For example, women make up 52 percent of the general population and 58 percent of Evangelicals. While Protestants make up 58 percent of the population, they make up 87 percent of all Evangelicals. Catholics, who account for 27 percent of the general population, make up 13 percent of Evangelicals. Mormons make up 2 percent of the total population and 1 percent of Evangelicals.

Evangelicals are older than the general population. Among the general population, 26 percent of adults are under 30, 36 percent are 30–49 and 33 percent are over 50. Among Evangelicals, 23 percent are under 30, 37 percent are 30–49 and 40 percent are over 50.

Evangelicals are less well educated than Americans as a whole. Nineteen percent of all Americans but only 13 percent of Evangelicals are college graduates; 25 percent of the general population and 22 percent of Evangelicals have had some college or technical school training; 34 percent of the population and 36 percent of Evangelicals are high school graduates; 22 percent of the population and 29 percent of Evangelicals have not graduated from high school.

While blacks make up 11 percent of the general population, they make up 15 percent of Evangelicals. Whites make up 87 percent of the population and 82 percent of Evangelicals. Hispanics account for 7 percent of the population and 6 percent of Evangelicals.

Almost half of all Evangelicals—46 percent—live in the South, while 30 percent of the general population lives there. Twenty-five percent of each group lives in the Midwest. Twenty-five percent of the general population, but only 13 percent of Evangelicals, live in the East; 20 percent of all Americans and 15 percent of Evangelicals live in the West.

Politically, Evangelicals are more evenly divided than the nation at large. In the general population, 31 percent are Republicans and 38 percent Democrats. Among Evangelicals, 36 percent are Republicans and 39 percent are Democrats.

In recent years, the political conventional wisdom has held that Evangelicals are considerably more conservative than non-Evangelicals. In fact, however, while Evangelicals are clearly more conservative on matters of sex and lifestyle, they are no more conservative on many domestic and foreign policy issues; they are actually slightly more liberal on some economic issues[2].

The major differences in attitudes toward public issues between Evangelicals and non-Evangelicals center on issues of traditional values, an area where Evangelicals are considerably more conservative. This cultural conservatism is largely responsible for the fact that President Reagan, a strong backer of traditional values, was considerably more popular among Evangelicals than among non-Evangelicals. But Evangelicals' broad personal support for the president did not always translate into support for his policies.

There are sharp differences between Evangelicals and non-Evangelicals on issues related to sex and lifestyle:

- Only 19 percent of Evangelicals, compared to 42 percent of non-Evangelicals, approve of making homosexual relations legal. The negative attitude of Evangelicals toward homosexuality seems to influence their attitude toward AIDS, a fatal disease, which in this country was at first found primarily, though not exclusively, in the homosexual community. Evangelicals are more likely than others to favor mandatory testing for the AIDS virus among specific groups and for the population at large.

- Almost twice as many Evangelicals (70 percent) as non-Evangelicals believe that premarital sex is wrong.
- Evangelicals are considerably more conservative in their attitudes toward alcohol—33 percent still support Prohibition, a national law to ban the sale of alcohol. Only 11 percent of non-Evangelicals support such a proposal.
- Religious faith is a key factor for Evangelicals in approaching politics: 75 percent say they would not vote for a qualified candidate of their own political party if he or she were an atheist, while only 17 percent would vote for such a candidate. In contrast, non-Evangelicals say, by a 55 to 38 percent margin, that they would vote for a qualified atheist.
- Evangelicals tend to focus their discontent on the Supreme Court because of its controversial decisions in areas like abortion and school prayer. For example, while 54 percent of non-Evangelicals express a "great deal" or "quite a lot" of confidence in the court, only 46 percent of Evangelicals do so.

The difference between Evangelicals' and non-Evangelicals' attitudes toward President Reagan can be seen, for example, in a November 1987 poll that found that 56 percent of Evangelicals approved of Reagan's performance in office and 36 percent disapproved; non-Evangelicals were more evenly divided, with 48 percent approving and 44 percent disapproving.

But Evangelicals' support for Reagan did not extend to all of his policies. For example, in June 1987, 64 percent of Evangelicals and 72 percent of non-Evangelicals said they believed that when all the information on the Iran-Contra affair came out, Reagan would be found to be more involved in the affair than he had claimed. On a related matter, Evangelicals were as likely as non-Evangelicals to believe that Congress should play a stronger role in making foreign policy: 38 percent of Evangelicals and 34 percent of non-Evangelicals say the congressional role is too weak.

- While Evangelicals were more likely than non-Evangelicals to support President Reagan's nomination of Judge Robert Bork to the U.S. Supreme Court, they remained almost evenly divided. As national opinion shifted against Judge Bork during his confirmation hearings, so did opinion among Evangelicals. Just before the Senate rejected his nomination, Evangelicals tilted against him by a 43 to 40 percent margin, while non-Evangelicals opposed him by a 56 to 28 percent margin. Asked if the president should nominate someone else like Bork, 40 percent of Evangelicals said he should and 38 percent said he should not; non-Evangelicals were opposed by 52 to 31 percent.
- Evangelical support for the president did not translate into support for his policies in Central America, however. The Reagan administration had been somewhat cool to a Central American peace plan offered by presidents of countries in that region. But 65 percent of Evangelicals and 70 percent of non-Evangelicals support the plan; 16 percent of Evangelicals and 15 percent of non-Evangelicals oppose it.

- A November 1987 survey asked respondents whether they supported continuing military aid to the Contras or waiting to see how the peace process develops, 69 percent of Evangelicals and 72 percent of non-Evangelicals said to give the peace process a chance; 22 percent of Evangelicals and 18 percent of non-Evangelicals favored continuing aid. But Evangelical opposition to Contra aid does not depend upon the peace proposal. In July 1987, Evangelicals opposed Contra aid by 61 to 26 percent, while non-Evangelicals opposed it by 65 to 26 percent.
- Another issue on which Evangelicals refute their conservative stereotype is defense spending. While Evangelicals are regarded as more hawkish than other Americans, they are not significantly more likely to support increased defense spending. In an April 1987 survey, 13 percent of Evangelicals and 14 percent of non-Evangelicals said the United States was spending too little on defense; 42 percent of Evangelicals and 46 percent of non-Evangelicals said the nation was spending too much and 38 percent of Evangelicals and 36 percent of non-Evangelicals said it was spending the right amount. In a July 1987 survey, 36 percent of Evangelicals and 35 percent of non-Evangelicals opposed cutting defense spending to reduce the budget deficit; 55 and 60 percent, respectively, supported such cuts.
- In a March 1987 survey, 62 percent of Evangelicals and 68 percent of non-Evangelicals said their sympathy in South Africa was with the blacks; 11 and 13 percent, respectively, said their sympathy was with the South African government.
- 55 percent of Evangelicals and 58 percent of non-Evangelicals support a United States presence in the Persian Gulf.

The fact that Evangelicals are sometimes more liberal than non-Evangelicals on some economic issues is related to the fact that Evangelicals have lower incomes—38 percent of Evangelicals and 24 percent of non-Evangelicals have family incomes below $15,000 a year. Here are views of the two groups on key domestic issues:

- 83 percent of Evangelicals and 74 percent of non-Evangelicals favor raising the minimum wage to $4.65 an hour.
- 11 percent of Evangelicals and 18 percent of non-Evangelicals favor raising taxes to reduce the budget deficit.
- 24 percent of Evangelicals and 20 percent of non-Evangelicals support cutting social programs to reduce the deficit.
- 8 percent of Evangelicals and 9 percent of non-Evangelicals support cutting entitlement programs like Social Security and Medicare to reduce the deficit.
- 58 percent of Evangelicals and 65 percent of non-Evangelicals favor a law that would force Congress to raise new funds for each new program it funded.
- 61 percent in each group believe that blacks are treated as well as whites in their communities.

- 33 percent of Evangelicals and 30 percent of non-Evangelicals believe the government is doing all it can to assure airline safety.
- 66 percent of Evangelicals and 69 percent of non-Evangelicals say AIDS is the top health care crisis facing the nation.

So far, we have treated all Evangelicals, black and white, as a unit. But there are important differences in attitudes between black and white Evangelicals[3]. Both race and self-identification as a Born-Again Christian serve as predictors of religious activity and orthodoxy among American Protestants, but the patterns are complex. There are three basic trends:

- Black and white Evangelicals hold virtually identical views on a series of religious questions; they are considerably more traditional in those views than are non-Evangelical Protestants. In other words, on religious issues, white Evangelicals have more in common with black Evangelicals than they do with white non-Evangelicals.
- Black non-Evangelical Protestants are more religiously active and traditional in their views and practices than are white non-Evangelicals.
- Black Protestants, both Evangelical and non-Evangelical, are considerably more likely to be Democrats and to favor government spending on domestic programs. In these areas, historic black ties to the Democratic Party and support for government social programs outweigh religious differences.

One example of the similarity between white and black Protestant Evangelicals can be seen in their responses to a question about whether they view themselves as "a religious person." Respondents were asked to respond on a scale of 1 to 10, with 10 indicating that the description was "perfect," and 1 indicating that it was "completely wrong." Responses of 8, 9 and 10 were grouped together as "strong" identification with the phrase "a religious person." Seventy-five percent of both white and black Evangelicals strongly identified themselves as "a religious person." In contrast, 36 percent of white non-Evangelicals and 38 percent of black non-Evangelicals did so.

The same survey gave five statements on religious belief and practice with which to agree or disagree. Again, white and black Evangelicals were identical in their overall scores, with each averaging 95 percent agreement with the statements. While scores among non-Evangelicals were lower, blacks (87 percent agreement) scored higher than whites (77 percent agreement). Table 4.1 shows the statements and the percentage in each group agreeing with them.

The same pattern can be seen in church attendance. Forty-five percent of white Evangelicals and 44 percent of black Evangelicals say they attend church at least once a week. Among non-Evangelicals, however, only 13 percent of whites and 16 percent of Blacks attend weekly. Overall, 79 percent of white Evangelicals and 89 percent of black Evangelicals attend church at least once a month; 38 percent of white non-Evangelicals and 56 percent of black non-Evangelicals attend at least monthly.

Table 4.1

RELIGIOUS VIEWS, BY RACE AND EVANGELICAL STATUS

	White Evan.	White Non-Evan.	Black Evan.	Black Non-Evan.
Prayer Is an Important Part of My Daily Life	93%	68%	96%	86%
We All Will Be Called Before God at the Judgment Day to Answer for Our Sins	96	79	96	90
Even Today Miracles Are Performed by the Power of God	96	78	97	84
I Am Sometimes Very Conscious of the Presence of God	95	72	93	82
I Never Doubt the Existence of God	97	87	95	93

In terms of political affiliation, white Evangelical Protestants are somewhat more Republican-oriented than are white non-Evangelical Protestants. Among white Evangelicals, 51 percent are Republicans or lean Republican. Among white non-Evangelicals, 46 percent are Republicans or lean Republican and 42 percent are Democrats or lean Democratic. Among black Protestants, however, only 11 percent of Evangelicals and 10 percent of non-Evangelicals are Republican oriented, while 85 and 83 percent, respectively, are Democratic oriented.

On questions concerning government spending, blacks are consistently more likely—often by a wide margin—to favor higher government spending. For example, while 35 percent each of white Evangelicals and white non-Evangelicals support increased government assistance for college tuition, 72 percent of black Evangelicals and 67 percent of black non-Evangelicals favored such an increase.

This pattern holds up even on programs that are extremely popular among white Protestants. For example, 72 percent of Evangelicals and 71 percent of non-Evangelicals favor increased spending on programs for the elderly. Among black Protestants, however, 86 percent of Evangelicals and 87 percent of non-Evangelicals favor an increase.

CATHOLICS

American Catholics give Pope John Paul II high ratings personally, but three in four say they are more likely to rely on their own consciences rather than papal teachings when they must deal with difficult moral questions. At the same time, three Catholics in ten believe the pope is too conservative in his positions[4].

American Catholics view Vatican officials considerably less favorably than they view Pope John Paul. But one-third of American Catholics say they are willing to increase their contributions to their church to help the Vatican overcome its budget deficit.

Seventy-seven percent of American Catholics say they are more likely to follow their consciences rather than the pope's teachings. Only 14 percent say they are more likely to follow the pope; another 7 percent volunteered the view that they would follow both.

There was no significant difference in opinion between men and women, with women choosing conscience by 79 to 12 percent and men by 74 to 16 percent. The most resistance to following the pope came from those age 30–49; only 7 percent said they were more likely to follow the pope, while 82 percent said they would follow their conscience. Those under 30 and over 50 opted for conscience by similar margins, 73 to 19 percent for the former and 74 to 15 percent for the latter.

Thirty-one percent of American Catholics said the pope was too conservative in his positions, while only 7 percent said he was too liberal; 57 percent said his views were just right. An amazing finding is that there was so little difference in attitudes toward the pope between Catholics and non-Catholics. A much higher percentage of non-Catholics (23 percent) than Catholics (5 percent) had no opinion. But among those who did have an opinion, 33 percent of Catholics and 32 percent of non-Catholics said the pope was too conservative, 7 percent of Catholics and 10 percent of non-Catholics said he was too liberal and 60 percent of Catholics and 57 percent of non-Catholics said his views were just right.

In 1987, Pope John Paul regained some of the popularity he lost among American Catholics in 1986, but he still ranked below his peak popularity level. On a scale with −5 representing the lowest rating and +5 the highest, 69 percent of American Catholics gave the pope the highest rating (+4 or +5). This marked a slight increase from 65 percent in 1986, but that figure marked a dramatic decline from 79 percent in 1985.

Overall, 94 percent of American Catholics gave the pope a positive rating in 1987, while only 2 percent gave him a negative one. College graduates were the least enthusiastic, with only 60 percent in this group giving the pope a +4 or +5 rating.

Table 4.2 shows the percentage of Catholics giving Pope John Paul a +4 or +5 rating since his election in 1978. The 1981 survey was conducted after

Table 4.2

PERCENTAGE OF CATHOLICS RATING
POPE JOHN PAUL II +4, +5

1987	69%	1980	85%
1986	65	1979 (Oct.)	80
1985	79	1979 (Sept.)	73
1984	82	1978	67
1981	83		

the assassination attempt on the pope; the October 1979 survey was taken after his first visit to the United States.

Pope John Paul remains popular with non-Catholics in America. Overall, 81 percent gave him a positive rating and only 9 percent gave him a negative one. Four non-Catholics in ten (38 percent) gave him a +4 or +5 rating.

Vatican officials lag well behind the pope in the view of American Catholics. Only 33 percent of American Catholics give them a +4 or +5 rating. Overall, 77 percent give them a positive rating and 7 percent a negative one. Only 19 percent of Catholic college graduates, 22 percent of those with incomes above $40,000 a year, 24 percent of those in the professions or business and 26 percent of those 30–49 give Vatican officials a high rating.

Despite lower enthusiasm for Vatican officials, a significant minority of American Catholics say they are willing to donate more money to their church to help the Vatican overcome its budget deficit: 36 percent of American Catholics say they are willing to increase their contributions, while 58 percent say they are not willing to do so; 6 percent have no opinion. Women (32 percent) are less likely than men (41 percent) to say they are willing to give more. Catholics under 30 are the most supportive; they are evenly divided, with 45 percent saying they are willing to give more and 46 percent saying they are not. The most resistance comes from Catholics age 30–49; only 25 percent of those in this group are willing to give more, while 72 percent say they are not.

Seventy-nine percent of American Catholics say they are church members and 52 percent say they attended church in the past seven days. Church attendance dipped below 50 percent for the first time in 1986, but rose again and has been stable, fluctuating by only a few points, for a decade.

Fifty percent of American Catholics say religion is "very important" in their lives, compared to 60 percent of Protestants who make this claim. Thirty-six percent of Catholics and 31 percent of Protestants say religion is "fairly important," while 13 percent of Catholics and 8 percent of Protestants say it is "not very important."

Table 4.3
COMPARISON OF CATHOLIC/U.S. DEMOGRAPHICS

	U.S.	Catholic
Men	48%	49%
Women	52	51
18–29	27	30
30–49	37	38
50+	36	31
White	87	96
Nonwhite	11	4
Hispanic	7	17
College Grad.	19	17
Some College	25	27
High School Grad.	33	34
Less Than High School	23	22
$40,000+/Year	21	23
$25–40,000	23	25
$15–25,000	22	21
Less Than $15,000	29	25
East	25	38
Midwest	25	25
South	31	19
West	19	18
Republican	29	26
Democrat	39	42
Married	63	62
Single	20	23
Divorced/Sep.	8	7
Widowed	8	7

Table 4.3 compares a profile of American Catholics with that of the population as a whole.

BAPTISTS

Baptists, who make up 20 percent of the general population, are the second largest religious family in the country. They are the most religiously conservative and active Protestant group and have done the best job of retaining younger members. These trends are even stronger among Southern Baptists, who make up half of all Baptists in the United States[5].

For example, 54 percent of all Americans, 70 percent of Baptists and 72 percent of Southern Baptists say that religion is "very important" in their lives. While 68 percent of all Americans are church members, 72 percent of Baptists and 80 percent of Southern Baptists claim membership. There is not much difference between Baptists and the general population in terms of church attendance, however: 39 percent of all Americans and Baptists and 42 percent of Southern Baptists say they have attended church within the past seven days.

Baptists are highly conservative in their self-perception when it comes to "traditional values about such matters as sex, morality, family life and religion." A survey question asked respondents to rate themselves on a scale of 1 to 7, with one representing "very traditional, old-fashioned values" and 7 representing "very liberal, modern values." We grouped responses of 1 and 2 together as "conservative," 3 through 5 as "moderate" and 6 and 7 as "liberal." Using this scale, we found that 36 percent of all Americans, 44 percent of all Baptists and 46 percent of Southern Baptists are conservative on traditional values; 52 percent of all Americans, 49 percent of Baptists and 41 percent of Southern Baptists are moderate; 11 percent of all Americans, 9 percent of Baptists and 10 percent of Southern Baptists are liberal.

The high degree of religious activity among Baptists is related to the fact that Baptists are the most likely to describe themselves as Born-Again Christians; more than half (57 percent) use that self-description. Baptists are the most likely Christians to read the Bible daily; while 12 percent of all Americans read the Bible at least once a day, 24 percent of Baptists and 23 percent of Southern Baptists read it at least once a day. At the same time, 70 percent of Baptists, compared to 49 percent of the general population, say they watch religious television programs at least occasionally.

Politically, Baptists are both more conservative and more Democratic than the general population. While Americans as a whole are split between the two major parties by a margin of 39 percent Democratic to 29 percent Republican, Baptists are split 50 percent Democratic to 25 percent Republican. But, paradoxically, Baptists were also more likely than the national average to approve of the job Ronald Reagan did as president.

While mainline Protestants are considerably older than the general population, Baptists have almost the identical age distribution as the general pop-

Table 4.4

COMPARISON OF BAPTIST/U.S. DEMOGRAPHICS

	U.S.	Baptists
Men	48%	48%
Women	52	52
18–29	27	28
30–49	38	38
50+	35	34
White	87	70
Nonwhite	11	29
Hispanic	7	2
College Grad.	19	10
Some College	25	20
High School Grad.	33	37
Less Than High School	23	33
$40,000+/Year	21	14
$25–40,000	23	20
$15–25,000	22	23
Less Than $15,000	29	39
East	25	13
Midwest	25	16
South	31	61
West	19	10
Republican	29	25
Democrat	39	50
Married	63	64
Single	20	20
Divorced/Sep.	8	8
Widowed	8	9

ulation: 27 percent of all Americans, 28 percent of Baptists and 27 percent of Southern Baptists are 18–29; 38 percent of all three groups are 30–49; 35 percent of all Americans and Southern Baptists and 34 percent of Baptists are over 50. These figures indicate that Baptists are doing a better job than other Protestant churches in retaining young adults as members. Table 4.4 compares Baptists and the general population demographically.

METHODISTS

One of the stereotypes in religious circles is that Methodists make up the moderate middle of American faith. In this case, however, survey evidence actually tends to support the stereotype; Methodists as a group are greatly similar in outlook to the general population[6].

Overall, 9 percent of Americans are Methodists. Members of the United Methodist Church, the third largest denomination after Catholics and the Southern Baptist Convention, make up 7 percent of the population. Most other Methodists are members of black Methodist denominations. Table 4.5 shows a demographic comparison between UMC members and the general population.

For most surveys on which denominational findings are available, we have figures for all Methodists. But because UMC members make up about 80 percent of all Methodists, these findings are likely to represent them accurately. Figures compiled throughout 1986 show that 69 percent of Methodists and 68 percent of all Americans say they are church members; 36 percent of Methodists and 40 percent of all Americans said they had attended church within the past seven days.

There was no significant difference between Methodists and the total population in assessing the importance of religion in their lives: 53 percent of Methodists and 54 percent of all Americans said religion is "very important" in their lives; 33 and 31 percent, respectively, said it was "fairly important" and 14 percent in each group said it was "not at all important."

In 1987, 31 percent of all Americans and 32 percent of Methodists described themselves as Born-Again Christians. But Methodists are more likely than the general population to contribute to television evangelists. In an April 1987 survey, 4 percent of all Americans and 10 percent of Methodists said they had contributed in the past year.

In terms of their views on specific issues, the major difference between Methodists and other Americans comes on the question of abortion. For example, a January 1986 survey asked respondents whether they favor or oppose the 1973 Supreme Court rulings, which legalized abortion within the first three months of pregnancy. The general population was evenly divided, with 45 percent favoring and 45 percent opposing. Methodists, however, favored the decision by a 53 to 40 percent margin. Some Methodist leaders base their support for legal abortion on memories of their denomination's support for the failed social experiment of Prohibition; they believe that a similar legal prohibition against abortion would not work.

Table 4.5

**COMPARISON OF UNITED METHODIST/U.S.
DEMOGRAPHICS**

	U.S.	UMC
Men	48%	43%
Women	52	57
18–29	27	19
30–49	38	34
50+	35	47
White	87	97
Black	11	3
Hispanic	7	1
College Grad.	19	21
Some College	25	24
High School Grad.	33	35
Less Than High School	23	19
$40,000+/Year	21	22
$25–40,000	23	25
$15–25,000	22	22
Less Than $15,000	29	27
East	25	24
Midwest	25	33
South	31	32
West	19	11
Republican	29	37
Democrat	39	36
Married	63	63
Single	20	13
Divorced/Sep.	8	6
Widowed	8	10

On foreign policy, Methodists are more likely to believe that the Soviet Union is now militarily stronger than the United States; 32 percent believe the USSR is stronger, while 26 percent believe the United States is stronger. But Methodists are as likely as other Americans to support the U.S.-Soviet treaty on Intermediate Range Nuclear Forces (INF). Methodists support the treaty by 73 to 12 percent, all Americans by 76 to 13 percent. Fifty percent of Methodists and 48 percent of all Americans believe the treaty will improve U.S.-Soviet relations a "great deal" or "quite a lot."

A plurality of Methodists believe the United States is spending too much for the military: 46 percent believe the United States is spending too much, 12 percent believe it is spending too little and 36 percent believe it is spending the right amount. Nationally, 44 percent of Americans believe the United States is spending too much, 14 percent believe it is spending too little and 36 percent believe it is spending the right amount.

On other issues:

- 67 percent of all Americans and 69 percent of Methodists support the Central American peace plan offered by the presidents of several countries in the region.
- All Americans said, by a 51 to 32 percent margin, that the Senate was correct to defeat the nomination of Judge Robert Bork to the U.S. Supreme Court; Methodists approved of the Senate's decision by 55 to 29 percent.
- 77 percent of all Americans and 74 percent of Methodists support raising the minimum wage to $4.65 an hour.

LUTHERANS

In 1987, leaders of three Lutheran churches merged into a new denomination, the Evangelical Lutheran Church in America, representing about 60 percent of all Lutherans in the United States. Lutherans make up 5 percent of the U.S. adult population[7]. The new church brought together the American Lutheran Church (ALC) (2 percent of the population), the Lutheran Church in America (LCA) (1 percent) and the Association of Evangelical Lutheran Churches (AELC), with official membership of 109,000, too low to register in survey samples.

The other large Lutheran body, the Lutheran Church–Missouri Synod (LCMS, with 1 percent of the population) did not take part in the merger. The Missouri Synod has been more conservative theologically than the other three churches. The AELC split off from the Missouri Synod in a dispute in the early 1970s. In addition 1 percent of the population identify themselves as Lutherans, but do not cite affiliation with a specific church. Less than 1 percent cite small Lutheran denominations other than the ALC, LCA or LCMS.

One striking feature about Lutherans today is that they are considerably older than the general population. While 35 percent of the total population is over 50, 46 percent of all Lutherans and 49 percent of those in the ALC are

Table 4.6

COMPARISON OF LUTHERAN/U.S. DEMOGRAPHICS

	U.S.	Lutheran
Men	48%	48%
Women	52	52
18–29	27	17
30–49	37	37
50+	36	46
White	87	98
Black	11	1
Hispanic	7	2
College Grad.	19	24
Some College	25	29
High School Grad.	33	32
Less Than High School	23	16
$40,000+/Year	21	25
$25–40,000	23	27
$15–25,000	22	22
Less Than $15,000	29	22
East	25	16
Midwest	25	55
South	31	11
West	19	18
Republican	29	39
Democrat	39	29
Married	63	69
Single	20	16
Divorced/Sep.	8	8
Widowed	8	8

over 50. At the same time, while 27 percent of the general population is 18–29, only 17 percent of Lutherans—and only 11 percent of those in the American Lutheran Church—fall within this group. This pattern could reflect differences in birth rates, but it also suggests that Lutherans are having a problem keeping young people involved in their church.

Generally, members of the Lutheran Church in America are younger and better educated than members of the American Lutheran Church, although ALC members have higher family incomes.

The new merger brought together two churches with different political makeups. ALC members lean Democratic, with 38 percent identifying themselves as Democrats and 33 percent as Republicans. Among members of the Lutheran Church in America, however, 48 percent are Republicans, while only 25 percent are Democrats. Nationally, 43 percent of all Lutherans are Republicans and 29 percent are Democrats.

Lutherans are heavily concentrated in the Midwest, with 56 percent of all members of the church living in that region. Twenty percent live in the West, 13 percent in the South and 11 percent in the East. Sixty-one percent of ALC members and 54 percent of LCA members live in the Midwest. The LCA is better represented in the East and South, with 13 percent of its members in each region. Twelve percent of the population in the Midwest, including 20 percent in the West Central states, is Lutheran.

Lutherans parallel Protestants as a whole in church membership, but lag behind in church attendance. Seventy-three percent of Lutherans and 72 percent of all Protestants are church members; 41 percent of all Protestants and 36 percent of Lutherans say they have attended church in the past seven days.

On several key religious issues, Lutherans' views are actually closer to those of Catholics than those of other Protestants. For example, 61 percent of all Protestants, 54 percent of Lutherans and 53 percent of Catholics say religion is "very important" in their lives; 29 percent of Protestants, 36 percent of Lutherans and 37 percent of Catholics say religion is "fairly important"; 9 percent of Protestants and Lutherans and 10 percent of Catholics say religion is "not at all important."

Lutherans also fall between all Protestants and Catholics in their view of the Bible. In a 1983 survey, 49 percent of Protestants said the Bible is the actual word of God and should be taken word for word, while 40 percent said it was the inspired word of God but should not be taken word for word. Fifty-five percent of Catholics said the Bible was inspired and 28 percent said it was the actual word of God. Lutherans split evenly, with 46 percent holding each position.

Because the Lutheran Church–Missouri Synod has been the most conservative Lutheran denomination in terms of biblical interpretation, it seems likely that the new Evangelical Lutheran Church in America will be composed primarily of those who believe the Bible is the inspired, not the actual, word of God.

Lutherans also rank between Catholics and all Protestants in frequency of

Bible-reading. Seventeen percent of all Protestants, 6 percent of Lutherans and 3 percent of Catholics read the Bible daily. Twenty-seven percent of all Protestants, 28 percent of Lutherans and 16 percent of Catholics read it at least weekly. Thirty-five percent of Protestants, 49 percent of Lutherans and 63 percent of Catholics read the Bible several times a year or less.

Table 4.6 compares demographics for Lutherans and the general population.

EPISCOPALIANS

As Episcopal church leaders look to the future, recent survey results offer both good news and bad news. On the positive side, the decline in those citing affiliation with the church has stabilized, and Episcopalians give high ratings to the church's handling of their spiritual concerns. On the negative side, there are signs of tension and malaise within the laity and some important gaps between church leadership and laity in terms of priorities[8].

Two percent of all Americans identify themselves as Episcopalians. This has held steady since a decline from 3 percent in the mid-1970s. Seventy-two percent of Episcopalians say they are church members, the same as the figure for all American Protestants. But only 34 percent of Episcopalians say they attended church in the past seven days.

One explanation for this gap is that Episcopalians are less likely than members of other denominations to say that religion is "very important" in their lives. Overall, 55 percent of Americans and 61 percent of Protestants but only 41 percent of Episcopalians said that religion was "very important." Significantly, while all Protestants were twice as likely to say that religion was "very important" than to say it was "fairly important," a plurality of Episcopalians—46 percent—said religion was "fairly important." Thirteen percent of Episcopalians and 9 percent of all Protestants said religion was "not very important."

A survey conducted for the Prayer Book Society in 1985 offers a more detailed look at Episcopalians. The study found that 80 percent of Episcopalians said their church was meeting their spiritual needs, while only 16 percent said it was not. The survey also found that 75 percent of Episcopalians agreed with church leaders' decision to ordain women, while 21 percent disagreed.

Another positive sign for church leaders is the finding that Episcopalians have a great deal of confidence in their seminaries: 15 percent gave them an "excellent" rating, 46 percent rated them "good," while 13 percent rated them "fair" and only 4 percent rated them "poor."

But the survey found a number of indications of unrest as well. For example, while 48 percent of Episcopalians said their church's philosophy was "about right," almost as many—43 percent—found reasons to criticize it. This included 27 percent who said the church was "too trendy" and 16 percent who said it was "too old-fashioned."

The survey also found a sharp gap between laity and clergy on the question of church priorities. A majority of Episcopal clergy (61 percent) said the church

Table 4.7

COMPARISON OF EPISCOPALIAN/U.S. DEMOGRAPHICS

	U.S.	Episcopalian
Men	48%	40%
Women	52	60
18–29	27	17
30–49	38	40
50+	35	43
White	87	94
Black	11	3
Hispanic	7	1
College Grad.	19	44
Some College	25	28
High School Grad.	33	21
Less Than High School	23	8
$40,000+/Year	21	39
$25–40,000	23	20
$15–25,000	22	15
Less Than $15,000	29	18
East	25	33
Midwest	25	16
South	31	28
West	19	23
Republican	29	39
Democrat	39	33
Married	63	62
Single	20	20
Divorced/Sep.	8	10
Widowed	8	9

should give equal emphasis to "worship and spiritual matters" and to "social, political issues." But 76 percent of the laity said the top church priority should be worship and spiritual matters. Only 22 percent of the laity said the church should give equal or top priority to social and political issues.

Episcopalian laity said by a 3-to-1 margin that they were less active in the church than they used to be: 65 percent said they were less active, while 22 percent said they were more active.

The most frequently cited reason for being less active in the church was having moved; 26 percent of those who said they were less active cited this reason. The next most common reason cited—by 20 percent—was a general reference to "changes in general over the past decade."

This figure was higher than that for two specific controversial changes— 2 percent said they were less active because of women's ordination and 8 percent said they were less active because of the adoption of the new Prayer Book.

Among the 22 percent who said they were more active, 27 percent cited changes in the past decade, 9 percent cited women's ordination and 5 percent cited the new Prayer Book.

Eleven percent of those who were less active cited lack of interest "in me and my family" by clergy, but 41 percent of those who were more active cited positive clergy interest.

Table 4.7 compares the demographic makeup of Episcopalians and all Americans.

PRESBYTERIANS

Presbyterians are more likely than members of other denominations to say they are church members, but they are also less likely than others to say they actually attended church in the previous week. Some 83 percent of Presbyterians say they are church members, but only 36 percent say they attended in the past week[9].

Table 4.8 compares these figures for various denominations.

Fifty percent of Presbyterians say religion is "very important" in their lives. In terms of demographic characteristics, Presbyterians are more likely than members of other denominations to be over 50, have a college education and call themselves Republican:

- While 35 percent of the general population is over 50, half of all Presbyterians—51 percent—are in this age group. At the same time, while 27 percent of the general adult population is under 30, only 17 percent of Presbyterians are under 30.
- Among the general population, 19 percent are college graduates and 25 percent have had some college or technical education beyond high school; among Presbyterians, 29 percent are college graduates and 30 percent had some college or technical school education.
- While Democrats outnumber Republicans 39 to 29 percent in the general

Table 4.8

RATIO OF CHURCH ATTENDANCE TO MEMBERSHIP, BY DENOMINATION

	Church Membership	Weekly Attendance	Percent Attending
Catholic	81%	49%	60%
Mormon	81	46	57
Protestant	72	41	57
Baptist	72	39	54
Southern Baptist	80	42	53
Methodist	69	36	52
Lutheran	73	36	49
Jewish	44	21	48
Episcopalian	72	34	47
Presbyterian	83	36	43

population, among Presbyterians, 43 percent are Republicans, 27 percent Democrats.

- 97 percent of Presbyterians are white, 2 percent black and 1 percent Hispanic.
- 69 percent of Presbyterians are married, 15 percent single; 6 percent are separated or divorced and 11 percent widowed.
- 28 percent of Presbyterians live in the East, 24 percent in the Midwest, 28 percent in the South and 20 percent in the West.

OTHER PROTESTANTS

While most survey data produces information about larger religious groups and denominations, we can also profile some other Protestant groups—the United Church of Christ, 2 percent of the population; the Christian Church (Disciples of Christ), 2 percent; "other Protestants," 6 percent; and "unspecified" Protestants, those who describe themselves as Protestants without naming a denomination, 5 percent[10]. Table 4.9 profiles these groups. The United Church of Christ tends to resemble the Episcopal and Presbyterian churches. The Disciples of Christ are a bit younger and demographically bear some resemblance to Baptists. Those who identify as Protestants without naming a denomination are only loosely tied in to organized religion, because there is no

Table 4.9

DEMOGRAPHICS OF OTHER PROTESTANT GROUPS

	United Church of Christ	Disciples of Christ	Other	Unspecified
Men	45%	47%	42%	50%
Women	55	53	58	50
18–29	14	26	26	12
30–49	39	34	37	41
50+	47	40	37	34
White	95	94	86	90
Black	4	5	11	8
Hispanic	3	4	5	6
College Grad.	21	13	17	19
Some College	25	28	23	29
High School Grad.	32	34	26	32
Less Than High School	22	25	29	20
$40,000+/Year	27	15	17	20
$25–40,000	25	21	21	26
$15–25,000	17	27	22	21
Less Than $15,000	27	30	35	29
East	29	8	15	15
Midwest	42	34	27	28
South	19	29	38	28
West	10	30	20	29
Republican	42	35	35	31
Democrat	29	33	32	32
Married	64	63	66	63
Single	13	15	14	18
Divorced/Sep.	8	10	9	12
Widowed	14	11	10	7

such thing as a "generic" Protestant church; this group could well provide the next Americans to join the ranks of the unchurched.

MORMONS

The Church of Jesus Christ of Latter-day Saints (Mormons) is one of the fastest growing and most religiously active denominations in the United States. Mormons are generally younger and better educated than Americans as a whole, and are more likely to be married and to be affiliated with the Republican Party[11].

Mormons barely registered a blip in national surveys a generation ago, but now account for 2 percent of the population, and a considerably higher percentage in parts of the West.

Eight Mormons in ten, compared to seven in ten in the general population, are church members. While 40 percent of Americans say they attended church in the past seven days, 46 percent of Mormons make that claim. And while 55 percent of the general population rates religion as "very important" in their lives, 70 percent of Mormons say religion is "very important."

Mormons make up 2 percent of most demographic groups, paralleling their representation in the general population. There are, however, some exceptions: Mormons account for only 1 percent each of blacks and Hispanics, 1 percent of those with less than a high school education and 1 percent of Democrats; they make up 3 percent of Republicans.

Mormons are based predominantly in the West, reflecting their historic settling of the state of Utah. They account for less than 1 percent of the population in the East and Midwest and only 1 percent in the South. In the West, however, Mormons make up 7 percent of the population. In the Rocky Mountain states in the West—such as Utah, Idaho and Nevada—one in five persons (19 percent) is a Mormon.

Seventy-seven percent of all Mormons are located in the West, including 57 percent in the Rocky Mountain states. Twelve percent of the Mormons in the United States are located in the South, 6 percent in the East and 5 percent in the Midwest. In contrast, 25 percent of the general population is located in the East, 25 percent in the Midwest, 31 percent in the South and 19 percent in the West.

Women make up a higher proportion of Mormons (58 percent) than of the general population (52 percent). Mormons are also younger than the general population: 31 percent of all Mormon adults are under 29, compared to 27 percent of the general population; 30 percent of Mormons and 35 percent of the general population are over 50. Thirty-nine and 38 percent, respectively, are 30–49.

Mormons are also more likely than the general population to be married, with 68 percent of Mormons and 63 percent of all Americans currently being married. This is somewhat surprising given the Mormons' relative youth, and suggests that the church's emphasis on family life may be leading Mormons to

Table 4.10
COMPARISON OF MORMON/U.S. DEMOGRAPHICS

	U.S.	Mormons
Men	48%	42%
Women	52	58
18–29	27	31
30–49	38	39
50+	35	30
White	87	94
Black	11	5
Hispanic	7	3
College Grad.	19	15
Some College	25	35
High School Grad.	33	35
Less Than High School	23	15
$40,000+/Year	21	18
$25–40,000	23	28
$15–25,000	22	23
Less Than $15,000	29	29
East	25	5
Midwest	25	5
South	31	12
West	19	77
Republican	29	46
Democrat	39	27
Married	63	68
Single	20	17
Divorced/Sep.	8	8
Widowed	8	7

marry at an earlier age than other Americans. Seventeen percent of Mormons and 20 percent of the general population are single; 8 percent of each are divorced; 7 percent of Mormons and 8 percent of the general population are widowed.

Mormons are predominantly white—94 percent are white, 5 percent are black and 3 percent are Hispanic.

Mormons are somewhat better educated than the general population. While only 15 percent of Mormons are college graduates, compared to 19 percent of the general population, 35 percent have had some college or technical school education, compared to 25 percent of the general population. Only 15 percent of Mormons have had less than a high school education, compared to 23 percent of all Americans. Thirty-five percent of Mormons and 33 percent of all Americans have graduated from high school but not had any further education.

Mormons are considerably more likely than the general population to be Republicans: 46 percent of Mormons and 29 percent of the general population are Republicans; 27 and 39 percent, respectively, are Democrats.

Table 4.10 compares Mormons and the general population demographically.

JEWS

Religion is a relatively low priority for American Jews, who lag well behind the general population in membership in a congregation, worship attendance and the importance they place on religion in their lives. Only 44 percent of American Jews say they are members of a synagogue, while 69 percent of the general population cites membership in a church or synagogue. To some degree, this reflects the fact that "Jewish" represents an ethnic as well as a religious group, and not all ethnic Jews are religious[12].

In 1986, one Jew in five (21 percent) reported attending synagogue in the week before being interviewed, half the national rate for church attendance (40 percent). This rate has remained fairly stable for a generation. In 1964, 17 percent of American Jews said they had attended religious services in the past week; in 1976, the figure was 23 percent.

One-third of American Jews (35 percent) say that religion is "not very important" in their lives, compared to 14 percent of the general population. Thirty-four percent of Jews and 31 percent of the general population report that religion is "fairly important." But while 55 percent of all Americans say religion is "very important," only 30 percent of Jews make this statement.

Overall, 2 percent of Americans identify themselves as Jewish, the same percentage found since the early 1970s. In 1947, 5 percent of the general population was Jewish.

One major change in recent decades is the geographic distribution of American Jews. In 1966, Judaism was centered almost exclusively in the Northeast, home to 84 percent of American Jews. But this figure dropped to 65 percent in 1976 and 56 percent in 1986.

The percentage of American Jews living in the Midwest grew from 6 percent

Table 4.11

COMPARISON OF JEWISH/U.S. DEMOGRAPHICS

	U.S.	Jews
Men	48%	49%
Women	52	51
18–29	27	19
30–49	38	41
50+	35	39
White	87	99
Black	11	1
Hispanic	7	1
College Grad.	19	44
Some College	25	25
High School Grad.	33	24
Less Than High School	23	7
$40,000+/Year	21	36
$25–40,000	23	24
$15–25,000	22	17
Less Than $15,000	29	17
East	25	63
Midwest	25	8
South	31	12
West	19	18
Republican	29	15
Democrat	39	59
Married	63	59
Single	20	24
Divorced/Sep.	8	7
Widowed	8	9

in 1966 to 12 percent in 1986. The percentage of Jews living in the South grew from 3 percent in 1966 to 17 percent in 1986—15 percent in the Southeast and 2 percent in the Southwest. The percentage of Jews living in the West grew from 7 percent in 1966 to 15 percent in 1986, with 12 percent on the Pacific Coast and 3 percent in the Rocky Mountain states. Jews make up 5 percent of the total population in the East, 2 percent in the West and 1 percent in the South and Midwest.

Partly because of a lower birth rate, American Jews are somewhat older than the general population. Twenty-seven percent of all Americans, but only 22 percent of Jews, are under 30. Thirty-seven percent of all Americans and 43 percent of Jews are 30–49; 35 percent in both groups are over 50.

Jews are one of the most upscale American groups in terms of education and income. Sixty-six percent of American Jews have attended college or technical school, up from 44 percent in 1966. In the general population, 43 percent have attended college or technical school. A full 44 percent of American Jews—compared to 19 percent in the general population—have graduated from college. This high educational level is reflected in income: 17 percent of the general population and 32 percent of Jews have family incomes above $40,000 a year.

One way in which this upscale background is reflected is in marital status—Jews are more likely than other Americans to be single. Thirty-eight percent of Jews and 21 percent of the general population are single; 48 percent of Jews and 63 percent of all Americans are married. There is no significant difference in divorce rates, with 7 percent of Jews and 6 percent of the general population currently divorced. Six percent of Jews and 8 percent of the general population are widowed.

In terms of political affiliation, Jews continue to be one of the most Democratic groups in the country, although there has been some erosion over the past generation. In 1966, 64 percent of Jews were Democrats and 9 percent were Republicans; in 1976, 56 percent were Democrats and 8 percent Republican; in 1986, 50 percent were Democrats and 16 percent were Republicans.

Table 4.11 compares demographics for Jews and the rest of the population.

"NONES"

Eight percent of Americans state no religious preference in public opinion surveys, and these "nones" make up, in effect, the fourth largest denomination in the country. But the religiously unaffiliated are not necessarily atheists. Despite their lack of identification with specific religious groups, the "nones" express a surprising degree of interest in religion and religious belief[13].

Those who state no religious preference are more likely to be young, male, well educated and to live in the Northeast or the Pacific Coast region. They rank in number behind Catholics, Baptists and Methodists, but ahead of Lutherans, Presbyterians, Episcopalians, Jews, Mormons, members of the Orthodox Church and members of the smaller Protestant sects.

Only half (56 percent) of those with no religious preference say that religion is "not very important" in their lives. Twenty-four percent said it was "fairly important," while 16 percent said it was "very important." Among the total population, 55 percent said religion was "very important," 31 percent said it was "fairly important" and 14 percent said it was "not very important."

In a 1987 survey in which Americans were asked how accurately the phrase "a religious person" described them, with a 10 indicating a "perfect" description, 5 percent of those with no religious affiliation rated themselves a 10.

The religiously unaffiliated are not necessarily strangers to church or synagogue; some may be preparing to leave, and some may be preparing to return. In 1986, 13 percent of the unaffiliated described themselves as church members, and 10 percent said they had attended church in the past seven days. Among the total population, 69 percent said they were church members and 40 percent said they had attended in the past seven days.

In a 1987 survey, 2 percent of the unaffiliated said they attended church or synagogue every week and another 2 percent said they attended almost every week; 4 percent said they attended once or twice a month. Another 24 percent said they attended church or synagogue several times a year; 61 percent said they never attend, and the rest did not respond.

About six in ten of the unaffiliated (57 percent) agree with the statement "I never doubt the existence of God," while 49 percent say, "I am sometimes very conscious of the presence of God." Significant numbers of the religiously unaffiliated also believe in miracles: 42 percent believe that "even today, miracles are performed by the power of God."

A similar percentage of the unaffiliated believe in Judgment Day: 38 percent believe that "we all will be called before God at Judgment Day to answer for our sins." One-third of the unaffiliated—35 percent—also say that "prayer is an important part of my daily life."

The unaffiliated have increased their representation in the general population over the long term, but have remained steady for the past decade. The proportion of unaffiliated dropped after World War II and stayed quite low until the 1970s. Table 4.12 shows the percentage of the population citing no religious affiliation at key points over the past forty years. Table 4.13 compares the "nones" demographically to the general population.

ETHNICITY AND RACE

Today's Americans have their roots in a wide variety of countries all over the world. That ethnic diversity adds a wealth of diversity to American religion[14].

For example, Catholicism is the most cosmopolitan religion in America, the only major religious group whose numbers include Americans with roots in at least thirteen different nationalities. Only 33 percent of American Catholics have their roots in England, Germany and Ireland, the three largest ethnic groups represented in the United States. In contrast, 57 percent of white Protestants cite roots in those countries.

Table 4.12

**PERCENTAGE OF POPULATION WITH
NO RELIGIOUS AFFILIATION, BY YEAR**

Year	%	Year	%
1987	8%	1976	6%
1986	8	1975	6
1984	9	1974	6
1983	9	1972	5
1982	8	1967	2
1981	7	1962	2
1980	7	1957	3
1979	8	1952	2
1978	8	1947	6
1977	8		

The extensive Gallup survey conducted for the Times Mirror Corporation's study, "The People, Press and Politics," asked respondents, "From what nationality group are you mainly descended?" An analysis of responses allows us to see both the ethnic breakdowns of major religious groups and the religious breakdowns of major ethnic groups.

The thirteen areas of origin citied specifically were the British Isles (17 percent of Americans), Germany (14 percent), Ireland (10 percent), Africa (8 percent), Eastern Europe (7 percent), Scandinavia, Italy and "Hispanic" (5 percent each), American Indian (3 percent), France (2 percent), other Western European nations (2 percent), Portugal or Spain (1 percent) and Asia (1 percent). In addition, 9 percent of Americans cited the United States as their nationality group, 2 percent cited "other" groups, and 11 percent said they did not know. (Totals do not add up to 100 percent because of rounding.)

Ethnicity is an integral part of Catholicism, and there is no numerically dominant ethnic group in the American Catholic church. Four groups represent virtually identical constituencies—Hispanics and Italian Americans each make up 14 percent of American Catholics, while German and Irish Americans make up 13 percent each. Eastern Europeans trail only slightly behind, with 10 percent, followed by those whose roots were in the British Isles (7 percent), France (4 percent), Portugal or Spain (3 percent), Scandinavia (2 percent), and other Western European nations, Asia and American Indian (1 percent each). Six percent of American Catholics cite the United States as their nationality group.

Among white Protestants, the most cited area of origin is the British Isles

Table 4.13

COMPARISON OF UNAFFILIATED/U.S. DEMOGRAPHICS

	U.S.	"Nones"
Men	48%	61%
Women	52	39
18–29	27	38
30–49	38	44
50+	35	18
White	87	86
Black	11	10
Hispanic	7	5
College Grad.	19	22
Some College	25	28
High School Grad.	33	29
Less Than High School	23	21
$40,000+/Year	21	22
$25–40,000	23	23
$15–25,000	22	23
Less Than $15,000	29	27
East	25	24
Midwest	25	23
South	31	20
West	19	33
Republican	29	22
Democrat	39	34
Married	63	51
Single	20	36
Divorced/Sep.	8	10
Widowed	8	3

(27 percent), followed by Germany (19 percent), Ireland (11 percent), Scandinavia (7 percent), Eastern Europe (4 percent), American Indian and other Western European nations (3 percent each), France (2 percent) and Italy (1 percent). Eight percent cite the United States as their nationality group. There is no significant difference in ethnic makeup between Evangelical and non-Evangelical white Protestants.

Among black Protestants, 67 percent cite Africa as the source of their national roots, while 20 percent cite the United States and 9 percent say they don't know.

Sixty-two percent of all American Jews come from Eastern Europe, while 11 percent cite American as their nationality.

The ethnic breakdown of those with no religious affiliation mirrors the national distribution of ethnic groups almost exactly.

Some of the religious patterns among ethnic groups are particularly fascinating. For example, fewer than one American Indian in ten identifies with Native American religions—only 7 percent list their religion as "other," a category that would include Native American religions. In contrast, 57 percent of those who say they are mainly descended from American Indians identify themselves as white Protestants; 13 percent identify themselves as Catholics and 12 percent say they have no affiliation.

Among other findings:

- White Protestants dominate among those from the British Isles (73 percent), Scandinavia (66 percent), Germany (65 percent), Ireland (54 percent) and other Western European nations (54 percent).
- Catholics dominate among Italians (77 percent), Hispanics (75 percent), Spanish and Portuguese (60 percent) and French (53 percent).
- Eastern Europeans are divided primarily among Catholics (40 percent), white Protestants (24 percent) and Jews (21 percent).
- The least likely ethnic groups to identify themselves as Evangelicals or Born-Again Christians are Italians and Eastern European (3 percent each), Portuguese and Spanish (2 percent) and Hispanic (less than 1 percent).

BLACKS

American blacks are, by some measures, the most religious people in the world. In 1981, for example, Gallup International organizations conducted surveys on religious beliefs in twenty-three nations. One question asked respondents to rank the importance of God in their lives, with 10 the top score. The highest score recorded was by American blacks—9.04[15].

Blacks rank above the average in the United States in assessing the importance of religion in their lives. In 1987, 54 percent of all Americans rated religion as "very important" in their lives, while 69 percent of blacks said it was "very important."

The importance that blacks attach to religion is related to the confidence they have in religion and religious institutions. In a March 1988 survey, 57 percent of the general population and 75 percent of blacks agreed with the statement that "religion can answer all or most of today's problems," while 20 percent of all Americans and only 7 percent of blacks agreed that "religion is largely old-fashioned and out-of-date."

Not surprisingly, blacks are more likely than other Americans to have high levels of confidence in the church or organized religion. In a 1987 survey, 69 percent of blacks and 61 percent of all Americans expressed a "great deal" or "quite a lot" of confidence in the church or organized religion.

Blacks translate their feelings about the importance of religion and their confidence in the church into church membership and attendance—they are more likely than other Americans to be church members and to attend church weekly. In 1987, 69 percent of all Americans and 72 percent of blacks said they were church members. Forty percent of all Americans and 42 percent of blacks said they had attended church in the past seven days. Blacks are happy with their churches. While 42 percent of all Americans say there was a time of two or more years when they stayed away from church, only 34 percent of blacks stayed away that long. And while 83 percent of all church members say they would invite someone to attend their church, 95 percent of black church members say they would extend an invitation.

The religious beliefs and practice of American blacks are closely tied to the Bible—blacks are more likely than other Americans to read the Bible frequently, and half (48 percent) read it at least once a week. A November 1986 survey found that 17 percent of blacks and 12 percent of all Americans read the Bible daily; 32 percent of blacks and 22 percent of all Americans read it once a week or more; 13 and 14 percent, respectively, read it at least once a month; 21 and 26 percent read it less than once a month; only 15 percent of blacks, compared to 22 percent of the general population, never read the Bible.

Blacks are more likely than other Americans to view the Bible as the literal word of God. According to a 1988 survey, 45 percent of blacks and 31 percent of all Americans interpret the Bible literally; while 17 percent of all Americans believe the Bible is not even inspired by God, only 8 percent of blacks hold this view.

Prayer is another area of religious life where blacks are more involved than the general population. While 88 percent of Americans say they sometimes pray to God, 93 percent of blacks pray. And while 32 percent of all Americans say they pray more than once a day, 38 percent of blacks pray that often.

A 1985 survey found that blacks are considerably more likely to be involved in religious activities outside of church attendance than are other Americans. Two-thirds of blacks (65 percent) and less than half of the general population (41 percent) took part in at least one listed religious activity. On specific items:

- 43 percent of blacks and 26 percent of the general population took part in Bible study.

- 32 percent of blacks and 18 percent of the general population took part in prayer and meditation groups.
- 27 percent of blacks and 21 percent of the general population took part in religious education programs.

In terms of denominational affiliation, 77 percent of blacks are Protestants, 11 percent are Catholic, 2 percent cite "other" religions and 10 percent have no affiliation. More than half of all American blacks—52 percent—are Baptists. Eight percent are Methodists, mostly members of black Methodist denominations.

Blacks make up 15 percent of all Protestants and 4 percent of all Catholics. They account for 29 percent of all Baptists, 8 percent of all Methodists, 3 percent of Episcopalians, 2 percent of Presbyterians and 1 percent of Lutherans.

HISPANICS

Hispanics offer a major irony—they are more pious than the general population, but they are also less likely to have formal church ties[16]. The weakness of these ties is apparently one reason why Hispanics are also more likely than the general population to report that they have been approached by people asking them to join a new church. While 34 percent of all Americans say they had been asked to join a church within the past year, 43 percent of Hispanics said they had been approached.

These findings come from "Unchurched Americans—1988," a Gallup study conducted for Congress "88, a coalition of twenty-two religious groups. The study included a larger than usual sample of Hispanics.

Hispanics show greater than average interest in religion on a number of indicators:

- They are more fundamentalist in their approach to interpretation of the Bible: 40 percent of Hispanics and 31 percent of all Americans believe that the Bible is the actual word of God and should be interpreted literally.
- While 58 percent of all Americans say they pray at least once a day, 67 percent of Hispanics say they pray at least once daily.
- 22 percent of all Americans and 29 percent of Hispanics said they had attended a Bible study, prayer or similar group over the past two years.
- While 42 percent of all Americans say there was a period of two or more years when they did not attend church, only 27 percent of Hispanics made that claim.
- Among those who were away from their church for two or more years, 47 percent of all Americans and 52 percent of Hispanics say they eventually went back to church.
- While 76 percent of all Americans believe that it is possible to be a good Christian or Jew without attending church or synagogue, only 64 percent of Hispanics held this view.

• 84 percent of all Americans and 89 percent of Hispanics said they believe Jesus was God or the Son of God.

But, despite this evidence of strong piety on the part of Hispanics, only 57 percent are church members, compared to 64 percent of the general population. And while Hispanics are more likely to believe in the divinity of Christ, they are less likely to say they have made a commitment to Christ—66 percent of all Americans and 58 percent of Hispanics make that claim.

Hispanics are also less likely than the general population to provide religious instruction for their children. This is particularly significant because Hispanics are more likely to have children—43 percent of Hispanics and 33 percent of all Americans say they have children age 4–18.

Among those with children in this age group, 69 percent of all Americans and 61 percent of Hispanics say they are providing religious training for their children. This corresponds to the fact that fewer among Hispanics (80 percent) than among the general population (86 percent) say they want such training for their children.

These figures echo the finding that Hispanics were less likely than other Americans to have had religious training as a child: 82 percent of all Americans and 76 percent of Hispanics say they had such training; significantly, 81 percent of all Americans and only 65 percent of Hispanics said they attended Sunday school or weekly religious instruction.

Lack of religious education reflects lower education levels among Hispanics in general. For example, while 44 percent of all Americans have had some education beyond high school, only 23 percent of Hispanics have had such education.

In terms of affiliation three Hispanics in four (74 percent) are Catholic; 18 percent are Protestant, 1 percent belong to "other" religions, and the rest have no affiliation. Two percent of Hispanics are Baptists and 2 percent are Methodists; 1 percent belong to the United Church of Christ; 1 percent describe themselves as "Protestant" without specifying a denomination; 5 percent are members of the Christian Church (Disciples of Christ).

CHARISMATICS/PENTECOSTALS

Eight percent of Americans describe themselves as "charismatic" or "Pentecostal" Christians[17]. These Christians believe in the "gifts of the spirit," including healing, speaking in tongues and receiving "words of wisdom" from the Holy Spirit. Generally, the term "Pentecostal" is used to describe those who belong to denominations, like the Assemblies of God, that officially hold these beliefs; "charismatic" is used to describe those who participate in Pentecostal-style practices, but belong to denominations, such as the Catholic church, that have not traditionally used those practices.

A separate survey found that 9 percent of Americans have taken part in a charismatic religious service in the past two years, with one in three attending regularly.

Nationally, one in five (22 percent) Evangelicals describe themselves as charismatics or Pentecostals. Only 2 percent of non-Evangelicals describe themselves that way. Baptists (6 percent) and mainline Protestants (5 percent) are less likely to describe themselves as charismatics or Pentecostals, but 18 percent of all other Protestants identify with one of those labels. Overall, 12 percent of Protestants describe themselves as charismatics or Pentecostals.

Four percent of Catholics call themselves charismatics. While this percentage is low, given the size of the Catholic population—28 percent of all Americans—this translates into approximately 2.5 million people.

Regionally, one person in ten in the West (11 percent) and South (10 percent) is a charismatic or Pentecostal, while only 2 percent of those in the East use that label; 8 percent of midwesterners are charismatics or Pentecostals.

When we look at a profile of charismatics/Pentecostals, we find that 85 percent are Protestants and 15 percent are Catholics; 81 percent are Evangelicals; 16 percent are Baptists, 15 percent are mainline Protestants and 54 percent are "other Protestants."

Four in ten (41 percent) of all charismatics/Pentecostals live in the South; 28 percent live in the West, 25 percent live in the Midwest and only 7 percent live in the East.

In terms of race and ethnicity, charismatics/Pentecostals mirror the general population—88 percent are white, 9 percent are black and 8 percent are Hispanic.

Women (55 percent) are more likely than men (45 percent) to be charismatics/Pentecostals. This group is a little younger than the general population—32 percent are 18–29, 29 percent are 30–49 and 37 percent are over 50.

In terms of education, 15 percent of charismatics/Pentecostals are college graduates, 28 percent have had some college, 28 percent are high school graduates and 26 percent have not graduated from high school.

In terms of income, 16 percent make more than $40,000 a year; 27 percent make $25,000–40,000; 17 percent make $15,000–25,000; and 28 percent make less than $15,000.

Thirty-five percent of those attending charismatic services in the past two years say they attend regularly, 48 percent say they attend occasionally and 17 percent say they attended only once.

Charismatic services are more popular with blacks, Hispanics and Protestants than with whites and Catholics. Thirteen percent of blacks and 11 percent of Hispanics, compared to 8 percent of whites, attended such services in the past two years. Eleven percent of Protestants and 6 percent of Catholics attended.

There was no difference in involvement by sex, age, education or marital status, although different patterns emerge among those who attended charismatic services regularly. Almost two-thirds (63 percent) of those who attended regularly are women. Forty-four percent are over 50, 35 percent are 30–49 and only 21 percent are adults under 30.

Seventy-seven percent of regular attenders are white, 18 percent black and 12 percent Hispanic.

Eighty-one percent of those who regularly attend charismatic services are Protestant; only 11 percent are Catholic. The rest belong to other religions. About one in ten of those who regularly attend these services are "unchurched," defined for purposes of this survey as those who have not attended church in the past six months except for special religious holidays or occasions like weddings or funerals.

Charismatic services are most popular in the South, least popular in the East. Almost half of all those who regularly attend such services (45 percent) live in the South; 25 percent live in the Midwest, 23 percent live in the West and only 7 percent live in the East.

Sixteen percent of those who regularly attend charismatic services are college graduates, and another 18 percent had some college or attended technical school; 39 percent graduated from high school and 27 percent have less than a high school degree.

In terms of marital status, 73 percent of those who regularly attend charismatic services are married, 12 percent are single and 15 percent are separated, divorced or widowed.

Those most likely to attend charismatic services regularly were southerners, those over 50 and those with less than a high school education (42 percent each), and the churched, women and Hispanics (42 percent each).

Those most likely to have attended only once are Catholics (33 percent), midwesterners (29 percent), singles (26 percent), high school graduates (25 percent), the unchurched (23 percent), Hispanics (22 percent) and men (21 percent).

Table 4.14 shows the frequency of attendance at charismatic services over the past two years.

RELIGION AND AMERICAN TEENAGERS

American teenagers (13–17) are considerably less likely than adults to say that religion is "very important" in their lives. They also say, by a 2-to-1 margin, that religion is less important to them than it is to their parents[18].

The largest gap between teens and adults in rating the importance of religion high comes among Catholics. The gap is smallest among southerners.

An April 1987 survey asked "How important would you say religion is in your life?" Fifty-four percent of adults ranked it "very important," 31 percent said it was "fairly important" and 15 percent said it was "not very important." Just a month earlier, teens were asked a comparable, but differently worded, question: "How important to you are your religious beliefs?" Only 39 percent

Table 4.14

FREQUENCY OF ATTENDANCE AT CHARISMATIC SERVICES, LAST TWO YEARS

	Regularly	Occasionally	Once
Churched	41%	44%	15%
Unchurched	16	62	23
Men	28	50	21
Women	41	45	14
18–29	29	52	19
30–49	32	47	20
50+	42	45	13
White	34	48	17
Black	35	49	16
Hispanic	41	37	22
East	17	68	16
Midwest	33	37	29
South	42	48	11
West	38	46	16
Less Than High School	42	49	9
High School Grad.	34	41	25
Some College	31	55	12
College Grad.	32	51	17
Married	40	44	15
Single	20	54	26
Divorced/Sep./Widowed	32	52	16
Protestant	39	47	13
Catholic	22	45	33

of teens said their religious beliefs were "very important"; 42 percent said they were "fairly important" and 20 percent said they were "not too important" or "not important at all."

While 58 percent of Catholic adults said religion was "very important," only 28 percent of Catholic teens said their religious beliefs were "very important" to them. In contrast, 59 percent of Protestant adults and 45 percent of Protestant teens ranked religion "very important."

Almost as many southern teens as adults ranked religion high in importance: 66 percent of adults and 62 percent of teens in the South rated religion "very important." In the East, 45 percent of adults and 26 percent of teens rated religion "very important"; 50 percent of adults and 31 percent of teens in the Midwest and 49 percent of adults and 30 percent of teens in the West ranked religion "very important."

The surveys also suggest that black teenagers rate religion as high as do black adults. Seventy-two percent of black adults rank religion as "very important"; so do 72 percent of black teens. Unfortunately, the number of black teens surveyed (thirty-nine) is too small to provide reliable information. Fifty-one percent of white adults and 34 percent of white teens rank religion as "very important."

The same pattern of gender differences in attitudes toward religion as among adults is found among teens. Among adults, 61 percent of women and 45 percent of men rate religion "very important." Among teens, 42 percent of females and 35 percent of males do so.

Forty-nine percent of teens say that religion is less important to them than it is to their parents, while 26 percent say it is more important and 24 percent say it is equally important to them and their parents. One percent had no opinion. Even among teenagers who attend church regularly—about half the sample—45 percent say religion is less important to them than to their parents, while only 28 percent say it is more important.

While southern teens are less likely than those in other regions to say religion is less important to them than to their parents, a plurality (42 to 30 percent) say religion is less important: 55 percent of teens in the East, 48 percent in the Midwest and 52 percent in the West say religion is less important to them than to their parents; 22 percent in the East, 27 percent in the Midwest and 25 percent in the West say it is more important.

Fifty-four percent of Catholic teens say religion is less important to them than to their parents, while 24 percent say it is more important. Among Protestant teens, 45 percent say religion is less important and 29 percent say it is more important to them than to their parents.

Fifty percent of teenage boys and 47 percent of teenage girls said religion was less important to them than to their parents; 23 percent of boys and 30 percent of girls said it was more important.

In a separate question, teens ranked religious faith last of eight values they said it was "very important" for them to learn. Table 4.15 lists the values mentioned and the percentages citing them as "very important."

Table 4.15

PERCENTAGE OF TEENAGERS CALLING VALUES "VERY IMPORTANT"

Honesty	89%	Independence	65%
Responsibility	89	Patience	61
Self-Respect	87	Obedience	60
Hard Work	70	Religious Faith	44

BABY BOOMERS

America's "Baby Boomers"—those born in the twenty-year period after the end of World War II—are less involved in religion and rate it less highly than do other Americans. But there are signs that their level of interest in religion will increase with age[19].

The Baby Boomers now make up 43 percent of the general population. Religious leaders have seen a pattern of involvement in which Americans move away from religion in their teens and early 20s and begin returning in their late 20s and 30s, with participation increasing with age. This pattern is visible among the Baby Boomers themselves, with older Boomers showing more interest than younger ones in religion.

The major unanswered question is the degree to which the Baby Boomers will return to church and synagogue as they grow older. If they return in the same numbers as earlier generations, it would mean that America's churches and synagogues will face a major increase in religious participation in coming years. If they return in lower numbers, it would mean a serious decline in church membership and involvement.

Overall, 65 percent of Baby Boomers are church members, compared to 73 percent of non-Boomers. Thirty-four percent of Boomers, compared to 43 percent of non-Boomers, say they attended church or synagogue in the past seven days.

Baby Boomers are less likely than others to say that religion is "very important" in their lives: 46 percent of Boomers make this statement, compared to 60 percent of non-Boomers. Thirty-six percent of Boomers and 25 percent of non-Boomers say religion is "fairly important," while 16 percent of Boomers and 12 percent of non-Boomers say it is "not very important."

The Baby Boomers are also less likely to have a high level of confidence in the church and organized religion. Thirty percent of Boomers and 40 percent of non-Boomers express a "great deal" of confidence in the church, while 25 percent of Boomers and 27 percent of non-Boomers express "quite a lot" of confidence. Thirty-four percent of Boomers and 25 percent of non-Boomers express "some" confidence in the church, 11 percent of Boomers and 1 percent of non-Boomers express very little confidence and 1 percent of each express no confidence.

The fact that there is no significant difference between Baby Boomers and non-Boomers in saying that religion is "not very important" or in expressing no confidence in the church indicates that the Boomers are not necessarily hostile to religion.

This pattern is reinforced by another finding. A July 1987 survey asked Americans if they were more interested in religion than they were five years ago, less interested or about equally interested. Baby Boomers were actually more likely than other Americans to say they were more interested in religion than they were five years ago; 45 percent of Boomers and 34 percent of others said they were more interested. Seventeen percent of Boomers and 12 percent of others said they were less interested in religion, and 37 percent of Boomers and 49 percent of others said their level of interest had not changed.

There are other notable areas of difference in attitudes toward religion between Boomers and non-Boomers:

- 27 percent of Boomers and 32 percent of others describe themselves as Born-Again Christians.
- 50 percent of Boomers say they would vote for an otherwise qualified atheist for president if their political party nominated one, while 42 percent say they would not. Non-Boomers reject an atheist presidential candidate by 53 to 39 percent.
- 13 percent of Boomers say they would be more likely to vote for a presidential candidate who described himself or herself as an Evangelical Christian, while 32 percent say they would be less likely to vote for such a candidate and 50 percent say it would make no difference. Among non-Boomers, 16 percent say they would be more likely to vote for an Evangelical, 26 percent said they would be less likely and 55 percent say it would make no difference.

CHAPTER

5

Case Studies

1. THE UNCHURCHED

ONE OF the most important and longest lasting discussions involving religion centers on the identity of unchurched Americans and the factors and dynamics that cause some people to be active in church life and others to stay away. One problem is finding a suitable definition for the unchurched.

The simplest approach is to define the unchurched as those who are not members of a church or synagogue. Since about 69 percent of Americans say they belong to a church or synagogue, this means that 31 percent—three Americans in ten—are not church members. This group includes many people who identify with a specific denomination[1].

Using this definition, the group with the largest number of unchurched members—56 percent—is American Jews; this figure may be misleading, however, because many Jews identify as Jews ethnically, not religiously. Among Christian groups, Methodists have the most unchurched members—32 percent. They are followed by Episcopalians and Baptists (28 percent each), Lutherans (27 percent), Catholics (21 percent), Southern Baptists and Mormons (20 percent each) and Presbyterians (17 percent).

We refined this definition of the unchurched as part of an effort to determine degrees of religious activity by combining responses for church membership, church attendance in the past seven days and attitudes toward the importance of religion. Using this system, we analyzed some 6,000 responses throughout

132

1986. We defined "churched" Americans as those who say they are church members or who attended church in the previous week. This includes a group who might be described as the "superchurched"—in addition to being church members or having attended in the past week, these people also say religion is "very important" in their lives.

The "unchurched" Americans are those who say they are not members of any church or synagogue and did not attend church or synagogue in the week before being interviewed. Many in this group, however, either expressed a religious preference or said that religion was at least "fairly important" in their lives. Those classified as "totally nonreligious" said they had no religious preference, were not church members, had not attended church in the previous week, and, in addition, said that religion was "not very important" in their lives.

Using this system we found that 72 percent of Americans are churched, including about three in ten Americans who are superchurched; 28 percent are unchurched, including 4 percent who are totally nonreligious[2].

In general, the unchurched and totally nonreligious are more likely to be young, male, college educated, single or divorced and live in the West. The churched and superchurched are more likely to be female, elderly, married or widowed and live in the South.

Men are considerably more likely than women to be unchurched or totally nonreligious. Thirty-four percent of men and 23 percent of women are unchurched. Six percent of men and 3 percent of women are totally nonreligious. Twenty-three percent of men and 38 percent of women are superchurched.

There is also a large gap between those over age 50 and those under 50, with older Americans more likely to be both churched and superchurched. Thirty-eight percent of those over 50 are superchurched and 78 percent are churched; only 2 percent are totally nonreligious.

There is no significant difference between those 18–29 and those 30–49. Thirty-three percent of those in the first group and 30 percent of those in the second are unchurched; 6 percent in each group are totally nonreligious.

Regional differences also appear. The East and Midwest reflect the national pattern, but the South is considerably more churched and the West considerably less churched than the average. Only 23 percent of those in the South, but 39 percent of those in the West, are unchurched. Similarly, 2 percent of those in the South and 7 percent of those in the West are totally nonreligious.

The South (34 percent) and the Midwest (33 percent) have the most superchurched Americans, with 28 percent of those in the East and 27 percent of those in the West being superchurched.

Whites and Hispanics reflect the national average, but blacks are more likely to be both churched and superchurched. Seventy-eight percent are churched and 37 percent are superchurched. Three percent of Blacks, 4 percent of whites and 5 percent of Hispanics are totally nonreligious.

There are notable differences by educational level. Those with less than a high school education are slightly more likely (31 percent) to be unchurched.

College graduates (6 percent) and those with some college (5 percent) are slightly more likely to be totally nonreligious.

Some of the most dramatic differences are related to marital status. Those who are married closely fit the national average. But single and divorced or separated Americans are considerably more likely to be unchurched, while the widowed are considerably less likely. Thirty-seven percent of single Americans are unchurched, 9 percent are totally nonreligious and only 19 percent are superchurched. Forty-four percent of the divorced are unchurched, 7 percent are totally nonreligious, while 23 percent are superchurched. Only 19 percent of the widowed are unchurched and only 2 percent are totally nonreligious, while 42 percent are superchurched.

Unchurched Americans show a surprising degree of support for religion, even though they lag well behind the churched in their approval of religion. At the same time, there are indications that the unchurched are less connected than the churched to all major institutions in American society.

Two-thirds of churched Americans (67 percent) said religion was "very important" in their lives, while 29 percent said it was "fairly important" and only 4 percent said it was "not very important." But half of the unchurched (48 percent) said religion was "very important" to them; another 44 percent said it was "fairly important."

One-third of the unchurched (35 percent) believe that "religion can answer all or most of life's problems," while 65 percent of the churched and 80 percent of the superchurched hold this view.

The unchurched are only somewhat less likely than the churched to want American school children to learn about religion: 84 percent of the super-churched, 82 percent of the churched and 74 percent of the unchurched say they would not object to public schools teaching about the major religions of the world.

Differences in perception between the churched and unchurched about the role of religion in society are not sharp: 41 percent of the unchurched, 51 percent of the churched and 55 percent of the superchurched believe religion's influence is increasing; 40 percent of the unchurched, 38 percent of the churched and 36 percent of the superchurched believe it is decreasing.

Differences are sharper, however, on the question of the level of confidence in the church or organized religion: 83 percent of the superchurched, 69 percent of the churched and 30 percent of the unchurched say they have "a great deal" or "quite a lot" of confidence in the church. While fewer than one in ten of the churched report having little or no confidence in the church, the figure rises to three in ten (29 percent) among the unchurched.

But the unchurched are also somewhat less likely than the churched to have "a great deal" or "quite a lot" of confidence in other major institutions. The average proportion of the churched showing high level of confidence in banks, the military, the public schools, newspapers, television, the Supreme Court, Congress, organized labor and big business was 40 percent; the average for the unchurched was 36 percent. An average of 18 percent of the churched and 22 percent of the unchurched reported very little or no confidence in those institutions.

The unchurched are less likely than the churched to be registered to vote: 75 percent of the unchurched, 79 percent of the churched and 82 percent of the superchurched are registered. The unchurched are also less likely than the churched to be involved in charity or social service activities such as helping the poor, sick or elderly: 28 percent of the unchurched, 39 percent of the churched and 46 percent of the superchurched take part in such activities.

Churched and unchurched Americans reflect differences in lifestyle and attitudes toward lifestyle. For example, 47 percent of the superchurched, 59 percent of the churched and 68 percent of the unchurched drink alcoholic beverages at least occasionally.

The unchurched also prefer smaller families: 78 percent of the unchurched, 62 percent of the churched and 56 percent of the superchurched view two or fewer children as the ideal family size. Thirty-six percent of the superchurched, 32 percent of the churched and only 16 percent of the unchurched view three or more children as the ideal.

While unchurched Americans view themselves as more moderate politically than churched Americans, there are very few issues on which the two groups differ. The issues over which they do differ tend to involve sex. Twenty percent of the unchurched describe themselves as liberals, 51 percent as moderates and 23 percent as conservatives. Among the churched, 21 percent describe themselves as liberals, 44 percent as moderates and 29 percent as conservatives. Among the superchurched, 15 percent describe themselves as liberals, 45 percent as moderates and 35 percent as conservatives.

The sharpest differences among the three groups surfaced on the restriction of pornography and the legalization of homosexual relations. Among the unchurched, 35 percent said laws regulating the sale of pornography should be more restrictive, 8 percent said they should be less restrictive and 49 percent said they should remain the same. But 49 percent of the churched favored more restrictive laws, 3 percent less restrictive ones and 40 percent said they should remain the same. Among the superchurched, 60 percent favored more restrictive laws, 3 percent favored less restrictive ones and 31 percent said they should remain the same.

The unchurched were about equally divided on the question of legalizing homosexual relations, with 42 percent supporting it and 45 percent opposing. The churched, however, opposed legalization by 62 to 28 percent; the superchurched opposed it by 71 to 20 percent.

There was no significant difference among the three groups in approval of the way President Reagan handled his job or specific problems: 51 percent of the unchurched, 50 percent of the churched and 53 percent of the superchurched approved of his overall job performance. Differences were small or nonexistent in attitudes toward Reagan's handling of specific issues.

The unchurched, churched and superchurched hold similar views on a number of highly visible public issues.

- 66 percent of the unchurched say they support the blacks in South Africa, while 10 percent say they support the South African government; the churched support the blacks by a 64 to 12 percent margin, the superchurched by 63 to 13 percent.
- 58 percent of the unchurched, 60 percent of the churched and 63 percent of the superchurched support stricter handgun laws.
- 78 percent of the unchurched, 77 percent of the churched and 76 percent of the superchurched support raising the minimum wage to $4.65 an hour.

The 1978 and 1988 "Unchurched American" Studies

Viewing the unchurched only in terms of those who say they are not church members misses the fact that many Americans are nominally church members, but are for all practical purposes religiously inactive. In 1978, a broad coalition of religious organizations came together to sponsor a study, "The Unchurched American," which defined the unchurched as those who are not members of a church or have not attended services in the previous six months other than for special religious holidays, weddings, funerals or the like. A similar coalition of religious groups sponsored an updated study in 1988.

Trying to analyze the findings of "The Unchurched American—1988" is a little like trying to decide whether the glass is half-full or half-empty—there's evidence to support both views. For those who believe the glass is half-empty, the evidence is that the churches have not made any advances in attracting the unchurched over the past decade: in 1978, 41 percent of all American adults were unchurched; in 1988, that figure rose to 44 percent. The percentage of unchurched adults, based on the Bureau of Labor Statistics population estimate, projected to 61 million in 1978 and 78 million in 1988. Overall, 64 percent of all respondents said they were church members, including 18 percent of the unchurched[3].

The same survey, however, also supports the contention that the glass is half-full. One might maintain that the churches have done well to keep slippage at a minimum in light of the continued high mobility among Americans during the last decade, the distractions of modern life and the apparent growing appeal of nontraditional religious movements.

The 1988 study also discovered an intriguing fact—while the proportion of unchurched Americans has increased, the unchurched are, by many measures, more religious than they were in 1978. We will look at those findings in depth shortly.

Just as was the case a decade ago, the new survey finds that there is considerable movement between the churched and unchurched categories— 25 percent of the churched and 65 percent of the unchurched say there was a period of two years in their lives when they had stayed away from their church. One-fourth (23 percent) of the unchurched who said they had left church for two years or more said they later went back.

Discontinuing church attendance is clearly related to youth—but so is returning to church. Three in four (73 percent) of those who said they had stopped attending church for at least two years did so before they were 30, and nearly half (48 percent) did so before they were 20. At the same time, half (51 percent) of those who went back to church after two or more years did so before age 30 and another 25 percent went back between 30 and 39.

Half (48 percent) of the unchurched have been away from church for more than a decade; 4 percent have been away less than a year, 9 percent one to two years, 16 percent three to five years, and 22 percent six to ten years.

In general, the unchurched are more likely to be male, under 30, to live in the West, to be single or married to a spouse with a different religious background. Table 5.1 compares the demographics of churched and unchurched Americans.

Table 5.1

DEMOGRAPHIC PROFILES OF CHURCHED AND UNCHURCHED AMERICANS

	Total	Churched	Unchurched
U.S.	100%	56%	44%
Men	48	44	54
Women	52	56	46
18–24	14	12	17
25–29	11	10	13
18–29	25	22	30
30–49	39	39	40
50 +	35	39	29
White	85	85	85
Black	12	13	11
Hispanic	8	8	8
East	25	25	25
Midwest	24	25	24
South	31	35	25
West	20	15	26
Less Than High School	23	21	26
High School Grad.	39	41	36

Table 5.1 (CONT.)
DEMOGRAPHIC PROFILES OF CHURCHED AND UNCHURCHED AMERICANS

	Total	Churched	Unchurched
Some College	19	19	19
College Grad.	19	19	18
Married	62	69	53
Single	21	16	29
Divorced/Sep./ Widowed	17	15	18
Protestant	59	65	51
Catholic	27	30	22
Jewish	3	2	3
Other	3	3	5
None	8	0	18
Children's Ages 4–18	34	36	31
4–9	19	20	18
10–14	15	16	13
15–18	12	12	10
None	66	64	69

There are some important differences in attitude between the churched and unchurched. Unchurched Americans are more likely to believe "it is possible to be a good Christian or Jew without attending church or synagogue." Eighty-eight percent of the unchurched and 67 percent of the churched believe this, while 9 percent of the unchurched and 29 percent of the churched do not. Overall, 76 percent of the total sample agreed with this statement, down 2 percent since 1978.

There was a sharper difference on a related question. Asked to respond to the statement, "I don't have to belong to an organized religion because I lead a good life," the churched rejected it by 59 to 32 percent; the unchurched, on the other hand, agreed with the statement by 64 to 23 percent.

Large majorities of churched and unchurched Americans agree that "one should arrive at their religious beliefs independent of any church or synagogue."

The churched agreed by 75 to 17 percent, the unchurched by 86 to 6 percent and the total sample by 80 to 12 percent.

There was a surprising degree of agreement between the churched and the unchurched on the statement, "It doesn't matter what church a person attends—one church is as good as another." The churched agreed by 53 to 37 percent, the unchurched by 62 to 24 percent and the total sample by 57 to 31 percent.

The unchurched are more likely to be critical of organized religion on some issues, but not all. The unchurched are also highly critical of organized religion for being too concerned with organizational matters and not concerned enough about social justice. Table 5.2 shows this pattern.

Differences on morality and sex continue to separate churched and unchurched Americans:

- The unchurched believe by 37 to 34 percent that "the rules about morality preached by the churches and synagogues today are too restrictive," while the churched disagree by 56 to 28 percent, a 2-to-1 margin.
- 28 percent of the unchurched and 17 percent of the churched say they would welcome a greater emphasis on sexual freedom in the future.
- 43 percent of the churched but only 19 percent of the unchurched believe that premarital sex is always wrong.

The unchurched (45 percent) are less likely than the churched (61 percent) to have had confirmation training, or special training for full membership in

---

Table 5.2

ATTITUDES OF CHURCHED AND UNCHURCHED TOWARD CHURCHES

	Total	Churched	Unchurched
Most Churches and Synagogues Today Are . . .			
Warm and Accepting of Outsiders	64%	73%	53%
Too Concerned With Organizational Issues	59	58	60
Not Concerned Enough About Social Justice	41	39	44
Effective in Helping People Find Meaning in Life	67	75	57

their church or synagogue, during their youth. This suggests that those who have had special or confirmation training are more likely to remain with their church.

The unchurched are considerably less active than the churched in other areas as well as church involvement. Table 5.3 compares the churched and unchurched on their degree of activity in civic, social and charitable activities.

The unchurched today are, by many measures, more religious than they were a decade ago. This suggests that some may be ready to move into the churched category. If only 5 percent of the unchurched become more active, it would mean increased involvement in American churches and synagogues by about four million people. The unchurched show an increased interest in religion on a variety of issues:

- 44 percent of the unchurched say they have made a "commitment to Christ." This is an increase over the 38 percent of the unchurched who made that statement in 1978. Among churched Americans, those making a commitment to Christ increased from 78 percent in 1978 to 83 percent in 1988.
- 72 percent of the unchurched said they believed that Jesus was God or the Son of God, up from 64 percent in 1978. Belief that Jesus was God or the Son of God increased among the churched from 89 to 93 percent.
- 48 percent of the unchurched are providing religious training for their children, up from 43 percent in 1978. There is still a considerable gap, however, between the percentage of unchurched actually providing religious education and the percentage—73 percent—who say they want such training for their children.
- 58 percent of the unchurched said they would "definitely," "probably" or "possibly" return to church, up from 52 percent in 1978. Thirty-seven percent in 1988 and 36 percent in 1978 said they would "definitely" or "probably" not return. Table 5.4 shows the way these figures break down.

Table 5.3

INVOLVEMENT IN SOCIAL AND CHARITABLE ACTIVITIES

	Churched	Unchurched
Very Active	13%	4%
Fairly Active	22	10
Only Somewhat Active	29	25
Not Active at All	34	55

Table 5.4		
POSSIBILITY OF RETURNING TO CHURCH		
	1988	**1978**
Definitely Yes	11%	16%
Probably Yes	17	11
Possibly Yes	30	25
Probably No	25	23
Definitely No	12	13
Don't Know	5	12

• 68 percent of the unchurched say they would invite others to join their religious congregation.

The level of traditional religious belief among the unchurched remains high:

• 82 percent cite a religious affiliation.
• 77 percent pray to God at least occasionally, and 41 percent do so at least once a day.
• 63 percent believe the Bible is the literal or inspired word of God.
• 58 percent believe in life after death.
• 31 percent say religion is "very important" in their lives, while 38 percent say it is "fairly important."
• 25 percent say they have had a powerful "religious experience."

"The Unchurched American—1988" provided important new information about the state of evangelism in the United States today. Invitation and evangelism are virtually ignored by the mainline churches, certainly an important reason why they have lost members in the last few decades. However, one American in three (34 percent) said they had been asked to become active in a church or synagogue other than their own in the past year; of this group, 79 percent were asked more than once.

Thirty-one percent of the churched and 38 percent of the unchurched reported being approached. Half (55 percent) of the total who were approached, including 51 percent of the churched and 60 percent of the unchurched, were invited by a relative, friend or neighbor. The vast majority of evangelizing in the United States is done by conservative and evangelical churches. Table 5.5 shows the groups cited by those who were approached.

It is likely that many of the Baptist and "other Protestant" churches ap-

Table 5.5

RELIGIOUS GROUP CITED BY THOSE RECEIVING CHURCH INVITATIONS

Baptist	19%	Protestant (Unspecified)	3%
Methodist	4	Other Protestant	44
Lutheran	2	Mormon	6
Presbyterian	2	Other	6
Christian Church	2	Don't Know	11
United Church of Christ	1		

proaching people to join are fundamentalist and evangelical churches, which, by their very nature, stress evangelization. In contrast, mainline Protestant churches (and Catholics, included among the "other") are all but invisible in inviting others to join their churches. This is significant, because about half of those approached to join a church say their response to the invitation was favorable. Overall, 38 percent of the total sample, 39 percent of the churched and 41 percent of the unchurched said they were favorably impressed; 40, 38 and 41 percent, respectively, were unfavorably impressed,

Members of minority groups are particular targets of evangelization. Blacks receive invitations to join a church at the rate of the national average, but Hispanics were more likely than the average to be approached—43 percent said they had received an invitation in the past year. Significantly, members of minority groups do not feel alienated from the churches. Only 8 percent of blacks and 3 percent of Hispanics say they have ever felt unwelcome or excluded from any church because of their race or ethnicity. Blacks and Hispanics are no more likely than whites to be unchurched. This response from Hispanics, who are primarily Catholic, appears to be particularly good news for the Catholic church. It is also possible, however, that blacks and Hispanics feel welcome in church because they go primarily to churches with other blacks and Hispanics. It is also important, however, that among the unchurched, religion is more important to Hispanics than to blacks or whites, suggesting that unchurched Hispanics are likely to become churched.

Americans who say they left their church or synagogue for at least two years were more likely to cite personal or lifestyle changes than particular problems with their church as the reason for leaving. Those who returned to church after such an absence were more likely to be motivated by an inner personal need to return than by external factors such as marriage or having children.

Forty-two percent of those surveyed said there had been a period in their lives of two years or more when they had not attended church except for special events or holidays. Only 22 percent cited specific problems with their church as the reason for this absence. Table 5.6 shows the reasons cited for lack of church attendance.

Of those who said they left the church for two years or more because of other interests, spending time with family or friends and work were the major interests cited. Only 4 percent cited conflicting commitments to community, political or volunteer organizations.

The unchurched who left the church for specific reasons were most likely to cite "excessive concern with money" and "narrow religious beliefs." Table 5.7 shows the reasons cited for leaving.

About half (47 percent) of those who had stayed away from church for two years or more eventually returned. Most cited feelings of a personal need to return. Table 5.8 shows the reasons cited for returning to church.

Almost half (44 percent) of those who said they left church after moving said they "never got around to looking for a new church," while another 8 percent said they "didn't want to get involved." But others cited more concrete reasons: "no church of preferred denomination close to new home" (18 percent); "didn't like any church near new home" (16 percent); "no one approached me"

Table 5.6
REASONS CITED FOR LACK OF CHURCH INVOLVEMENT

Reason	Total	Churched	Unchurched
Found Other Activities	26%	34%	21%
Started Making My Own Decisions	25	20	28
Moved to New Community	22	26	19
Specific Problems with Church	22	15	25
Lifestyle No Longer Compatible	13	12	14
Church No Longer a Help	13	10	15
Work Schedule	12	16	10
Divorced or Separated	6	8	5
Poor Health	4	5	3
Felt Out of Place	3	3	3
Other Reasons	18	15	19
Don't Know	5	5	6

Table 5.7

REASONS FOR LEAVING CHURCH

Reason	Total
Too Much Concern for Money	38%
Teachings About Beliefs Too Narrow	32
Want Deeper Spiritual Meaning	23
Moral Teachings on Sex and Marriage Too Narrow	19
Poor Preaching	18
Dislike Traditional Form of Worship	13
Personal Dispute With Members	12
Church Unwilling to Work for Social Changes	12
No Longer Believe in Supernatural Being	11
Dissatisfied With Pastor or Rabbi	11
Dislike Changes From Traditional Forms of Worship	10
Dislike Church's Social or Political Involvement	9
Teachings About Beliefs Too Broad and Inclusive	9
No One in Church Cares About Me	6
Moral Teachings on Sex and Marriage Too Loose	2
Other Problem	18
Don't Know	10

(4 percent); "didn't like presentation of local church representatives" (2 percent); "other" (25 percent).

The unchurched were more likely than they were a decade ago to cite family reasons as a factor that could bring them back to the church; in fact, they were more likely to cite a variety of factors as likely to bring them back. Table 5.9 shows these shifts.

Practical Steps

"The Unchurched American—1988" suggests a number of practical steps that churches can take both to attract the unchurched back to active participation and to prevent others on the borderline from becoming inactive.

1. Broadly speaking, it would appear that churches need to be still more responsive to the growing public belief in, and commitment to, Jesus Christ.

Table 5.8

REASONS CITED FOR RETURNING TO CHURCH

Factor in Return	Total	Churched	Unchurched
Felt Inner Need to Go Back	40%	44%	32%
Felt Inner Need to Rediscover My Religious Faith	27	31	20
Wanted Child to Receive Religious Training	23	23	21
Felt Guilty About Not Going	19	18	19
Got Older and Thought More About Eternal Life	18	21	12
Went With Spouse or Relative	17	15	20
Invited to Church	14	13	17
Got Married	12	13	10
Had an Important Religious Experience	8	9	5
Moved Back Home	5	5	6
Divorced or Separated	3	3	3
Recovered From Illness	2	2	2
Another Reason	9	8	12
Never Attended Again	2	2	1
Don't Know	3	3	2

They also need to listen more closely to people's inner spiritual journeys and religious experiences—33 percent of adults say they have had a particularly powerful religious insight or awakening—and help them build on those experiences.

2. Churches should encourage religious education programs, particularly by forming a partnership with parents to foster religious training in the home. The fact that the churched were more likely than the unchurched to have had confirmation training, or similar training bringing them into full church membership, certainly indicates that an emphasis on such education for young people will have a long-term impact on church activity.

3. Churches, particularly mainline churches, which have shied away from the practice in the past, should intensify programs of invitation and evangelization. Invitation, if done in a friendly, nonthreatening manner ("pro-

Table 5.9

CIRCUMSTANCES THAT COULD LEAD TO RETURN TO CHURCH

Circumstance	1988	1978
There Is a Change in My Family Situation	22%	12%
I Find a Pastor or Rabbi With Whom I Can Openly Discuss My Spiritual Needs	21	15
I Find a Church or Synagogue With a Good Youth Program	19	13
I Find a Church or Synagogue That Is Serious About Working for a Better Society	17	14
I Find a Church or Synagogue With Good Preaching	17	14
There Is a Crisis in My Life and a Church or Synagogue Demonstrates Genuine Interest in Me	16	12
I Find a Pastor or Rabbi With Whom I Can Openly Discuss My Religious Doubts	15	17
I'm Invited by a Member and I Like the People	15	13
A New Congregation of My Denomination Is Started in My Area	8	4
Other Circumstances	27	10
Don't Know	9	1

pose, not impose"), is one of the best ways to bring about church growth. The lack of evangelization and invitation appears to be one reason contributing to the steady membership decline within mainline Protestant churches.

4. Small groups, particularly prayer and Bible study groups that meet outside of church, offer a way to both attract people to church and sustain current members.

5. Churches should understand the "life cycle effect"; people tend to leave the church in their late teens and early 20s, but begin returning in their late 20s. Americans are also far less likely to be active in church or synagogue when they are single; they tend to become more active when they are married. The unchurched are also less likely than the churched to be

involved in any civic, social or charitable activity. The pattern is that people who are not involved in any community activities are less likely to be active in church; as they become more rooted in the community, however, church activity increases.

6. Churches need to develop different strategies for attracting college graduates than for approaching those with less education. College graduates view religion as less important in their lives; but they are more likely than the average to provide religious training for their children, more likely to take part in independent Bible study and discussion groups, and more likely to say they are interested in church-sponsored cultural activities. They are more likely to be attracted by adult education groups, discussion groups, theater trips, etc.

7. One in five Americans who are married (18 percent) is in a religiously mixed marriage. People in this category consistently lag behind those whose spouses have the same religious affiliation in levels of religious activity; they are less likely to be church members and to provide religious education for their children; they are more likely to become religiously inactive and less likely to return; and they are more likely to react unfavorably to invitations to join a church. These families present a real challenge to American churches, because an invitation to rejoin a church may be interpreted as an effort to drive a wedge between husband and wife. Churches must learn how to minister to their members who become involved in religiously mixed marriages in a way that will make both partners feel welcome.

8. Among the unchurched, those most likely to respond favorably to invitations to return to or join a church are those who belong to the demographic groups that are most religiously active. For example, women are more likely than men to return to church; married people are more likely than single people to return; blacks are more likely than whites to return.

While churches are interested in reaching out to the unchurched, this study suggests another fruitful approach—preventing people from leaving the church by anticipating and dealing with situations that are likely to cause people to leave. For example:

- While this study supports the belief that those over 50 are more religiously active than those under 50, it also shows that Americans who are over 50 are not immune to becoming inactive. Churches should guard against complacency with their members in this age group. Churches should also be particularly attuned to the needs of older members who have health problems. A significant number of those over 50 report that they were inactive for a period of two or more years because of health problems.

- When people become separated or divorced, they are more likely to drift away from their church. Improved ministry to those in broken marriages can retain their involvement in church. The study also shows that single parents are less likely to provide religious education to their children; this may reflect less interest in religion, but it may also reflect the difficulties in providing religious training along with meeting the many conflicting demands one-parent families face.

- A significant number of people who leave church and then return are people who have relocated; this is particularly true for people in their late 20s. This problem could be reduced by strategies to help people stay in touch with their churches when they move. For example, pastors should make an effort to keep track of their parishioners who move and help them contact churches in their new homes. Another approach would be for interfaith agencies to provide a "Welcome Wagon" to insure that new residents receive information about available churches and synagogues. The study found that Catholics are significantly less likely than Protestants to become religiously inactive when they move. This may reflect the fact that the Catholic Church, for the most part, uses a geographic parish; Catholics who live in a particular neighborhood are expected to attend a particular church. Because Protestants, for the most part, are more likely to pick and choose their church, it takes them longer to become familiar with the possibilities in their new homes.

- People with children age 15–18 are more likely than the national average to say that religion is important in their lives, but are also more likely to say that there have been times in their lives when they were more active than they are now. Families coping with older teenagers need more pastoral support from their churches.

RELIGIOUS TELEVISION

One of the major topics of interest within the world of religion for more than a decade has been religious television. The 1980s saw an explosion of interest in big-name religious broadcasters like Jerry Falwell, Jimmy Swaggart, Pat Robertson and others; the combination of colorful personalities, the influence of the "Electronic Church" and the vast amounts of money involved made the subject irresistible. The Gallup Organization has studied religious television at several key points in the past, obtaining a solid basis for understanding this phenomenon.

The major Gallup survey in this area was conducted in 1983 as part of a wide-ranging study of religious television sponsored by a broad coalition of religious organizations, which included both religious broadcasters and their critics. The Annenberg School of Communication at the University of Pennsylvania conducted part of the study, but we will examine only the Gallup data. While it is likely that some of the figures would change if we were to replicate the entire study today, there is no reason to believe that a new study would come to significantly different conclusions. In fact, as we shall see, later studies reinforce the baseline conclusions in the earlier study.

The survey found that about one in three adults (32 percent) had watched some kind of religious television program in the previous thirty days and 18 percent had watched in the previous seven days. (This was somewhat smaller than the figure found in previous surveys and later surveys, but the other surveys were conducted close to religious holidays, so they probably reflected higher than average viewing.) Two-thirds of those who watched religious programs did so before noon on Sunday; 44 percent watched between 6 and 10 A.M., and another 20 percent watched between 10 A.M. and noon[4].

The major reason cited for watching religious programs (22 percent) was simply that people said they enjoyed them, but one in seven (14 percent) did admit that they watched as a substitute for attending church. Another 13 percent said they were inspired or uplifted by the programs; 10 percent said they watched programs because they shared the same religious beliefs; 9 percent cited spiritual growth and 8 percent each cited the sermons and information as reasons for watching. Asked what they liked specifically about the programs, 52 percent cited the preaching, 41 percent cited the music, 40 percent cited "having your spirits lifted" and 36 percent said the programs made them feel closer to God.

Religious television is important to its viewers—three in ten said it contributed as much or more than the church to their spiritual life: One viewer in five (18 percent) said religious television contributes more to their religious life than the church, while half (54 percent) chose the church; 13 percent said they played an equal role.

Religious television scored even better when it comes to providing information about "the moral and social issues that are crucial in America today" —half of the viewers said religious television provides as much or more information than the church: 34 percent said religious television does more to inform them, 39 percent picked the church and 14 percent said they played an equal role.

Demographically, religious-television viewers are more likely to be Protestant, Evangelical, female, older, widowed or divorced, to have low levels of education and to live in the South or in rural areas. Almost half are over 50; one in five is widowed or divorced; more than a third never advanced beyond eighth grade. Table 5.10 compares the profiles of viewers and nonviewers.

There are several other key factors that distinguish viewers from nonviewers:

- Viewers are more likely to be dissatisfied with "the way moral standards have been changing in America," but are no more dissatisfied with the religious climate in general; they are also more satisfied with the way things have been going in their own local church.
- Viewers are more likely to see evangelism and mission work and less likely to see working for social justice as a priority for the church.
- A 1982 Gallup survey found that among those over 50, viewers were in poorer physical health than nonviewers; 56 percent of nonviewers and only 39 percent of viewers in this age group said they were in good physical health.

Table 5.10
DEMOGRAPHIC PROFILES OF RELIGIOUS TV VIEWERS AND NONVIEWERS

	Viewers	Nonviewers
Men	44%	51%
Women	56	49
18–29	17	31
30–49	35	38
50+	48	31
Married	66	63
Single	12	26
Divorced/Widowed	21	11
White	81	89
Nonwhite	19	11
East	18	31
Midwest	29	27
South	37	23
West	16	19
Central City	29	34
Suburb	35	29
Rural	36	27
Protestant	72	51
Catholic	19	40
Other	9	9
Baptist	15	8
Southern Baptist	15	6
Methodist	10	8
Lutheran	6	5
Presbyterian	3	3

Table 5.10 (Cont.)
DEMOGRAPHIC PROFILES OF RELIGIOUS TV VIEWERS AND NONVIEWERS

	Viewers	Nonviewers
Episcopalian	1	3
Evangelical	37	9
Church Member	77	66
Church Attendance		
Once a Week or More	48	33
2–3 Times a Month	11	12
Once a Month	17	11
Special Occasions	13	24
None	11	20
Believe Bible Is the Literal Word of God	58	28
Have Tried to Encourage Someone to Believe in Jesus Christ or Accept Him as Their Savior	68	37
Born-Again Christian	55	24
Had a Religious Experience	49	26
Religion Very Important	71	44
Fairly Important	23	34
Not Very Important	5	22

The 1983 survey asked differently worded questions to get a sense of which religious television programs were the most popular. One asked, "Which religious television program do you watch most often?" The most frequently cited (by 16 percent) was Billy Graham; although Graham does not have a regular program, his Crusades are frequently televised. Several other programs were bunched closely behind: Jimmy Swaggart (13 percent); Oral Roberts (12 percent); "The 700 Club," with Pat Robertson (11 percent); "The PTL Club," with Jim Bakker (10 percent); "The Hour of Power," with Robert Schuller (8 percent); and "The Old-Time Gospel Hour," with Jerry Falwell (5 percent). Six percent mentioned unspecified "religious services."

Those who said they had watched religious programs within the past seven days gave a different response: Jimmy Swaggart was the most watched in this group, cited by 25 percent, followed by Oral Roberts (20 percent), Pat Robertson (18 percent), Jim Bakker (16 percent), Billy Graham (14 percent), Robert Schuller (13 percent) and Jerry Falwell (12 percent). Nine percent cited "religious services." (Some viewers cited more than one program.)

There were enough viewers (more than 100) for each of four programs, plus "local programs" to be useful in developing a profile of the different audiences for the most-viewed programs:

- Billy Graham. Of the five programs, Graham had the highest percentage of female viewers, the highest percentage of viewers age 50 and over and the largest proportion of white viewers. His viewers were relatively less likely to be Evangelicals, but did not stand out on any of the other religious measures.
- Jimmy Swaggart. His viewers include the highest percentage of men (although women are still the majority), the highest proportion in the South (nearly half), and one of the highest proportions of rural dwellers. He has the largest percentage of Protestant viewers and the smallest percentage of Catholic viewers; his viewers are the most likely to say religion is "very important" to them and the most likely to hold evangelical views.
- Oral Roberts. Roberts had the highest percentage of viewers under age 30, but also one of the highest percentages of viewers past age 50. His audience is particularly likely to be divorced, widowed or single—nearly half are not married. He had by far the least educated audience. His audience includes a relatively large proportion of nonwhites and rural dwellers, but he also has the largest proportion of viewers in the East of any of the programs. He has the highest proportion of non-church members, people who do not attend church regularly, and people who consider religion only fairly important.
- Pat Robertson. Robertson has the highest percentage of viewers age 30–50, the highest percentage who are married, the lowest percentage with only a grade school education, the lowest share in rural areas and the highest share in the Midwest. His viewers also score highest on being church members and attending church regularly.
- Local Programs. This category is more diverse; it includes all those who cited watching "religious services" most often, or "generic" programs sponsored by Baptists or Catholics. Viewers of these programs are somewhat better educated than average viewers, more racially diverse, better represented in the West and better represented among Catholics.

On the whole, similarities among these audiences outweigh differences when they are compared with nonviewers. But it is also clear from these comparisons that somewhat differentiated markets have been developed by the different content and style of the programs. For example, Jimmy Swaggart seems to have the greatest appeal to the traditional, conservative Protestant in the southern Bible Belt. Oral Roberts, in contrast, attracts more viewers from outside the church, particularly the dispossessed who may gain hope from the type of message he presents. Pat Robertson, on the other hand, appears more successful at capturing a churched audience from Middle America, Billy Graham's audience is relatively diverse. But the most diverse audience is that of the local programs, which are themselves more diverse in denominational sponsorship, region, race and theology.

Table 5.11 compares the social characteristics of the audiences for these five programs.

Most religious television programs stay on the air by soliciting money from their viewers, and one viewer in three has contributed to a program. The mean (average) gift was $95, while the median gift was $30. Viewers who contribute to religious television are slightly more likely to be female and over 50, but other than that, the demographic profiles of givers and nongivers are virtually identical. In terms of religious characteristics, however, viewers who contribute were more likely to be Protestant, Evangelical, church members, frequent church attenders and to say that religion is "very important" to them. Giving

Table 5.11
PROFILES OF AUDIENCES OF LEADING RELIGIOUS TV PROGRAMS

	Billy Graham	Jimmy Swaggart	Oral Roberts	Pat Robertson	Local Programs
Men	38%	44%	43%	41%	42%
Women	62	56	57	59	58
18–29	16	12	17	15	10
30–49	24	44	27	47	32
50+	59	43	56	37	57
Married	64	68	53	72	68
Single	9	7	15	12	11
Divorced/Widowed	27	25	32	16	21
Grade School	47	42	58	29	39
High School	38	45	31	46	33
Some College	7	10	5	15	16

Table 5.11 (Cont.)
PROFILES OF AUDIENCES OF LEADING RELIGIOUS TV PROGRAMS

	Billy Graham	Jimmy Swaggart	Oral Roberts	Pat Robertson	Local Programs
College Grad.	8	3	5	10	12
White	87	80	76	82	76
Nonwhite	13	20	24	18	24
Central City	24	21	26	36	32
Suburb	31	32	28	30	39
Rural	45	46	46	34	29
East	19	14	22	16	18
Midwest	32	23	32	40	26
South	38	49	37	38	33
West	11	14	9	6	23
Protestant	81	83	80	71	68
Catholic	17	6	14	18	24
Other	2	11	6	11	8
Evangelical	43	52	43	47	42
Church Member	81	78	74	84	84
Religion Very Important	74	83	70	72	82

is related to frequency of viewing: 35 percent of those who watched two hours or more of religious television each week contributed, compared to only 15 percent of those who had watched less than one hour.

A question that has long concerned church leaders is the impact that religious television has on church attendance, activity and contributions. The "Religious Television in America" study approached these questions in several ways. First, it simply asked viewers whether watching religious television had changed their involvement in their local church. Only 10 percent said it had changed their involvement, and 7 percent said it had increased it. Among those who had watched one hour or more in the past seven days, 17 percent said it had changed their church involvement, with 14 percent saying they had increased their church activity.

Another approach was more complicated. We have already seen that viewers are more likely than nonviewers to attend church regularly, but that reflects the fact that religion is more important to viewers than to nonviewers. Analysts then controlled for attitudes toward the importance of religion and found that of those who say that religion is "very important," 59 percent of viewers and 57 percent of nonviewers attend church once a week or more. By this test, watching religious television does not seem to be associated with reduced levels of attendance at religious services.

A similar analysis found that among those for whom religion was "very important," 50 percent of viewers and 41 percent of nonviewers had done volunteer work several times during the previous year. Finally, religious-television viewers were actually somewhat more likely to contribute to their church, and they contributed higher amounts.

Some religious leaders tend to view the church and religious television as competitors. The study compared the views of those who watched an hour or more of religious television each week with those who attended church once a week (there was some overlap) on the gratifications they received from their activity. While the findings were almost the same for many gratifications, the church was rated considerably higher for providing closeness to God, worship and fellowship. Table 5.12 shows this pattern.

The overall pattern was that watching religious television did not weaken church ties. Within small subgroups, however, religious television does seem to be associated with lower religious activity. These subgroups include persons requiring assistance in going places, persons over 50, the divorced, those with low levels of education and those who have become dissatisfied with their local church.

The 1987 Study

Religious television became one of the biggest stories of the year in 1987 in the wake of two developments. One was the revelation of financial and sexual scandals involving Jim Bakker of the PTL Club that resulted in his leaving the organization and, a year later, being indicted for fraud. The other development was controversy surrounding Oral Roberts' claim that God would "call me home" if he could not raise $8 million for his medical school.

An extensive survey conducted in April 1987 found that these events had taken a dramatic toll on public attitudes toward television evangelists. The public overwhelmingly favored full economic disclosure by television ministries and more than 40 percent even favored federal regulation. While the scandals did not lower the overall viewing audience for religious television, it seemed that the percentage of those contributing to television ministries had declined[5].

The survey found that 49 percent of Americans had watched religious television at some time in their lives; 39 percent had watched within the past

Table 5.12

COMPARISON OF GRATIFICATIONS FROM CHURCH, RELIGIOUS TV

	Gratification From Religious TV	Gratification From Church
Percentage Saying They Especially Liked:		
The Preaching or Sermon	61%	66%
Having Your Spirits Lifted	54	62
Feeling Close to God	50	77
The Music	49	52
General Enjoyment	44	41
Knowing More About What's Happening in the World	31	23
The Experience of Worshiping	30	60
Feeling That You Are a Better or Stronger Person	28	50
Information About Important Moral or Social Issues	24	32
Sense of Companionship or Fellowship	20	54

thirty days, and 25 percent had watched within the past seven days. Table 5.13 compares the profiles of all viewers and those who watched religious television within the past seven days (frequent viewers).

Overall, 4 percent of Americans said they had contributed money to a television evangelist in the past twelve months; this figure rose to 8 percent for those who said they watched religious television and 12 percent for those who had watched in the past seven days. In 1983, however, about one-third of religious-television viewers, or about 10 percent of the population as a whole, said they had contributed to a religious television program they watched. There was some difference in question wording, but it appears that the percentage of viewers who contribute to religious television dropped between 1983 and 1987. Those who did contribute in 1987 gave more than those who said they gave in 1983. About half of those who said in 1987 that they had contributed

Table 5.13

PROFILES OF ALL RELIGIOUS TV VIEWERS AND FREQUENT VIEWERS

	Viewers	Past 7 Days
U.S.	49%	25%
Men	44	21
Women	56	29
Whites	46	23
Blacks	68	39
18–29	39	18
30–49	47	22
50+	58	33
College Grad.	42	18
Some College	45	20
High School Grad.	46	22
Less Than High School	64	21
East	36	17
Midwest	46	21
South	62	37
West	48	21
Evangelical	79	46
Non-Evangelical	36	15
Catholic	34	17
Protestant	60	74

in the past twelve months gave more than $100; in 1983 half gave more than $30.

Nine in ten (92 percent) of those surveyed agreed that "religious organizations should make full disclosure of the funds they receive and how they are spent"; only 5 percent disagreed. This reflected an increase from an 86 to 7 percent margin favoring full disclosure in 1980.

A smaller percentage (14 percent), however, agreed in 1987 that "giving money to religious causes or organizations is more important than giving money to other causes"; in 1980, 28 percent of Americans held that view.

In 1980, Americans rejected the statement that "the federal government should regulate the fund-raising activities of religious organizations" by a 54 to 35 percent margin. In 1987, however, that margin fell to only 49 to 43 percent.

The 1987 study also echoed another finding from 1983—90 percent of religious-television viewers said viewing did not change their involvement in their local church. Eight percent said it did change their involvement; two-thirds said watching religious television increased their involvement.

The biggest change from the past, however, was a dramatic decline in public confidence in television evangelists:

- In the 1987 survey, 63 percent of Americans viewed television ministers as "untrustworthy" with money, while only 23 percent said they were "trustworthy." In 1980, a 41 percent plurality had positive views, with 36 percent holding negative ones.
- In 1987, 53 percent of Americans called television ministers "dishonest" and 34 percent called them "honest"; in 1980, "honest" outweighed "dishonest" by 53 to 26 percent.
- In 1987, 51 percent of Americans said television ministers were "insincere," while 34 percent said they were "sincere"; in 1980, "sincere" outweighed "insincere" by 56 to 25 percent.
- In 1987, 48 percent said television ministers "care about people," while 38 percent said they did not; in 1980, "caring" outweighed "not caring" by almost a 3-to-1 margin, 59 to 21 percent.
- In 1987, 56 percent rejected the idea that television ministers have a "special relationship with God," while 30 percent said that they did; in 1980, half of all Americans (47 percent) believed they had such a relationship, while 33 percent disagreed.

These negative attitudes about television ministers in general carried over to attitudes toward specific ministers. Respondents were asked to rate eight evangelists on a 10-point scale, with 1 to 5 indicating favorable ratings and −1 to −5 indicating negative ratings. With the exception of Billy Graham, who received favorable ratings from 76 percent of Americans in both the 1980 and 1987 surveys, the ratings of the evangelists, especially those involved in current scandals, were lower than they were in 1980. Ratings are based on responses by those who say they recognize the men in question.

Jim Bakker, for example, received only 23 percent positive ratings and 77 percent negative ratings; in 1980, he had a 58 to 42 percent favorable rating. Oral Roberts' positive ratings also dropped sharply, from 66 percent in 1980 to 28 percent in 1987, while his negative ratings increased from 34 to 72 percent. Jimmy Swaggart's favorable ratings dropped from 76 to 44 percent, while his negative ratings rose from 24 to 56 percent. (Swaggart was involved in the 1987 scandals because of his efforts to get Bakker, a fellow minister in the Assemblies of God, to resign; news of Swaggart's relationship with a Louisiana prostitute did not become public until 1988 and did not affect his 1987 ratings.)

Other evangelists had less falloff in their favorable ratings: Robert Schuller fell from 78 to 61 percent favorable, Rex Humbard from 73 to 55 percent favorable and Pat Robertson from 65 to 50 percent favorable.

Jerry Falwell, who was not rated in 1980, had 38 percent positive and 62 percent negative ratings. Falwell became chairman of PTL in an attempt to rescue the ministry after Bakker left, and apparently suffered a loss of popularity because of his involvement. In October 1986, 45 percent of Americans gave him a favorable rating.

Table 5.14 shows the pattern in detail.

Frequent viewers of religious television programs—those who say they watched within the past seven days—have a much more positive view of television evangelists than do other Americans. But even among this group, a plurality (47 percent) believe that television evangelists are not trustworthy with money; 37 percent said they are trustworthy.

Frequent viewers gave the evangelists positive ratings on only one of five areas about which they were asked: 60 percent of frequent viewers said the evangelists care about people, while 26 percent said they do not.

On three questions, frequent viewers differed sharply from the general population in their attitudes:

- A majority of frequent viewers (by 53 to 34 percent) said television evangelists were honest, while the general population said by the same margin (53 to 34 percent) that they were dishonest.
- Frequent viewers said the evangelists were sincere (by 51 to 33 percent), while the general population said they were not sincere (by 51 to 34 percent).
- Frequent viewers said the evangelists have "a special relationship with God" (by 48 to 37 percent), while the general population rejected this view by 56 to 30 percent.

Frequent viewers were also considerably more likely than the general population to give a favorable rating to individual evangelists. This was true even for the one evangelist—Billy Graham—given high marks by the general population: 76 percent of all Americans and 85 percent of frequent viewers who recognized Graham's name gave him a favorable rating. Table 5.15 compares the favorable ratings given by the general population and frequent viewers who recognize the television ministers' names.

Evangelical Christians are the major supporters of television evangelists and Catholics are among their sharpest critics. Members of mainline Protestant churches occupy a middle ground between the two. This pattern partly reflects the fact that five of the six most prominent TV evangelists on the air at least

Table 5.14
RATINGS OF LEADING TELEVISION MINISTERS

Favorable	Highly Favorable (+5, +4)	Mildly Unfavorable (+3, +2, +1)	Mildly Unfavorable (−1, −2, −3)	Highly Unfavorable (−4, −5)
Graham				
1987 (90%)	35%	41%	13%	11%
1980 (92%)	35	41	14	10
Roberts				
1987 (89%)	8	20	25	47
1980 (83%)	21	45	21	13
Bakker				
1987 (78%)	5	18	28	49
1980 (28%)	18	40	22	20
Falwell				
1987 (78%)	9	29	24	38
Swaggart				
1987 (76%)	16	28	26	30
1980 (23%)	31	45	15	9
Robertson				
1987 (72%)	13	37	24	26
1980 (25%)	21	44	16	19
Schuller				
1987 (53%)	20	41	19	20
1980 (19%)	29	49	10	12
Humbard				
1987 (50%)	10	45	22	23
1980 (43%)	22	51	20	7

once a week—Jim Bakker, Jerry Falwell, Oral Roberts, Pat Robertson and Jimmy Swaggart—are themselves Evangelicals. The sixth, Robert Schuller, is a minister in the Dutch Reformed Church, a mainline church.

The negative reaction of Catholics toward television evangelists is most evident in responses to five pairs of terms used to describe them: 62 percent of Catholics believe TV evangelists are "dishonest," while 24 percent believe

Table 5.15

COMPARISON OF FAVORABLE RATINGS OF TV MINISTERS BY U.S., FREQUENT VIEWERS

	U.S.	Frequent Viewers
Graham	76%	85%
Bakker	24	28
Robertson	50	73
Schuller	61	75
Swaggart	45	69
Roberts	28	45
Falwell	38	61
Humbard	50	75

they are "honest"; 70 percent believe they are "untrustworthy with money," while only 17 percent believe they are "trustworthy"; 64 percent believe they do not have a "special relationship with God," while 20 percent believe they do; and 61 percent believe they are "not sincere," while 24 percent believe they are. A plurality of Catholics—by 46 to 40 percent—even believe that the TV evangelists "do not care about people."

In contrast, 57 percent of Evangelicals believe the TV evangelists care about people, while 26 percent believe they do not; 50 percent believe they are sincere, while 33 percent believe they are not; 48 percent believe they are honest, while 35 percent believe they are not; 45 percent believe they have a special relationship with God, while 38 percent believe they do not. Even a plurality of Evangelicals, however, believe—by 47 to 36 percent—that the TV evangelists are untrustworthy with money.

Mainline Protestants are more critical than Evangelicals and less critical than Catholics: 45 percent believe the TV evangelists are honest while 44 percent believe they are not; 28 percent believe they are trustworthy with money, while 61 percent believe they are not; 36 percent believe they have a special relationship with God, while 55 percent believe they do not; 56 percent believe they care about people, while 32 percent believe they do not; 44 percent believe they are sincere, while 46 percent believe they are not.

Evangelicals, Catholics and mainline Protestants also differ in their attitudes toward individual television evangelists. Those Evangelicals who recognized the television ministers' names gave these favorable ratings: Graham (82 percent), Schuller (74 percent), Robertson (68 percent), Swaggart (67 percent),

Humbard (61 percent), Falwell (57 percent), Roberts (41 percent) and Bakker (37 percent).

A majority of Catholics gave favorable ratings to only two TV ministers—Graham (68 percent) and Schuller (55 percent). They were followed by Robertson (43 percent), Humbard (40 percent), Swaggart (31 percent), Roberts and Falwell (24 percent each), and Bakker (19 percent).

Mainline Protestants also ranked Graham the highest (82 percent), followed by Schuller (72 percent), Humbard (61 percent), Robertson (53 percent), Falwell (42 percent), Swaggart (41 percent), Roberts (29 percent) and Bakker (23 percent).

Despite basic differences in attitudes toward the TV evangelists, 91 percent of Evangelicals, 90 percent of Catholics and 96 percent of mainline Protestants believe they should all make full financial disclosure.

Evangelicals are strongly opposed to government regulation of the TV evangelists, with 56 percent opposing such regulation and 36 percent supporting it. Catholics were about evenly divided on this question, with 45 percent supporting government regulation and 46 percent opposing it. Among mainline Protestants, 42 percent support government regulation and 52 percent oppose it.

Evangelicals are more likely than the two other religious groups to agree that "giving money to religious causes or organizations is more important than giving money to other causes." Twenty-eight percent of Evangelicals agree with this statement, while only 10 percent of Catholics and 13 percent of mainline Protestants agree.

Despite the scandals and negative publicity surrounding several well-known television evangelists during 1987 and 1988, the percentage of Americans who say they gave money to such evangelists remained stable between April 1987 and April 1988. In April 1987, 4 percent of all Americans said they had contributed to television evangelists in the past year. In March 1988, 5 percent of all Americans said they had contributed. There is no statistical significance in the 1-point difference between these two figures[6].

Several major television evangelists reported a dramatic decrease in contributions between 1987 and 1988. The contrasting stability in the percentage of contributors nationally suggests that viewers are either giving less money to evangelists they have supported in the past, or are shifting their donations to different television evangelists. While major figures like Jerry Falwell, Jimmy Swaggart and Oral Roberts receive the bulk of publicity, there are more than sixty nationally syndicated television evangelists, as well as a large number of evangelists who broadcast only to a local audience.

The profile of contributors remained essentially the same in 1988 as in 1987. Basically, those who contribute to television evangelists are more likely to be Evangelicals, older and less well educated than the general population, and to live in the South.

In terms of religion, 12 percent of Evangelicals, and only 2 percent of non-

Evangelicals, said they had contributed to television evangelists in the past year in 1988. This represented no change since 1987, when 11 and 2 percent, respectively, said they had contributed.

Six percent of Protestants and 2 percent of Catholics in both surveys said they had contributed. Because Evangelicals make up almost half of all Protestants, these figures indicate that non-Evangelical Protestants are no more likely than Catholics to contribute to television evangelists.

Regionally, 9 percent of those living in the South said they had given money to a television evangelist in the past year, up from 6 percent. Other regions were more stable: in the East, 3 percent in 1987 and 3 percent in 1988 had contributed; in the Midwest, it was 3 percent in both surveys and in the West (4 percent in 1987 and 5 percent in 1988).

Those over 50 are most likely to contribute to television evangelists; 7 percent contributed each year. In 1988, 5 percent of those 30–49 and 3 percent of those 18–29 contributed, up slightly from 4 and 1 percent, respectively, in 1987.

Eleven percent of those with less than a high school degree said in the 1988 survey that they gave money to television evangelists. Four percent of high school graduates, 5 percent of those with some college and 3 percent of college graduates said they had contributed. Figures for 1987 were 6 percent (less than high school), 4 percent (high school graduates), 3 percent (some college) and 3 percent (college graduates), respectively.

There were no real differences along gender and race lines: in 1987, 4 percent of whites and 5 percent of blacks were contributors; in 1988, 5 percent of whites and 4 percent of blacks said they had made donations. Four percent of men in 1987 and 6 percent in 1988 said they had contributed, as did 5 percent of women in each year.

In 1987, 8 percent of Republicans, 2 percent of Democrats and 3 percent of Independents said they were contributors; in 1988, it was 5 percent, 5 percent and 6 percent, respectively.

Observations on Religious Television

As we noted earlier, many church leaders have regarded religious television as a competitor. The fact is, however, that for the vast majority of viewers, religious television is far more a supplement to church life than a replacement for it. To the degree that religious television affects church involvement, it probably encourages more than it discourages.

Different television ministers attract different audiences. If a particular minister becomes involved in scandal or loses his audience, it is likely that his viewers will not leave religious television altogether; instead, they are more likely to find another minister—or ministers—who offer the same style or message. For example, those who watched Jimmy Swaggart, a fire-and-brimstone Pentecostal, but lost confidence in him personally will not turn to the mainline Robert Schuller or the fundamentalist Jerry Falwell—they will look for another minister who mirrors Swaggart.

Even frequent viewers of religious television are affected by scandals involving major TV ministers; but they do not appear to have lost their faith in the institution of religious television. For a significant proportion of Americans—older, female, lower income, poorly educated, Evangelical—religious television has become part of their religious routine.

PART
II

CHAPTER

6

Religion and Public Issues

R ELIGION is a key factor in the way in which Americans view social and political issues. Some issues, like abortion and peace, have an inherently religious aspect. But on many issues, whether or not the religious component is clear, different religious groups hold different views; on many occasions, differences related to religion are more pronounced than differences related to factors such as gender, age or education. This chapter will examine the differences among religious groups in their attitudes toward a wide variety of major contemporary issues.

ABORTION

Few issues in American life are as controversial as abortion. Feelings, usually rooted in religious beliefs, run deep on both sides of the issue. American attitudes toward abortion are marked by ambiguity and, often, by outright contradictions. One of the most interesting sides of the question of attitudes toward abortion is that slight differences in the wording of questions produce wide differences in responses. We will go into unusual detail in examining these attitudes in order to draw the best picture possible of the views of all Americans on abortion, particularly the views of key religious groups.

The dividing line in the current debate is the Supreme Court's action in legalizing most abortions in its January 22, 1973, decisions in the *Roe* and *Doe* cases. The court held that states cannot place restrictions on a woman's right to an abortion during the first trimester of pregnancy. In the second trimester, the states have no authority to prevent abortion, but can regulate certain medical aspects involved. Only during the third trimester, when medical experts generally agree that the fetus is capable of living outside the womb, can states impose restrictions on a woman's right to have an abortion.

Since 1974, Gallup surveys have periodically asked the identical question: "The U.S. Supreme Court has ruled that a woman may go to a doctor to end pregnancy at any time during the first three months. Do you favor or oppose this ruling?" Responses have fluctuated within a narrow range over that period. Support has ranged between 45 and 50 percent, opposition between 43 and 46 percent. In January 1986, Americans were split 45 to 45 percent.

The demographic patterns in response to this question are somewhat unexpected. There is no difference in attitude between men and women. But age, education and religion are significant factors. Younger Americans are more likely to favor the Supreme Court decisions—those under 30 support the decisions by 49 to 41 percent, while those over 50 oppose them by 48 to 38 percent.

There are major differences in attitude by educational levels—59 percent of college graduates support the court's decisions, compared to only 36 percent of those with less than a high school education and 27 percent of those with only a grade school education.

There are some unexpected patterns along religious lines. Catholics, whose church condemns abortion, oppose the court's decisions by 49 to 41 percent, but they are not the denomination with strongest opposition—55 percent of all Baptists and 59 percent of Southern Baptists oppose the decisions. Evangelicals are even more opposed to legal abortion. The strongest support for legal abortion comes from mainline Protestants, Jews and those with no religious affiliation.

Another set of questions has probed attitudes about support for a constitutional amendment that would bar legal abortion except in the case of rape, incest, or danger to the mother's life. There has been more fluctuation on this question. In October 1984, Americans favored such an amendment by a 50 to 46 percent margin. In that survey, the biggest gap in support was not between Catholics (59 percent) and Protestants (51 percent), but between Evangelicals (66 percent) and Methodists (44 percent). Sixty percent of Southern Baptists supported such an amendment. A Gallup-*Newsweek* Poll conducted in early 1985 found 58 to 36 percent support for the amendment overall. This shift was apparently due to a burst of publicity for the antiabortion movement at the time, including publicity about the film *The Silent Scream*, which depicted an abortion.

The *Newsweek* poll uncovered a piece of information that underscores the emotion and confusion surrounding abortion—four Americans in ten (38 percent) said that they wonder whether their position on abortion is the right one. Significantly, equal percentages of those who favor or oppose a ban on abortion wonder about the correctness of their own decisions.

Further evidence of the conflict in people's minds about abortion is found in the fact that while 58 percent favored a ban on abortion in most cases, the vast majority—with similar percentages among those on both sides of the issue—felt that if abortions were illegal, a wide variety of negative consequences would occur. For example, 87 percent said many women would be harmed by abortions performed by unqualified people and 81 percent said wealthy women would still be able to get safe abortions. At the same time, only 26 percent said an abortion ban would improve the moral tone of America[1].

By June 1988, opinion on a constitutional amendment was again more evenly divided, with 45 percent of Americans opposing an amendment to bar abortion except in the cases mentioned, and 44 percent supporting such an amendment[2]. Table 6.1 shows responses by key demographic groups.

Table 6.1
VIEWS ON CONSTITUTIONAL AMENDMENT TO RESTRICT ABORTION

	Support Amendment	Oppose Amendment
U.S.	44%	45%
Men	42	46
Women	47	45
18–29	47	47
30–49	42	47
50 +	45	43
65 +	49	37
East	43	46
Midwest	48	44
South	45	41
West	40	51
College Grad.	34	59
Some College	45	43
High School Grad.	47	42
Less Than High School	52	38
$50,000 + /Year	37	56

Table 6.1 (CONT.)
VIEWS ON CONSTITUTIONAL AMENDMENT TO RESTRICT ABORTION

	Support Amendment	Oppose Amendment
$30,000–49,999	40	53
$15,000–29,999	46	45
Less Than $15,000	53	34
Major Metropolitan Area	41	51
Over 150,000 Population	41	44
Less Than 150,000	50	40
White	44	46
Black	40	48
Republican	48	41
Democrat	43	47
Independent	42	47
White Protestant	47	44
White Catholic	46	44
White Evangelical	56	36
Non-Evangelical	39	50

Two new questions about abortion were included in the Times Mirror Corporation's study, "The People, Press and Politics," in a survey conducted in April and May 1987[3]. One asked whether respondents supported changing the nation's laws "to make it more difficult for a woman to get an abortion"; the other asked them to rank themselves as supporters of the "antiabortion movement." The question used a scale of 1 to 10, with 1 indicating that the description was "totally wrong," and 10 indicating that it was "perfect." The survey found that Americans rejected making it more difficult to get an abortion by a 5-to-4 margin. But one-third of Americans can be classified as strong supporters (with scores of 8–10) of the antiabortion movement and one-third can be classified as strong opponents (with scores of 1–3).

Along religious lines, the strongest opposition came from Evangelical Protestants, while the strongest support came from non-Evangelical Protestants,

Jews and those with no religious affiliation. American Catholics are evenly divided on the question of making it more difficult to obtain an abortion.

Overall, 51 percent of all Americans are opposed to making it more difficult to get an abortion, while 41 percent favor such a change. Among Catholics, 48 percent oppose more restrictions on abortion, while 46 percent support them. Jews oppose further abortion restrictions by 76 to 20 percent and those with no religious affiliation are opposed by 72 to 15 percent.

Evangelical and non-Evangelical Protestants hold dramatically different views on abortion. White Evangelical Protestants support restrictions on abortion by 62 to 32 percent, while white non-Evangelical Protestants are opposed by 60 to 32 percent. Identification as an Evangelical is also a factor in attitudes of black Protestants. Black Evangelical Protestants are evenly divided, with 44 percent supporting abortion restrictions and 46 percent opposing. But black non-Evangelical Protestants oppose restrictions by 62 to 26 percent.

Those who belong to "other" religious groups are evenly divided, with 46 percent supporting restrictions and 47 percent opposing.

Table 6.2 shows how various groups feel about abortion restrictions.

Table 6.2
ATTITUDES ON PLACING MORE RESTRICTIONS ON ABORTION

	Support Restrictions	Oppose Restrictions
Men	38%	54%
Women	44	49
18–29	38	56
Men	35	58
Women	40	55
30–49	40	53
Men	38	54
Women	42	53
50+	45	46
Men	39	50
Women	50	41
White	42	51
Black	36	53
Hispanic	47	48

Table 6.2 (CONT.)

ATTITUDES ON PLACING MORE RESTRICTIONS
ON ABORTION

	Support Restrictions	Oppose Restrictions
College Grad.	29	67
Some College	39	55
High School Grad.	44	49
Less Than High School	48	41
Less Than $10,000/Year	45	44
$10–19,999	44	47
$20–29,999	44	50
$30–39,999	38	57
$40–49,999	40	55
$50,000+	29	67
East	37	55
Midwest	44	50
South	47	44
West	34	60
Republican	48	46
Democrat	40	52
Independent	38	55

Using this scale of 1 to 10, 33 percent of Americans were strong supporters of the antiabortion movement and 36 percent were strong opponents. In general, the pattern of response paralleled the responses to the question about making it more difficult to get an abortion. The one group showing a significant difference was Catholics—39 percent were strong supporters of the antiabortion movement, while 29 percent were strong opponents. The fact that Catholics consider themselves strong supporters of the antiabortion movement, but are evenly divided on the question of legal restrictions, suggests that to some Catholics, being antiabortion does not necessarily mean bringing about legal restrictions. They may see their goal as convincing women not to choose abortion, even though it is legal.

Table 6.3 shows responses by key groups.

By one key measure, however, public opinion has remained virtually un-changed since the Supreme Court abortion decisions. In September 1988, a 57 percent majority favored legal abortion only under certain circumstances, while 24 percent back unlimited access and 17 percent an outright ban[4]. This

Table 6.3

SELF-DESCRIPTION AS SUPPORTER OF ANTIABORTION MOVEMENT

	Totally Wrong 1	2	3	4	5	6	7	8	9	Perfect 10
U.S.	23%	6%	7%	6%	11%	6%	6%	7%	7%	19%
Men	23	7	7	6	13	6	6	6	7	16
Women	23	6	6	5	10	6	6	7	7	21
White	24	6	7	5	11	6	6	8	7	18
Black	20	5	5	6	14	7	7	6	6	20
Hispanic	20	7	7	5	8	11	8	6	11	16
College Grad.	35	8	9	6	9	5	5	5	5	11
Some College	27	6	8	5	10	7	6	4	5	20
High School Grad.	19	6	6	6	13	6	7	8	7	19
Less Than High School	17	5	5	5	11	6	6	8	8	23
$50,000+/Year	33	6	10	5	14	7	3	4	4	12
$40–49,999	27	7	7	5	11	5	7	7	8	14
$30–39,999	25	7	7	6	12	6	6	6	5	19
$20–29,999	22	6	8	7	13	7	7	6	6	18
$10–19,999	20	6	5	5	10	6	7	7	8	22
Less Than $10,000	20	7	5	5	11	6	4	7	7	20
18–29	22	6	6	7	12	7	8	5	7	17
30–49	26	6	8	5	10	6	5	6	6	19
50+	20	6	5	5	13	6	6	8	7	19

Table 6.3 (CONT.)

SELF-DESCRIPTION AS SUPPORTER OF ANTIABORTION MOVEMENT

	Totally Wrong 1	2	3	4	5	6	7	8	9	Perfect 10
Married	22	6	7	5	11	6	6	7	7	19
Single	25	8	7	8	11	7	6	4	6	16
Divorced/Sep.	30	7	4	5	13	4	5	6	6	17
Widowed	18	5	5	5	13	4	5	9	7	22
East	23	6	6	6	12	7	6	6	6	18
Midwest	20	5	8	5	13	5	6	8	8	21
South	22	6	5	5	11	6	6	7	7	20
West	28	10	8	6	9	6	5	6	7	13
Republican	22	6	6	6	11	8	7	7	7	20
Democrat	22	6	7	5	11	6	7	7	7	19
Independent	25	7	7	6	12	5	5	7	7	17
Protestant										
White/Evan.	14	4	6	5	11	5	6	8	10	27
White/Non-Evan.	29	8	8	7	13	5	6	6	5	10
Catholic	16	6	7	5	11	6	7	8	8	23
Jewish	50	7	3	2	10	3	2	3	1	14
None	45	9	5	3	9	9	3	4	2	8

represents little change from 1975, when 54 percent approved of abortion in certain circumstances, 21 percent thought it should be legal in all circumstances and 22 percent thought it should be illegal in all circumstances.

Large majorities of those who approve of abortion only in certain circumstances think it should be legal if the woman's life is endangered (by 94 to 2 percent), if the pregnancy results from rape or incest (by 85 to 11 percent), if the woman's physical health will be severely impaired (by 84 to 11 percent) and if there is a chance the baby will be born deformed (by 60 to 29 percent). They reject legal abortion on economic grounds—if the woman cannot afford to have the child—by 75 to 19 percent.

Table 6.4 shows the long-range trend on attitudes toward legal abortion. Table 6.5 shows attitudes by demographic groups.

Significantly, support for legal abortion grew over the previous decade in all of these cases except danger to the mother's life, which has had a high degree of support for a long time. We added the responses of those saying abortion should be legal in each instance to the 24 percent of Americans saying abortion should be legal in all cases to obtain the percentage of Americans supporting legal abortion in each circumstance. Table 6.6 shows the trend.

Two other findings related to abortion are relevant:

- Americans rejected a Reagan administration policy to withhold federal funds from family planning clinics that provide abortion-counseling by 66 to 27 percent. Even Evangelicals rejected this position by 57 to 34 percent[5].
- When Americans are asked to name the most important problem facing the nation, barely 1 percent cite changing abortion laws. Traditionally, economic and peace issues top the most important list, but dozens of others are usually also mentioned.

Finally, there are important shifts taking place among American Catholics when it comes to abortion—Catholics are becoming more accepting of legal abortion. Consider the following:

- Catholics were less likely in 1988 than in 1984 to support a constitutional amendment to restrict abortion.
- They are more likely than a decade ago to believe that abortion should be legal in a variety of specific cases.

Table 6.4

WHEN SHOULD ABORTION BE LEGAL?

| | Legal | | Illegal |
	All Cases	Certain Cases	All Cases
1988	24%	57%	17%
1983	23	58	16
1981	23	52	21
1980	25	53	18
1979	22	54	19
1977	22	55	19
1975	21	54	22

Table 6.5

WHEN SHOULD ABORTION BE LEGAL?—BY GROUPS

	Legal		Illegal
	All Cases	Certain Cases	All Cases
U.S.	24%	57%	17%
Men	24	56	17
Women	23	58	17
Whites	25	57	15
Nonwhites	15	55	28
18–29	22	60	16
30–49	28	54	17
50+	19	60	17
College Grad.	39	50	19
Some College	23	61	14
High School Grad.	20	59	17
Less Than High School	13	59	26
East	28	53	17
Midwest	20	62	16
West	32	48	16
Republican	23	57	17
Democrat	23	55	19
Independent	26	60	12
Protestants	20	60	17
Catholics	17	62	18
Evangelicals	12	62	24
Non-Evangelicals	31	55	12

Table 6.6

CHANGES IN ATTITUDES TOWARD ABORTION IN SPECIFIC CASES

	1977	1979	1988
Life of Mother	77%	78%	77%
Physical Health	54	52	72
Rape/Incest	65	59	72
Deformed Fetus	42	44	58
Can't Afford	16	15	35

· Catholics disapproved of the Reagan policy of withholding federal funds from family planning clinics that provide abortion-counseling by 66 to 28 percent.

In October 1984, a Gallup survey asked Americans whether they supported a constitutional amendment that would bar abortion except in the case of rape, incest or a threat to the life of the mother. Catholics supported the amendment by 59 to 38 percent. But when the same question was repeated in June 1988, a major shift was visible. Exact comparisons are impossible because the 1988 survey categorized Catholics differently. But it found that white Catholics supported the amendment by only 46 to 44 percent. Hispanics supported the amendment by 51 to 34 percent. Seventy percent of Hispanics are Catholics, and about one Catholic in five is Hispanic. Combining these figures suggests that there was about a 10-point drop in support for the amendment among Catholics.

An October 1988 survey found that Catholics are more likely today than a decade ago to support legal abortion in the case of rape, incest, severe risk to the mother's physical health, the chance that a baby will be born deformed and when the mother cannot afford to have the child. Seventy-seven percent of Catholics believe abortion should be legal when the mother's life is in danger. This is about the same as the 77 percent who gave this answer in 1977 and the 82 percent who gave it in 1979.

Differences were sharper on other issues. On the question of a severe threat to the mother's physical health, 71 percent in 1988 said abortion should be legal, up from 51 percent in 1977 and 46 percent in 1979.

Similarly, 71 percent said abortion should be legal in the case of rape or incest, up from 68 percent in 1977 and 57 percent in 1979.

For the first time, a majority of Catholics (57 percent) said in 1988 that abortion should be legal when there is a risk that the baby will be born deformed; 40 percent held this view in 1977 and 41 percent in 1979.

The least support is found for legal abortion when the mother cannot afford to have a child. Only 28 percent of Catholics support legal abortion in this case. But this represents an increase from 15 percent in 1977 and 1979.

What patterns emerge from all of these figures on attitudes toward abortion? There are several. First, it is easy to understand the level of intensity that surrounds the issue—four Americans in ten have very strong feelings about abortion, with 19 percent saying the phrase "a supporter of the antiabortion movement" describes them perfectly, and 23 percent saying that description is "totally wrong." The correlation between views on abortion and religious affiliation strengthens the emotional intensity surrounding the issue.

Despite this intensity, however, there is more consensus on abortion than first meets the eye. Whatever their responses to questions about the Supreme Court's decisions or proposed constitutional amendments, large majorities of Americans, as many as three in four, want abortion to be available legally in the "hard" cases—danger to the mother's life or health, pregnancy resulting from rape or incest, or risk of a deformed child. The opposition to legal abortion for purely economic reasons may reflect two concerns. First, Americans may feel that money should be found somewhere to care for a child. Second, they may question the sincerity of some claims of poverty, which may be a cover for abortion for the sake of convenience. These findings also lend support to the belief that support for easy abortion is seen as a symbolic attack on family values even among those who support legal abortion in many cases.

The demographic patterns on attitudes toward abortion are fascinating.

- There is no gender gap on abortion.
- Young people are considerably more supportive of legal abortion, older people considerably more opposed, although the differences even out when it comes to specific cases.
- College graduates are the most likely to favor legal abortion, those with less than a high school degree the least likely; the same pattern holds up in terms of income, with those with higher incomes most likely to support legal abortion.
- The West is the most pro-choice region, followed by the East; the South is marginally more pro-choice than the Midwest.
- The backbone of the antiabortion movement comes increasingly from white Evangelicals, not Catholics, who have become more accepting of legal abortion in the past decade. In fact, the heavy antiabortion feeling among Hispanics to some degree masks the increasing acceptance of legal abortion among white Catholics.
- There may be no other issue that so clearly differentiates the views of white Evangelical and white non-Evangelical Protestants.

What does the future hold? Given the growing acceptance of legal abortion in specific cases and the gap in attitudes between those under 50 and those over 50, it would seem that as more time passes, the public will become increasingly accepting of legal abortion unless there is a dramatic change in attitude among younger Americans.

EDUCATION

Education clearly will be one of the top domestic priorities of the 1990s; parents, educators, business leaders, religious leaders, and government leaders at the state and local levels have been focusing on education as necessary for both teaching young Americans the skills they need to have in order to compete economically and the values they need to know in order to be good citizens. Questions of religion and values are present throughout the education debate, including questions related to the role of church-run private schools. The following section will discuss important attitudes toward education, along religious lines.

A perennial issue is the controversial case of aid to church-run schools, an issue over which Americans are sharply divided. Americans support tax credits for tuition paid to private schools by 50 to 45 percent[6]. Catholics support tuition tax credits by 65 to 31 percent, while Protestants oppose them by 49 to 46 percent. This is an issue on which there is a sharp difference between Evangelical and mainline Protestants—for example, Evangelicals support tax credits by 53 to 40 percent, while mainline Protestants are sharply opposed. The increased Evangelical support for tuition tax credits reflects support for the Christian schools that have emerged in the past decade.

At the same time, a plurality of Americans—by 45 to 40 percent—support a voucher system, in which the government would give parents an educational voucher to be used at the school of their choice, public or private. In 1986, by 46 to 41 percent, they supported a plan to give parents a voucher worth $600 in tuition at the public, private or parochial school of their choice. This was down slightly from a 51 to 38 percent majority in 1983. Majorities of Catholics, blacks, people under 30 and those dissatisfied with the public schools support vouchers[7].

Fourteen percent of public school parents say that if they had such a voucher, they would use it to send a child to a church-run school. Another 13 percent would shift a child to a private school, while 6 percent would shift to another public school. Nineteen percent of women and only 9 percent of men say they would send a child to a church-run school if they had a $600 voucher.

If money were not a factor, about half of parents of public school students (49 percent) say that they would send one of their children to a private or parochial school, while 46 percent say they would not. Women are far more supportive of private and parochial schools—57 percent of women and only 38 percent of men say they would send a child to private or parochial school if they could.

While Americans are split on the question of government aid to nonpublic schools, they believe the existence and growth of those schools is a good thing—in 1985, they approved this growth by a 2-to-1 margin. Not surprisingly, Catholics, who have a well-established nonpublic school system, are more likely than Protestants to believe that the increase in the number of private schools is a good idea. Support for growth in this area is highest among private school parents. But even public school parents support the trend by a 2-to-1 margin. Table 6.7 shows responses on this issue.

At the same time, there is a strong consensus that the increase in "home schools"—parents teaching their children at home—is a bad idea, although there has been an increase in support for home schools in the past few years[8]. Table 6.8 shows this pattern.

Why do Americans reject home schools while they support private schools? One reason may well be concern that parents teaching their children at home will not meet the academic standards Americans believe are necessary for a proper education. Another reason might be that children educated at home do not receive the benefit of the socialization that students receive by dealing with others, including people from different backgrounds than their own, in either public or private schools.

By an overwhelming majority, almost unanimously, parents of private school students want their children's schools to meet the same teacher certification and accreditation standards as public schools[9]. There is no difference in views among nonpublic school parents, public school parents, Catholics, Protestants and the total population; more than 90 percent in each group support such standards. The percentage of those favoring the use of public school standards for home schools is only a few points lower across the board.

These findings, from the seventeenth annual Gallup–Phi Delta Kappa survey of educational attitudes, come at a time when state legislatures are under pressure from some fundamentalist groups to exempt home schools and church-run schools from state teacher certification and accreditation standards. But

Table 6.7

ATTITUDES TOWARD GROWTH OF PRIVATE SCHOOLS

	Good Idea	Bad Idea
U.S.	55%	27%
Catholics	64	18
Protestants	54	30
Public School Parents	56	28
Nonpublic School Parents	71	21

Table 6.8

**SHIFT IN PERCENTAGE SAYING GROWTH OF
HOME SCHOOLS IS A "GOOD IDEA"**

	1985	1988
Total	16%	28%
Catholics	14	29
Protestants	17	27
Public School Parents	14	30
Nonpublic School Parents	22	30

our findings make it clear that whatever else parents want from nonpublic schools, they also want strong academic standards.

Much of the discussion of the needs of public and private, mostly parochial, schools suggests that supporters of private education are hostile toward the public schools. But the twentieth annual Gallup–Phi Delta Kappa survey of attitudes toward public education found no such hostility among parents of children in private schools[10]. In fact, half (52 percent) of parents with children in private schools also have children in public schools. At the same time, 14 percent of parents with children in public schools also have children in private schools. According to national studies, perhaps three-quarters of those in private schools attend church-run schools.

Parents of children in private schools are almost as likely as public school parents to support tax increases to help the public schools and are as likely to support increased government spending on specific programs. While 73 percent of public school parents support increased taxes to pay for public education, so do 68 percent of private school parents.

Table 6.9 shows support of public school parents and private school parents for specific programs in the public schools.

Despite these areas of agreement, there are some important differences in attitudes toward the public schools between public school parents and private school parents. Private school parents give lower grades to public schools both locally and across the country and to express less confidence in their ability to deal with problems like alcohol and drug abuse and teenage pregnancy.

For example, 41 percent of public school parents give their local schools an "A" or a "B" grade, while only 33 percent of private school parents give them such grades; 8 percent of public school parents, but 21 percent of private school parents, give local schools a "D" grade. Four percent in each group give their local public schools a failing grade.

One explanation for this difference may be lack of contact with public

Table 6.9

ATTITUDES OF PUBLIC AND PRIVATE SCHOOL PARENTS

	Public School Parents	Private School Parents
Increase Spending For Students With Learning Disabilities	48%	44%
Increase Spending for Gifted and Talented Students	27	25
Establish Before- and After-School Programs for "Latchkey" Children	77	76
Develop AIDS Education Programs	94	95

school students by private school parents. While 57 percent of public school parents said they get some of their information about the public schools from their students, only 41 percent of private school parents made this statement.

On issues related to race, private school parents appear less supportive than public school parents of integration in the public schools, but they are more supportive of other efforts to provide education for minorities. Among public school parents, 36 percent believe more should be done to integrate the public schools, while 24 percent believe less should be done. Among private school parents, the margin favoring more efforts toward integration was narrower, 30 to 26 percent.

Fifty-seven percent of public school parents and 49 percent of private school parents said integration has improved the quality of education for black students; 31 percent and 34 percent, respectively, said it has been bad for them. Thirty-seven percent of public school parents and 36 percent of private school parents said integration has improved the quality of education for white students, while 47 percent and 48 percent, respectively, said it had not.

But 59 percent of private school parents and 54 percent of public school parents favor government efforts to give special financial aid to schools that prove they can increase academic achievement among minorities, as measured by standardized tests. And 57 percent of private school parents, compared to 48 percent of public school parents, believe public colleges should adopt a tuition plan that takes account of minority students' ability to pay.

Despite these differences in attitude, there is no significant difference in the racial makeup of the two groups of parents: 16 percent of public school parents and 15 percent of private school parents are nonwhite.

There are some demographic differences between the two groups, however.

In public schools, 57 percent of the parents are Protestant and 27 percent are Catholic. In private schools, 44 percent of the parents are Catholic and 41 percent are Protestant.

Private school parents are more likely to live in cities with populations above one million (47 percent versus 33 percent of public school parents), to live in the East (30 percent versus 23 percent), to be college graduates (29 percent versus 17 percent), and to have family incomes above $50,000 a year (24 percent versus 16 percent).

There are important differences between Catholics and Protestants in attitudes toward education[11]. The twentieth annual Gallup–Phi Delta Kappa survey of attitudes toward education found that while Protestants support the use of physical discipline—spanking—in the schools by a margin of 58 to 38 percent, Catholics oppose it by 56 to 41 percent. Overall, 50 percent of Americans support physical discipline in the schools, while 45 percent oppose it.

Overall, however, there is a considerable amount of agreement between the two groups on educational issues despite the fact that Catholics are twice as likely as Protestants to have children in parochial or private schools: 12 percent of Catholics and 6 percent of Protestants with school-age children have children in such schools. Fifty-seven percent of Protestants and 27 percent of Catholics with school-age children have children in public schools.

Agreement between Catholics and Protestants includes issues related to education about AIDS. The U.S. Catholic bishops have been involved in a major debate over whether Catholic morality permits discussion of the use of condoms to reduce the spread of AIDS, with some prominent bishops charging that such education weakens the church's ban on the use of artificial means of birth control. But American Catholics seem unconcerned about this debate. When asked whether public schools should include information about "safe sex" in AIDS education programs, 80 percent of Catholics said it should be taught; only 15 percent disagreed. Protestants approved teaching about "safe sex" by 76 to 18 percent, while all Americans approved by 78 to 16 percent.

Overall, 91 percent of Catholics, 90 percent of Protestants and 90 percent of all Americans said the public schools should develop AIDS education programs, with almost half saying the programs should begin with students under the age of 10. Only about four in ten in all groups, however, expressed a high level of confidence in the schools' ability to provide such programs. On another AIDS-related issue, 60 percent of Catholics, 56 percent of Protestants and 57 percent of all Americans said that students who are AIDS victims should be allowed to attend school.

There were other differences between Catholics and Protestants:

- Catholics (75 percent) were more likely than Protestants (68 percent) to support the use of public schools for before- and after-school programs for "latchkey" children who would otherwise be home alone. This difference reflects generally higher support among Catholics for government social programs.

- Catholics are less likely to believe that their children are getting a better education than they did themselves: 43 percent believe their children are getting a better education, but 39 percent believe their children's education is worse than their own. Protestants, on the other hand, believe that their children are getting a better education than they did by a 52 to 33 percent margin. This difference could reflect the fact that today's Catholic adults were significantly more likely than their children to have attended a parochial school.
- Catholics were less likely to support a recent Supreme Court decision giving public school officials more power to censor student newspapers. Protestants approved of the decision by 64 to 24 percent, Catholics by 57 to 31 percent.

There were no significant differences between Catholics and Protestants on key education issues:

- 64 percent of Catholics and 65 percent of Protestants said they would be willing to pay higher taxes to improve the quality of the public schools.
- 74 percent of each group supported the requirement that high school students pass a standardized national test in order to graduate.
- 87 percent of each group supported competency testing for teachers.
- Both groups gave virtually identical grades to the performance of local public schools, although Catholics gave a slightly lower rating to public schools nationally. Table 6.10 shows the grades they gave to the schools.

Parents who send their children to church-run schools do so largely to have them taught religious values. But parents who send their children to public schools also want them to learn moral values. Six in ten parents of children in public schools favor courses on values and ethical behavior and seven in ten believe it would be possible to develop subject matter for such a course that is acceptable to most people in the community[12].

Table 6.10
GRADES GIVEN PUBLIC SCHOOLS, BY RELIGIOUS GROUP

	Protestants	Catholics		Protestants	Catholics
Local			National		
A	9%	9%	A	3%	2%
B	33	32	B	21	18
C	34	35	C	47	52
D	9	10	D	13	12
F	4	4	F	3	3

These findings are based on the 1987 Gallup–Phi Delta Kappa survey on education, the nineteenth such poll. The survey asked "Do you think courses on values and ethical behavior should be taught in the public schools, or do you think that this should be left to the students' parents and the churches?"

Among all Americans, 36 percent favored leaving values education to parents and churches; 43 percent favored courses in the schools and 13 percent favored both, for a total of 56 percent supporting values courses in the public schools.

Among public school parents, 38 percent favored leaving values education to parents and churches; 45 percent favored school courses and 13 percent favored both, for a total of 58 percent favoring school courses on values.

Those with no children in school were slightly less likely to favor values courses—36 percent favored leaving values education to parents and churches; 42 percent favored school courses and 13 percent favored both, for a total of 55 percent favoring school courses.

Parents of children in nonpublic schools were actually the most supportive of values education in the public schools: 31 percent favored leaving values education to parents and churches; 54 percent favored courses in public schools and 11 percent favored both, for a total of 65 percent favoring public school courses.

Half of the parents of nonpublic school students and one in nine parents of public school students had children in both types of school. The survey included 455 public school parents, 103 nonpublic school parents and 1,053 Americans with no children in school.

There was no significant difference in attitudes between Protestants and Catholics, between Republicans and Democrats or between whites and non-whites. But there were differences by age and region.

Americans age 18–29 were least likely to favor values courses in the public schools: 41 percent favored leaving such education to parents and churches, 37 percent favored school courses and 13 percent favored both. Among those 30–49, 36 percent favored parents and churches, 45 percent favored school courses and 13 percent favored both. Among those over 50, 33 percent favored parents and churches, 46 percent favored school courses and 13 percent favored both.

Regionally, the South was most likely to favor values education in the home and churches, although there was no significant difference in support for values courses in school as well. Table 6.11 shows responses by region.

Americans were somewhat more likely to believe that it was possible to develop acceptable subject matter for courses in values and ethics than they were to support such courses themselves: 62 percent said it was possible to develop such courses, 24 percent said it was not and the rest had no opinion.

Among public school parents, 68 percent said it was possible to develop such programs and 22 percent said it was not. Fifty-nine percent of those with no children in school said it was possible to develop such courses and 24 percent said it was not. Again, parents of students in nonpublic schools were more supportive, with 78 percent saying it was possible to develop acceptable values courses and 17 percent saying it was not.

Table 6.11

BEST SOURCE FOR TEACHING VALUES, BY REGION

	Schools	Parents, Churches	Both
East	46%	34%	13%
Midwest	45	34	11
South	38	39	16
West	44	38	11

There were fewer demographic differences on the question of whether it was possible to develop acceptable values courses. Table 6.12 shows responses by demographic groups.

RELIGION AND TOLERANCE

Catholics and non-Evangelicals are generally more tolerant of religious, racial, ethnic and social diversity than are Protestants and Evangelicals[13]. The difference is particularly great on the question of voting for an atheist for president. The long-range trend, however, has been toward greatly increased tolerance in America.

One traditional measure of tolerance in America has been attitudes toward potential presidential candidates. In 1958, for example, 34 percent of American Protestants said they would not vote for a Catholic for president. After John Kennedy's election in 1960, however, willingness to vote for a Catholic president rose dramatically. The last time the Gallup Poll asked that question, 1983, 89 percent of Protestants said they would vote for a qualified Catholic and only 7 percent said they would not.

The United States has not yet had a Jewish president, but 89 percent of Americans said in 1987 that they would vote for a qualified candidate who was Jewish, while only 6 percent said they would not. There was no significant difference along religious lines on this question.

There was considerable difference, however, on the question of voting for an atheist. A majority of Protestants (57 percent) said they would not vote for an atheist, while 35 percent said they would. In contrast, 55 percent of Catholics said they would vote for an atheist, while 38 percent said they would not.

All Baptists (by 68 to 22 percent) and Southern Baptists (by 65 to 24 percent) were the most strongly opposed Protestant denominations (by 68 to 22 percent), but mainline Protestants were evenly split, with 46 percent saying they would vote for an atheist and 48 percent saying they would not. Evangelicals were

Table 6.12

POSSIBILITY OF DEVELOPING VALUES COURSES IN PUBLIC SCHOOLS

	Possible	Not Possible
Men	62%	24%
Women	62	23
White	62	25
Nonwhite	65	16
18–29	57	24
30–49	67	23
50+	61	23
Republican	63	23
Democrat	63	22
Independent	61	25
College Grad.	65	29
Some College	65	24
High School Grad.	65	21
Less Than High School	54	22
Protestant	65	22
Catholic	62	24

strongly opposed to an atheist presidential candidate (by 75 to 17 percent), while non-Evangelicals would vote for a qualified atheist (by 55 to 38 percent).

There are no major differences along religious lines in attitudes toward voting for a qualified black for president. Catholics (82 percent) are the most supportive, followed by non-Evangelicals and mainline Protestants (80 percent each), Evangelicals and Southern Baptists (79 percent each), all Protestants (78 percent), Baptists (76 percent) and white Evangelicals (75 percent).

There is slightly higher support for voting for a qualified woman, led by Southern Baptists (86 percent); mainline Protestants (85 percent), Catholics and non-Evangelicals (84 percent each), all Protestants (80 percent), Baptists (78 percent), all Evangelicals (77 percent) and white Evangelicals (75 percent).

Religious differences emerge when Americans are asked what groups they would not like to have as neighbors. The greatest difference came on the question of having unmarried persons living together as neighbors: only 7 percent of non-Evangelicals, 10 percent of Catholics and 11 percent of mainline Protestants objected, while 25 percent of Evangelicals objected. Eighteen percent of Baptists and 16 percent of all Protestants objected.

The strongest objections across all groups was to having members of religious sects or cults as neighbors. Southern Baptists objected the most (53 percent), followed by all Baptists (49 percent), Evangelicals (48 percent), all Protestants and mainline Protestants (45 percent each), non-Evangelicals (42 percent) and Catholics (41 percent).

There was a large gap between Evangelicals and non-Evangelicals on the question of living next door to religious fundamentalists; 15 percent of non-Evangelicals and only 6 percent of Evangelicals objected. Mainline Protestants (17 percent) were most likely to object, followed by all Protestants (12 percent) and Catholics (11 percent).

Catholics and non-Evangelicals were the least likely to object to black neighbors (11 percent each), while Southern Baptists (20 percent) were the most likely, followed by all Baptists and Evangelicals (17 percent each), mainline Protestants (16 percent) and all Protestants (15 percent).

There was less opposition to Hispanics as neighbors, with the strongest objection coming from Baptists and Southern Baptists (15 percent each), followed by mainline Protestants and Evangelicals (11 percent each), Protestants (10 percent) and Catholics and non-Evangelicals (9 percent each).

No more than 4 percent in any group objected to Catholics, Jews or Protestants as neighbors.

Overall, there was a large gap between Catholics and Baptists in that 15 percent of Catholics did not object to having any of the groups named as neighbors, while only 6 percent of Baptists and 5 percent of Southern Baptists offered no objections. Thirteen percent of non-Evangelicals, 8 percent of Evangelicals, 12 percent of mainline Protestants and 10 percent of all Protestants offered no objections to any group.

Martin Luther King, Jr., and Civil Rights

A generation after the assassination of the Rev. Martin Luther King, Jr., three in four Americans hold a favorable opinion of the late civil rights leader. At the same time, half of all Americans can now be described as strong supporters of the civil rights movement[14]. Dr. King, who died in April 1968, was a Baptist minister who based his civil rights activities on nonviolence, modeled on the lives of Jesus and Mahatma Gandhi. These findings come from the Times Mirror Corporation's study, "The People, Press and Politics," conducted in April and May 1987.

In general, groups who had a more favorable view of Dr. King were more likely to be strong supporters of the civil rights movement. Among religious groups, Jews, Catholics, those with no religious affiliation and members of

"other" religions were most likely to view Dr. King and the civil rights movement favorably; white Protestants were the least likely to hold such views.
Young people and those with some college education were also more likely to
support the civil rights movement. While the South lagged slightly behind the
rest of the country, it still showed strong support for civil rights.

Overall, 74 percent of Americans had a favorable impression of Dr. King,
while 20 percent had a negative impression. Dr. King's popularity rating was
higher than that of several recent presidents. Among presidents mentioned in
the survey, John Kennedy received a favorable rating from 86 percent, Franklin
Roosevelt from 82 percent, Jimmy Carter from 70 percent, Ronald Reagan from
62 percent and Richard Nixon from 39 percent.

A separate survey question asked respondents to use a scale of 1 to 10 to
indicate how well the phrase "a supporter of the civil rights movement" described them, with 1 indicating that the description was "totally wrong" and
10 indicating that the description was "perfect." Table 6.13 shows the percentage of Americans found at each point along the scale.

Views at the extremes are the most revealing, so we designated the combined
1, 2 and 3 responses "as civil rights opponents" and the combined 8, 9 and 10
responses as "strong civil rights supporters." This grouping shows 47 percent
of Americans as strong civil rights supporters and only 12 percent as opponents.

It is not surprising that nonwhites are the most enthusiastic supporters of
civil rights—90 percent give Dr. King a favorable rating and 80 percent are
strong civil rights supporters. But whites also exhibit significant support—71
percent give Dr. King a favorable rating and 40 percent are strong civil rights
supporters. Hispanics fall in between whites and nonwhites: 76 percent give
King a favorable rating and 55 percent are strong civil rights supporters.

Ninety-eight percent of black Evangelical Protestants and 94 percent of
black non-Evangelical Protestants give Dr. King a favorable rating; 88 and 81
percent, respectively, are strong civil rights supporters.

While the margin of error for Jews in the survey is high—11 points—Jews
still emerge as the strongest white supporters of civil rights, a finding consistent

---

Table 6.13

SELF-DESCRIPTION AS SUPPORTER OF THE CIVIL RIGHTS MOVEMENT

Description Totally Wrong	1	6%		7	12%
	2	2		8	15
	3	4		9	10
	4	4			
	5	13	Description Perfect	10	22
	6	9			

with past polls. Sixty-two percent of Jews are strong civil rights supporters, while only 4 percent are opponents; 74 percent of Jews give Dr. King a favorable rating.

While not as supportive as are Jews, Catholics are considerably more supportive of civil rights than are white Protestants: 48 percent of Catholics are strong supporters, while only 9 percent are opponents, and 77 percent give Dr. King a favorable rating.

Among all white Protestants, 67 percent give Dr. King a favorable rating, 36 percent are strong civil rights supporters and 18 percent are opponents. White Evangelical Protestants are less likely to be supporters: while 64 percent have a favorable impression of Dr. King, strong civil rights supporters outnumber opponents by only 33 to 23 percent. Among white non-Evangelical Protestants, 70 percent hold a favorable view of Dr. King, 38 percent are strong civil rights supporters and 15 percent are opponents.

Table 6.14 shows findings for other groups.

Homosexuality and AIDS

Among American religious groups, attitudes toward AIDS and AIDS victims parallel attitudes toward homosexuality; generally, those who are least sympathetic to the rights of homosexuals are most likely to blame AIDS victims for their disease[15]. About eight in ten in all groups, however, say that AIDS victims should be treated with compassion.

The sharpest differences in attitude come between Evangelicals and non-Evangelicals. Catholics and mainline Protestants hold very similar views.

Evangelicals are the least likely group to favor legalization of homosexual acts or the hiring of homosexuals in a variety of jobs, while non-Evangelicals are the most supportive. Only 19 percent of Evangelicals support legalization of homosexuality, with 73 percent opposed. Non-Evangelicals are almost evenly split, with 42 percent favoring legalization and 46 percent opposing.

Among Catholics, 37 percent support legalization and 52 percent oppose it. Protestants oppose legalization by 61 to 29 percent. When we disallow Protestant Evangelicals (Evangelicals make up about 40 percent of all Protestants, and 90 percent of all Evangelicals are Protestant), we see that attitudes among mainline Protestants are close to those of Catholics.

Evangelicals are considerably more likely than members of other groups to oppose ordaining homosexuals. Only 25 percent support hiring homosexual clergy, while 69 percent are opposed. Non-Evangelicals support ordaining homosexuals by 54 to 40 percent. Catholics support ordination of homosexuals by 50 to 44 percent, while Protestants are split, with 47 percent supporting ordination and 44 percent opposing.

Table 6.15 shows attitudes toward allowing homosexuals to hold some other jobs.

Sixty-one percent of Evangelicals agree with the statement, "I sometimes think that AIDS is a punishment for the decline in moral standards"; only 25

Table 6.14

FAVORABLE RATING OF MARTIN LUTHER KING, JR., CIVIL RIGHTS SUPPORTERS

	King Favorable Rating	Strong Rights Supporters	Opponents
Men	73%	45%	14%
Women	75	48	11
18–29	82	55	8
30–49	78	49	12
50+	64	38	17
College Grad.	83	53	8
Some College	83	52	12
High School Grad.	69	43	11
Less Than High School	67	44	15
No Religion	73	49	8
Other Religion	81	52	9
Republican	65	34	18
Democrat	77	57	9
Independent	76	45	12
East	77	46	8
Midwest	79	46	12
South	67	45	17
West	75	51	10

percent disagree. In contrast, 50 percent of non-Evangelicals disagree, while 35 percent agree.

Catholics also disagree with the statement by 50 to 35 percent, while Protestants are more evenly divided, with 48 percent agreeing and 46 percent disagreeing. Baptists are twice as likely to agree (by 56 to 28 percent), while mainline Protestants (defined here as Methodists, Lutherans, Presbyterians and Episcopalians) disagree by 49 to 39 percent.

Table 6.15

ALLOW HOMOSEXUALS TO HOLD CERTAIN JOBS

	Protestant		Catholic		Evangelical		Non-Evangelical	
	Yes	No	Yes	No	Yes	No	Yes	No
Doctors	45%	46%	54%	39%	36%	53%	58%	35%
Sales	68	24	76	15	61	29	78	15
Armed Forces	52	40	57	35	45	47	62	31

Fifty-seven percent of Evangelicals agree that "most people with AIDS have only themselves to blame"; 31 percent disagree. Non-Evangelicals are evenly divided, with 42 percent agreeing and 43 percent disagreeing. Catholics are similarly split, with 44 percent agreeing and 43 percent disagreeing. All Protestants agree with the statement by 49 to 37 percent; Baptists agree by 52 to 35 percent and mainline Protestants by 46 to 41 percent.

A plurality of Evangelicals (40 to 33 percent) agree that "people with AIDS should be allowed to live in the community normally." Non-Evangelicals agree by 52 to 27 percent, Catholics by 53 to 27 percent, all Protestants by 45 to 30 percent, Baptists by 40 to 29 percent and mainline Protestants by 49 to 29 percent.

There is more division, however, on the question of whether "employers should have the right to dismiss an employee because that person has AIDS." Evangelicals support the employer by 42 to 34 percent, while non-Evangelicals oppose by 47 to 30 percent. Catholics are opposed to firing AIDS victims by 48 to 32 percent, and Protestants oppose by a narrower margin (40 to 35 percent). Baptists are evenly divided, with 37 percent supporting the employer and 39 percent supporting the employee. Mainline Protestants support the employee by 43 to 32 percent.

There is general agreement across religious lines that "people who have the AIDS virus should be made to carry a card to this effect." Evangelicals agree by 68 to 18 percent, non-Evangelicals by 56 to 28 percent. Catholics agree by 60 to 26 percent, Protestants by 61 to 21 percent, Baptists by 68 to 14 percent and mainline Protestants by 54 to 30 percent.

All groups agree by wide margins that "AIDS sufferers should be treated with compassion": Evangelicals (77 to 9 percent); Non-Evangelicals (79 to 7 percent); Catholics (78 to 8 percent); Protestants (78 to 7 percent); Baptists (77 to 9 percent); and mainline Protestants (80 to 6 percent).

FAMILY AND LIFESTYLE

One Catholic woman in five (22 percent) prefers a lifestyle that does not include having children and, in fact, Catholics today are more likely than Protestants to be childless[16]. This is due partly to the fact that Catholics as a whole are somewhat younger than the general population, but it also seems to be related to a greater desire for independence on the part of Catholic women. Thirty-one percent of Catholics and 27 percent of the general population are under 30.

At the same time, Catholics are no more likely than Protestants to believe that the ideal family size is large, with four or more children. Catholics were more likely to favor larger families for several decades, but the difference in attitudes disappeared in 1985 and has not reappeared since.

Despite the large numbers of women who, when asked about their own lives, said they prefer being childless, only 1 percent of Catholics and Protestants said the ideal family does not include children. This suggests that many women do not view their own preferences as "ideal."

Asked to choose "the most interesting and satisfying lifestyle for you personally," 10 percent of Catholic women cited being unmarried and holding a job; 7 percent preferred marriage and a job, but no children; and another 5 percent preferred marriage, but neither children nor a job. These figures add up to 22 percent of Catholic women preferring a lifestyle that does not include children.

In contrast, 17 percent of Protestant women make the same choice: 7 percent preferred being single and working; 6 percent preferred being married and working, with no children; and 4 percent preferred being married, with neither job nor children.

Eighteen percent of Baptist women and 15 percent of women in mainline churches (here defined to include Methodist, Lutheran, Presbyterian and Episcopalian churches) cited lifestyles that did not include children. Nine percent of Baptist and 5 percent of mainline church women preferred being single and employed; 7 and 6 percent, respectively, preferred being married and employed, without children; and 2 and 4 percent, respectively, preferred marriage without either children or a job.

Twenty-five percent of Catholic women and 17 percent of Protestant women say they have no children; 30 percent of Catholic men and 25 percent of Protestant men say they have not fathered any children. Twenty-nine percent of Baptist men and 15 percent of Baptist women say they are childless, as do 21 percent of mainline church men and 20 percent of mainline church women.

Table 6.16 shows the number of children claimed by Catholic and Protestant men and women.

Twelve percent each of Catholics and Protestants say the ideal family consists of four or more children. But there is a significant difference in attitudes among Protestants: Baptists are more likely to prefer large families,

Table 6.16
NUMBER OF CHILDREN, BY RELIGION, GENDER

	Catholic		Protestant	
	Men	Women	Men	Women
Number of Children:				
1	11%	16%	14%	19%
2	27	25	31	27
3	14	14	16	17
4	6	11	6	10
5	4	2	4	6
6 or More	7	7	4	6

with 17 percent saying the ideal family includes four or more children, while mainline Protestants are more likely to prefer small families, with only 8 percent citing four or more children as the ideal.

There has been an across-the-board preference for smaller families over the past generation. In 1968, for example, 50 percent of Catholics and 37 percent of Protestants said the ideal family included four or more children.

Table 6.17 shows the ideal family size preferences of Catholics, Protestants, Baptists and mainline church members.

WOMEN IN SOCIETY

American religion has always been closely identified with family life. Surveys show major differences among religious groups on key questions about the role of women in society[17]. In general, white Evangelical Protestants hold the most traditional views; Jews and the those with no religious affiliation hold the least traditional views and other groups are clustered together in the middle. These findings come from the Times Mirror Corporation's study, "The People, Press and Politics."

The survey asked respondents to agree or disagree with the statements that "women should return to their traditional role in society" and that "too many children are being raised in day care centers these days." Respondents were also asked to express their level of identification as "a supporter of the women's movement." The survey used a scale of 1 to 10, with 10 signifying that the

Table 6.17

IDEAL FAMILY SIZE, BY RELIGION

	Catholic	Protestant	Baptist	Mainline
Number of Children:				
1	3%	2%	3%	2%
2	57	62	58	65
3	21	19	18	21
4	9	8	10	6
5	2	3	4	1
6 or More	1	1	3	1

term was a "perfect" description, and 1 indicating that the description was "completely wrong." Those responding with an 8, 9 or 10 were classified as "strong supporters," and those responding with 1, 2 or 3 were classified as "weak supporters."

White Evangelical Protestants appear to view the women's movement as a threat to family life, while other groups do not. One reason may be that white Evangelicals more closely identify the women's movement with support for legalized abortion, and they are the only group that supports changes in the law to make it more difficult to get an abortion.

Among white Evangelicals, 31 percent were weak supporters of the women's movement and only 20 percent were strong supporters. Forty percent of white Evangelical Protestants—more than in any other group—said that women should return to their traditional role in society. White Evangelical Protestants were also the most likely to say that too many children are being raised in day care centers—78 percent agreed with that assessment.

The religiously unaffiliated were the least likely to believe that women should return to their traditional role—only 20 percent agreed. They were also the least likely (57 percent) to say that too many children were being raised in day care centers. Thirty-three percent were strong supporters of the women's movement, while 15 percent were weak supporters.

Jews were among the strongest supporters of the women's movement, with strong supporters outnumbering weak ones by 47 to 11 percent. Only 24 percent of Jews said that women should return to their traditional role in society; 64 percent said too many children were being raised in day care centers.

Four other religious groups fell in between the two extremes in their responses:

- White non-Evangelical Protestants were more lukewarm in their backing for the women's movement, with 26 percent strong supporters and 20 percent weak supporters. But only 23 percent said women should return to their traditional role. Sixty-four percent said too many children were being raised in day care centers.
- Black Evangelical Protestants showed some tension—they were the strongest supporters of the women's movement, by 48 to 17 percent, but were almost as likely as white Evangelical Protestants to support a return to traditional roles for women; 35 percent supported such a change. Sixty-six percent said too many children were being raised in day care centers.
- Among black non-Evangelical Protestants, 36 percent were strong supporters of the women's movement and 18 percent were weak supporters; 31 percent supported a more traditional role for women and 60 percent said too many children were being raised in day care centers.
- Among Catholics, 30 percent were strong supporters of the women's movement and 19 percent were weak supporters; 31 percent wanted a more traditional role for women and 68 percent said too many children were being raised in day care centers.
- White Catholics are more likely than white Protestants to support the Equal Rights Amendment. They back the ERA by 78 to 13 percent. All white Protestants support it by 67 to 20 percent; white Evangelicals support it by 67 to 21 percent, and non-Evangelicals support it by 73 to 16 percent.

AMERICANS SUPPORT "BABY M" DECISION

Americans, by an overwhelming 5-to-1 majority, support the judge's decision in the controversial "Baby M" case, awarding custody of the child to her natural father, and not to the surrogate mother who bore her[18]. There was remarkable agreement across demographic lines, with no differences emerging by sex, age, region, political affiliation or marital status. Slight differences did emerge along lines of education, income and race, with the strongest support coming from college graduates and upper-income families and the strongest opposition coming from blacks and lower-income families.

The consensus in attitudes toward the decision stands in contrast to attitudes toward the general question of surrogate motherhood, where sharp differences emerge by gender, age, race and education.

Ninety-three percent of Americans said they had heard about the case. Respondents who had were asked their reaction to the decision, which gave custody of Baby M "to her natural father and removed all parental rights from the surrogate mother who had signed a contract to bear her." Seventy-six percent of respondents approved of the judge's decision, while 15 percent disapproved. The rest had no opinion.

Eighty-two percent of college graduates supported the decision, while only 9 percent disapproved. Among those with less than a high school education, 71 percent approved and 21 percent disapproved. High school graduates supported the decision by 78 to 15 percent. Those with some college or technical school education beyond high school supported it by 73 to 16 percent.

The same pattern was reflected along income lines. Those with family incomes above $40,000 a year supported the decision by 80 to 11 percent; those in the $25,000–40,000 bracket approved by 78 to 14 percent; those making $15,000–25,000 a year supported it by 76 to 14 percent; among those making less than $15,000 a year, 72 percent approved and 21 percent disapproved the decision.

The strongest disapproval of the decision came from blacks, but even they supported the ruling by 69 to 24 percent. Whites supported the decision by 77 to 14 percent, Hispanics by 74 to 16 percent.

There was also surprising agreement across religious lines. There was no significant difference between Catholic and Protestant support, despite the recent Vatican declaration that condemned surrogate motherhood and urged national legislatures to bar the practice. Catholics supported the decision by 75 to 15 percent, Protestants by 77 to 15 percent. Members of mainline Protestant churches—combining responses for Methodists, Lutherans, Presbyterians and Episcopalians—supported the decision by 79 to 15 percent.

Similarly, there was no significant difference in views between Evangelicals and non-Evangelicals. Seventy-six percent of Evangelicals and 78 percent of non-Evangelicals supported the decision, while 15 percent in each group disapproved.

A Gallup Poll conducted for *Newsweek* asked whether Americans approve or disapprove of surrogate motherhood. Overall, 48 percent approved and 41 percent disapproved, with 11 percent having no opinion.

Men approved by 51 to 37 percent, while women were evenly divided, with 44 percent approving and 45 percent disapproving. Disapproval increased with age. Those 18–29 approved of surrogate motherhood by 68 to 24 percent, those 30–49 approved by 49 to 39 percent, while those over 50 disapproved by 57 to 30 percent. Whites approved by 49 to 40 percent, while nonwhites opposed by 48 to 41 percent.

Again, support was strongest among college graduates, with 55 percent approving and 32 percent opposing. On the other hand, those with less than a high school education opposed by 53 to 40 percent.

Support for surrogate motherhood rose significantly when specific circumstances were described in the *Newsweek* poll, however.

- When a woman is unable to bear children, 63 percent of Americans support surrogate motherhood, while 33 percent oppose it. Support rises to 81 percent of those 18–29, and 62 percent of nonwhites approve of surrogate motherhood in this situation. Those over 50 and those with less than a high school education are evenly divided.

- When pregnancy would result in a significant health risk to the wife, 54 percent of Americans support surrogate motherhood, while 39 percent oppose. Fifty percent of nonwhites approve, while 43 percent oppose. Those over 50 oppose by 53 to 39 percent and those with less than a high school education oppose by 51 to 40 percent.
- When birth defects are likely because of the wife's genetic makeup, 52 percent of Americans approve and 41 percent disapprove. A majority of those over 50 and those with less than a high school education disapprove, while nonwhites are evenly divided (49 percent approve and 45 percent disapprove).
- When the wife is afraid of pregnancy, only 14 percent of Americans approve of surrogate motherhood, while 81 percent disapprove.

AMERICANS DIFFER BY RELIGION
ON SMOKING, DRINKING

Americans of different religious affiliations differ sharply in the degree to which they drink alcohol and smoke and in their attitudes toward policies to restrict drinking and smoking[19]. In general, Catholics, mainline Protestants and non-Evangelicals are considerably more likely to drink than are Baptists and Evangelicals. Non-Evangelicals are more likely than Evangelicals to smoke.

Among major denominations, Lutherans (74 percent) and Catholics (73 percent) are the most likely to say that they drink alcohol at least occasionally and are not total abstainers; 59 percent of Methodists and 47 percent of Baptists say they drink. Our samples for Presbyterians and Episcopalians are too small to be definitive, but findings suggest that these groups are as likely as Lutherans and Catholics to drink.

There is a sharp difference in behavior between Evangelicals and non-Evangelicals; 73 percent of non-Evangelicals, but only 41 percent of Evangelicals, say they drink.

Among those who do drink, 33 percent of non-Evangelicals, 29 percent of Catholics, 27 percent of Protestants and 20 percent of Evangelicals say they sometimes drink too much. We do not have data by denomination on this question, but the gap between Protestants and Evangelicals (90 percent of whom are Protestant) indicates that non-Evangelical Protestants may be even more likely than Catholics to drink too much on occasion.

At the same time, however, Catholics (19 percent) and non-Evangelicals (22 percent) are less likely than Protestants (25 percent) and Evangelicals (29 percent) to report that drinking has been a source of trouble in their families.

There are also no significant differences along religious lines in attitudes toward two proposals aimed at restricting drinking. About three-fourths in all groups support "a federal law that would require TV and radio stations carrying beer and wine commercials to provide equal time for health and safety warning messages about drinking."

Similarly, about 80 percent in each group support "a federal law that would require health and safety warning labels on alcoholic beverage containers like those now required on cigarette packages."

But there are major differences on a proposal for "doubling the federal excise taxes on alcoholic beverages to raise revenues to fight drug and alcohol abuse." Sixty-one percent of Catholics, 64 percent of mainline Protestants (Lutherans, Methodists, Presbyterians and Episcopalians), 71 percent of all Protestants and 79 percent of Baptists support such a proposal.

Baptists (65 percent) were considerably more likely than mainline Protestants (53 percent) or Catholics (50 percent) to support all three proposals. Among all Protestants, 58 percent supported all three proposals.

There are no significant differences between Catholics (32 percent) and Protestants (29 percent) in the number reporting that they had smoked within the past week. But 35 percent of non-Evangelicals and only 23 percent of Evangelicals reported smoking.

Among those who do smoke, Evangelicals (85 percent) are more likely than non-Evangelicals (73 percent) to say that they want to quit smoking; 74 percent of Protestants and 77 percent of Catholics say they want to quit.

Religious groups are closely divided on a proposal to ban cigarette advertising. Protestants are evenly divided, supporting such a ban by 48 to 47 percent. Catholics oppose such a ban by 53 to 45 percent. Evangelicals support it by 50 to 44 percent, while non-Evangelicals oppose a ban on advertising by 50 to 48 percent.

Differences are sharper, however, on a proposal to ban smoking in public places. Evangelicals support such a ban by 60 to 38 percent and non-Evangelicals support it by 53 to 45 percent. Protestants support it by 57 to 41 percent. Catholics, on the other hand, are evenly divided, with 50 percent supporting such a ban and 49 percent opposing it.

GUN CONTROL

Gun control is another area in which there are significant differences in attitudes along religious lines. The strongest support for tougher gun control laws comes from Catholics, Jews, black Protestants and those with no religious affiliation. White Protestants, both Evangelical and non-Evangelical, are considerably more resistant to gun control[20].

One important measure of these religious differences can be seen in responses to a question asking those surveyed the degree to which they identify themselves as supporters of the National Rifle Association. The NRA is widely recognized as the major anti–gun control organization in the country. The question was contained in a survey conducted for the Times Mirror Corporation's study, "The People, Press and Politics."

Respondents were asked to use a scale of 1 to 10, with 1 indicating that the description of being an NRA supporter was "completely wrong," and 10 indicating that the description was "perfect." Responses of 1–3 were grouped together to indicate "weak support" for the NRA, while responses of 8–10 were grouped together to indicate "strong support."

The only religious group in which strong supporters (37 percent) outnumbered weak supporters (27 percent) was white Evangelical Protestants. This finding partly reflects the fact that a disproportionate number of white Evangelicals have less education and are more likely to live in rural areas than other Americans; people in those groups are less supportive of gun control.

White non-Evangelical Protestants were about evenly divided, with 35 percent weak supporters of the NRA and 31 percent strong supporters. Among black Protestants, however, both Evangelicals and non-Evangelicals were strongly anti-NRA: 45 percent of Evangelicals and 48 percent of non-Evangelicals were weak supporters, while only 15 percent and 16 percent, respectively, were strong NRA supporters.

Catholics were less supportive of the NRA than white Protestants and more supportive than blacks: 39 percent of Catholics were weak supporters of the NRA, while 24 percent were strong supporters.

The strongest opposition to the NRA came from Jews—only 4 percent were strong supporters, while 69 percent were weak supporters. Among those with no religious affiliation, 48 percent were weak supporters and 24 percent were strong supporters.

Catholics and Lutherans emerged as strong supporters of gun control in a separate survey in which responses were tabulated along denominational lines. One question, for example, asked respondents whether they favored or opposed the approach of some communities that had banned the sales and possession of handguns.

Catholics supported such a ban by 51 to 45 percent, Lutherans by 56 to 43 percent. Overall, Protestants opposed a ban by a slim 49 to 45 percent margin. Mainline Protestants (including Methodists, Lutherans, Presbyterians and Episcopalians) were evenly divided, with 48 percent supporting a ban and 48 percent opposing. Baptists, on the other hand, opposed a ban by 50 to 39 percent; Southern Baptists opposed by 51 to 35 percent.

All the denominations surveyed agreed by large margins that gun control laws should generally be made more strict. Only 7 to 10 percent in each group believed laws should be made less strict. The percentages of those supporting stricter gun control laws were Catholics (64 percent), Methodists (62 percent), mainline Protestants (61 percent), Lutherans (60 percent), all Protestants (58 percent), Baptists (57 percent) and Southern Baptists (51 percent). The rest had no opinion or said the laws should remain as they are now.

There was similar strong support across denominational lines for a continuation of a ban on the interstate sale of handguns. Catholics were strongest in support, backing the ban by 72 to 22 percent. They were followed by Lutherans (68 to 28 percent), Methodists (67 to 24 percent), mainline Protestants (67 to 26 percent), all Protestants (65 to 25 percent), Baptists (61 to 24 percent) and Southern Baptists (59 to 20 percent).

In another set of questions, Catholics and non-Evangelicals were more likely than Protestants and Evangelicals to favor gun control and regulation. Table 6.18 shows responses by major religious groups on key questions.

The same patterns that emerge in attitudes toward gun control and regulation are reflected in patterns of gun ownership: while 51 percent of all Americans say they own a gun, the figure is 59 percent for Protestants and only 38 percent for Catholics; 57 percent of Evangelicals and 48 percent of non-Evangelicals own guns.

GOVERNMENT SPENDING

White Catholics and Jews are more likely than white Protestants to support increased federal funding for a variety of domestic programs. The strongest support among religious groups for increased government spending comes from black Protestants, but this largely reflects the influence of race—blacks have historically been more likely than whites to support federal social programs. Religious views, however, do account for much of the remaining differences when only whites are considered. About 80 percent of Catholics and 99 percent of Jews are white[21].

These findings are contained in the Gallup survey conducted for the Times Mirror Corporation's study, "The People, Press and Politics." The survey asked about attitudes toward government spending in thirteen areas: improving the environment, financial aid for college students, Social Security, AIDS research,

Table 6.18
VIEWS ON GUN CONTROL, BY RELIGION

	U.S.	Protestant	Catholic	Evangelical	Non-Evangelical
Favor Registration of All Firearms	67%	64%	74%	64%	69%
Favor License for All Guns Carried Outside the Home	84	81	90	81	85
Favor National Law Requiring 7-Day Waiting Period Before a Handgun Could Be Purchased	91	89	94	90	91

aid for the unemployed, scientific research, programs for blacks and other minorities, health care, programs to reduce drug addiction, improving the public schools, aid for the homeless, aid for farmers and aid for the elderly.

An average of 76 percent of black Protestants supported increased government spending on these programs. They were followed by Catholics (62 percent), Jews (61 percent), white Catholics (59 percent), all Protestants and those with no religious affiliation (57 percent each), white non-Evangelical Protestants (54 percent), white Protestants (53 percent) and white Evangelical Protestants (52 percent).

Catholics and Jews have traditionally been more likely than white Protestants to support government social programs, partly because Protestantism has placed more emphasis on the individual, while Catholicism and Judaism place more emphasis on community. The three groups now hold similar views on some spending issues, but significant gaps remain in attitudes toward particular programs.

There was consensus among white Protestants, white Catholics and Jews on four issues—Social Security, health care, and aid for the homeless and the elderly. Table 6.19 shows the pattern on these issues.

While Catholics and Jews were more likely to support higher spending in virtually every area, there are also important differences in spending priorities between Catholics and Jews. The following differences emerged:

- Jews (73 percent) were most supportive of increased spending on the environment, followed by white Catholics (63 percent) and white Protestants (53 percent).
- Jews (46 percent) and white Catholics (45 percent) were more supportive

Table 6.19
SUPPORT FOR INCREASED GOVERNMENT SPENDING, BY RELIGION

	White Protestants	White Catholics	Jews
Support Increased Spending For:			
Social Security	58%	64%	62%
Health Care	67	70	74
Aid for the Homeless	62	67	67
Aid for the Elderly	71	74	71

than white Protestants (35 percent) of increased financial aid for college students.

- Jews (76 percent) were the strongest supporters of increased spending on the public schools, but large majorities of white Protestants (67 percent) and white Catholics (66 percent) also backed an increase.
- Jews (83 percent) were considerably more likely to support increased spending on AIDS research, although solid majorities of white Catholics (71 percent) and white Protestants (66 percent) also supported an increase.
- Jews (72 percent) were also the most likely to support increased spending on scientific research. A majority of white Catholics (52 percent) also supported an increase, but only 40 percent of white Protestants did so.
- White Catholics (40 percent) were most likely to support increased aid for the unemployed, while Jews (30 percent) and white Protestants (32 percent) lagged behind.
- White Catholics (61 percent) were the most likely to support an increase in spending on aid for farmers, followed by 55 percent of white Protestants and 40 percent of Jews. This finding is particularly interesting because a larger percentage of white Protestants than white Catholics live in rural areas, and one would expect them to have greater sympathy for struggling farmers. This response suggests greater willingness among Catholics to support government help for those in economic need.
- White Catholics (68 percent) were most likely to support increased funding to reduce drug addiction, followed by white Protestants (64 percent) and Jews (60 percent).
- White Catholics (32 percent) and Jews (29 percent) were more likely to support increased spending on programs for blacks and other minorities, while only 22 percent of white Protestants supported such an increase.

LABOR

Among religious groups, Catholics and black Protestants are the strongest supporters of unions, while white Protestants are more critical. At the same time, there is strong support across religious lines for a top priority of the labor movement—increasing the minimum wage to $5.05 an hour over the next four years[22].

The findings reflect historic patterns among the various religious groups. Working-class Catholic immigrants made up the backbone of the labor movement in the late nineteenth and early twentieth centuries. As Catholics became more affluent—there are now no differences in economic status between Catholics and Protestants—they retained their support for unions in principle, while becoming more critical of unions in practice. The lower economic status of blacks leads them to see unions as a potent ally in their effort to improve themselves economically.

In a May 1988 survey conducted for the Times Mirror Corporation's study, "The People, Press and Politics," 69 percent of all Americans agreed with the statement that "labor unions are necessary to protect working people," while 26 percent disagreed.

Agreement was highest among Catholics (74 percent) and black Protestants (71 percent), and lowest among white Protestants (65 percent). There was no significant difference between Evangelical and non-Evangelical Protestants, with 64 percent of the former and 66 percent of the latter agreeing. Among those with no religious preference, 67 percent agreed with the statement.

But while the survey showed support for the existence of unions, it also found that 58 percent of all Americans agreed with the statement that "labor unions have too much power"; 34 percent disagreed.

Only black Protestants—by 50 to 40 percent—rejected the claim that unions have too much power. Those with no religious affiliation were almost evenly divided, with 47 percent agreeing and 41 percent disagreeing.

Catholics (57 percent) were less likely than Protestants (61 percent) to say that unions have too much power. But 65 percent of white Protestants— including 67 percent of Evangelicals and 63 percent of non-Evangelicals— agreed.

An earlier survey conducted for the Times Mirror Corporation's study in May 1987 asked respondents to indicate their degree of identification as a "union supporter." On a scale of 1 to 10, a 1 indicated that the description was "completely wrong," and a 10 indicated that it was "perfect." We grouped responses of 1, 2 and 3 as "weak supporters" and responses of 8, 9 and 10 as "strong supporters."

Using this approach, black Protestants emerged as the strongest pro-union group, with 42 percent strong supporters and 21 percent weak supporters. Catholics were evenly divided, with 31 percent strong supporters and 30 percent weak supporters. Among those with no religious affiliation, 33 percent were weak supporters and 22 percent were strong supporters.

White Protestants were the least likely to identify as "union supporters," with 39 percent weak supporters and 22 percent strong supporters. Among white Evangelical Protestants, weak supporters outnumbered strong supporters by 41 to 21 percent; among white non-Evangelical Protestants, 37 percent were weak supporters and 24 percent were strong supporters.

On the question of increasing the minimum wage, there was strong support, with Catholics the most enthusiastic—82 percent backed an increase, while only 14 percent opposed. Among all Protestants, 73 percent supported an increase, while 23 percent opposed. White Evangelicals backed an increase by 76 to 18 percent. The sample of blacks was too small to provide reliable figures for black Protestants, but among all blacks, 89 percent supported an increase in the minimum wage, while only 10 percent opposed one.

THE SUPREME COURT

When President Reagan nominated Judge Robert Bork as an associate justice for the Supreme Court in 1987, the strongest support for Bork came from

Evangelicals, who gave the court lower ratings than the population as a whole and who strongly preferred that the court move in a more conservative direction. Bork's strongest opposition, on the other hand, came from Catholics and non-Evangelicals, who were more satisfied with the court's performance and were evenly divided between those who want a more conservative court and those who want a more liberal one[23].

These findings are based on attitudes toward the court expressed in a July 1987 survey and a question on Bork asked in an August survey. In August, before Bork's televised confirmation hearings, 31 percent of Americans said the Senate should confirm Bork, 25 percent said it should not and the remaining 44 percent were undecided.

There were sharp differences along religious lines. Evangelicals favored Bork's confirmation by a 2-to-1 margin (39 to 19 percent). Non-Evangelicals, on the other hand, were evenly divided, with 28 percent supporting Bork and 27 percent opposing him. Protestants supported Bork by 34 to 21 percent, while Catholics were evenly divided, with 29 percent opposing Bork's confirmation and 28 percent supporting him.

In general, Catholics were the most supportive of the Supreme Court, followed closely by mainline Protestants. Non-Evangelicals also rate the court highly, but Evangelicals and Baptists give the court lower ratings.

For example, 42 percent of Evangelicals and 44 percent of Baptists believe the court favors one group, while only 37 percent of Evangelicals and 35 percent of Baptists believe the court is impartial.

In contrast, 50 percent of Catholics believe the court is impartial, while 33 percent believe it is not. Mainline Protestants believe the court is impartial by 46 to 35 percent and non-Evangelicals believe it to be so by 47 to 36 percent. All Protestants are evenly divided, with 41 percent saying the court is impartial and 38 percent saying it is not.

There is little difference between Evangelicals and non-Evangelicals in their rating of the court: 49 percent of Evangelicals and 51 percent of non-Evangelicals rate it "excellent" or "good"; 35 percent of Evangelicals and 36 percent of non-Evangelicals rate it "fair" and 7 percent of Evangelicals and 6 percent of non-Evangelicals rate it "poor."

There is a notable gap between Catholics and Protestants: 56 percent of Catholics and 46 percent of Protestants rate the court "excellent" or "good"; 37 percent of Catholics and 44 percent of Protestants rate it "fair"; 4 percent of Catholics and 8 percent of Protestants rate it "poor."

Among Protestants, members of mainline churches hold views similar to those of Catholics—54 percent rate the court "excellent" or "good," 35 percent rate it "fair" and 5 percent rate it "poor." Among Baptists, however, only 41 percent give the court a high rating, while 44 percent rate it "fair" and 9 percent rate it "poor."

There are also important differences among religious groups in the degree of confidence they have in the Supreme Court as an institution: 61 percent of Catholics, 58 percent of mainline Protestants, 55 percent of non-Evangelicals,

48 percent of Protestants, 46 percent of Evangelicals and 41 percent of Baptists expressed "a great deal" or "quite a lot" of confidence" in the court.

Evangelicals, Baptists and Protestants are more likely to want the court to move in a more conservative direction, while Catholics and non-Evangelicals are more evenly divided. Table 6.20 shows attitudes on this question.

PUBLIC FIGURES

There are significant differences along religious lines in the way Americans view major public figures. These differences occur, however, within a framework of broad consensus.

The largest difference in attitudes involves a controversial religious figure, the Rev. Jerry Falwell, founder of the Moral Majority. While Evangelical Christians rate Falwell highly, he is actually less popular than Soviet Premier Mikhail Gorbachev among non-Evangelical Americans. Thirty-six percent of non-Evangelicals give Falwell a favorable rating and 50 percent give him a negative rating. Forty-seven percent of non-Evangelicals give Gorbachev a favorable rating, while 43 percent give him a negative rating[24].

Fifty-eight percent of Evangelicals give Falwell a favorable rating, while 39 percent give him a negative rating. Overall, Falwell receives a 45 percent favorable rating and a 43 percent negative rating among all Americans. Protestants give Falwell a narrow positive margin, by 48 to 41 percent. Catholics offer a similar assessment, with 45 percent giving Falwell a positive rating and 38 percent a negative rating.

One of Falwell's most controversial statements was his charge that black Anglican Archbishop Desmond Tutu of South Africa, winner of the 1984 Nobel Peace Prize, was a "phony." But Tutu is considerably more popular than Falwell

Table 6.20

SUPREME COURT—MORE LIBERAL OR MORE CONSERVATIVE?

	More Liberal	More Conservative	Neither
Evangelicals	24%	55%	10%
Non-Evangelicals	35	37	18
Catholics	36	41	16
Protestants	28	45	15
Baptists	32	46	9
Mainline Protestants	29	42	18

among Americans. Fifty-seven percent give him a favorable rating and 23 percent an unfavorable rating. (A large number of Americans had no opinion on Tutu, probably because of lack of information about him.)

Tutu rates highest among non-Evangelicals (61 percent favorable to 23 percent unfavorable) and Catholics (60 to 20 percent favorable). Among all Protestants, 55 percent view him favorably and 28 percent view him unfavorably. Fifty-one percent of Evangelicals view Tutu favorably and 29 percent view him unfavorably.

In terms of pure percentages, Falwell (58 percent favorable) is more popular than Tutu among Evangelicals. But he also has a higher negative rating. When we discard the undecideds, Archbishop Tutu is actually slightly more popular than Falwell among Evangelicals—64 percent of those expressing an opinion view him favorably, while 60 percent view Falwell favorably.

There is surprising agreement in rating of another major religious figure, Pope John Paul II. While the 91 percent of Catholics who give the pope a favorable rating is higher than the national average, four in five Americans (82 percent) give the pope a favorable rating. This includes 81 percent of Protestants and 78 percent of Evangelicals.

Another dramatic difference along religious lines concerns Gorbachev. Evangelicals view him most negatively, with 59 percent giving him an unfavorable rating and 36 percent a favorable rating. This is in sharp contrast to the small plurality of non-Evangelicals giving him a favorable rating and the even split among Catholics, with 46 percent giving Gorbachev a favorable rating and 46 percent an unfavorable rating.

There are some interesting differences along religious lines in attitudes toward the last four American presidents. President Reagan is slightly more popular among Catholics (86 percent) and Evangelicals (85 percent) than among non-Evangelicals.

There is no significant difference in attitudes of Evangelicals and non-Evangelicals toward President Jimmy Carter, despite the fact that Carter's Evangelical ties are well known. Seventy-two percent of Evangelicals and 70 percent of non-Evangelicals give him a favorable rating. There is also no real difference between Protestants and Catholics—70 percent of Protestants and 69 percent of Catholics give him a favorable rating.

Carter's predecessor, Gerald Ford, is slightly more popular among Evangelicals (78 percent) than among non-Evangelicals (73 percent) and slightly more popular among Protestants (76 percent) than among Catholics (72 percent).

There is a sharper difference in attitudes toward Richard Nixon. Non-Evangelicals view him negatively, with 56 percent rating him unfavorably and 41 percent rating him favorably. But Evangelicals are about equally divided, with 50 percent holding an unfavorable opinion and 47 percent a favorable opinion. Catholics give Nixon an unfavorable rating by a 56 to 39 percent margin, Protestants by a 51 to 46 percent margin.

One would-be president fares equally poorly with all groups. Lyndon LaRouche receives a favorable rating in the 13 to 15 percent range. LaRouche ranked ahead of only Libyan leader Khadafy among the ten figures about whom attitudes were solicited. Khadafy's favorable rating ranged from 3 percent among Catholics to 6 percent among Protestants and Evangelicals.

THE MOST ADMIRED MEN AND WOMEN

Similar patterns of difference are visible when it comes to naming the most admired men and women in the world. Protestants and Catholics often hold contrasting views, as do Evangelicals and non-Evangelicals. According to a January 1987 Gallup survey, the list of the ten most admired men was headed by President Reagan and Chrysler Corporation Chairman Lee Iacocca, followed by Pope John Paul II, the Rev. Jesse Jackson, the Rev. Billy Graham, former President Jimmy Carter, South African Archbishop Desmond Tutu, Sen. Edward Kennedy, Vice President George Bush and Terry Waite, the envoy of the Archbishop of Canterbury who had been negotiating for the release of American hostages in Lebanon. (The survey was conducted while Waite's efforts were in the news, but before he, himself, disappeared[25].)

Among American Protestants, President Reagan ranked first, followed by Iacocca, Jackson and Graham. Tutu, Pope John Paul and President Carter were tied at the next level, followed by Bush and Waite. While it is not surprising that Protestants are more likely to admire Protestant religious leaders than the pope, it is significant that they still rank the pope ahead of such American figures as George Bush.

Catholics, not surprisingly, ranked Pope John Paul first, but they also ranked Iacocca ahead of the president. Reagan was followed in popularity by a three-way tie consisting of Bush, Sen. Kennedy and New York Gov. Mario Cuomo.

President Reagan was the man most admired by Evangelicals, followed by Jackson and Graham. This reflects strong support for Jackson among black Evangelicals and strong support for Graham among white Evangelicals. Iacocca ranked fourth, followed by a tie between the pope and television evangelist Pat Robertson. Another TV evangelist, Jimmy Swaggart, followed, ranking ahead of Bush and Archbishop Tutu.

Among non-Evangelicals, Iacocca led, followed by Reagan, Pope John Paul, Jesse Jackson and a tie among Bush, Cuomo and Waite.

Among all Americans, the most admired woman is Mother Teresa, followed by Margaret Thatcher, Nancy Reagan, Philippine President Corazon Aquino, former Rep. Geraldine Ferraro, Coretta Scott King, Jane Fonda, Betty Ford, Queen Elizabeth II and Jacqueline Onassis.

Protestants ranked Margaret Thatcher slightly ahead of Mother Teresa, who was followed by Mrs. Reagan, Aquino, Ferraro and King. Among Catholics, however, Margaret Thatcher ranked third, following the overwhelming first choice, Mother Teresa, and Aquino. Nancy Reagan was fourth, followed by Geraldine Ferraro. Princess Diana, former United Nations Ambassador Jeanne Kirkpatrick, Betty Ford and Barbara Walters rounded out the list.

Evangelicals ranked Mother Teresa first, followed by Nancy Reagan, Margaret Thatcher, Corazon Aquino and Coretta Scott King. Non-Evangelicals also ranked Mother Teresa first, followed by Thatcher, Aquino, Reagan, Ferraro, Betty Ford and Jane Fonda.

Survey respondents are asked to cite their choices without the aid of a list of names. This procedure, while opening the field to all possible choices, tends to favor men and women who are currently in the news.

Questions about the most admired men and women have been asked since 1948. Religious leaders have appeared on the list of most admired men every year, but have appeared less frequently on the list of most admired women.

In 1986, for the first time, half of those on the list of most admired men were religious figures—Pope John Paul, Billy Graham, Jesse Jackson, Archbishop Tutu and Terry Waite. Tutu appeared on the most admired list after he won the 1984 Nobel Peace Prize. Billy Graham has appeared on the list every year since 1955. Jackson first appeared on the list in 1981, and has appeared every year since. In contrast, the Rev. Martin Luther King, Jr., who won the 1964 Nobel Peace Prize, appeared on the most admired list only in 1964 and 1965.

The reigning pope has appeared on the most admired list every year since 1948 except for 1958, 1960 and 1974. Pope John Paul has ranked in the top three ever since his election in 1978.

From 1952 to 1957, another Catholic leader, Bishop Fulton Sheen, appeared on the most admired list. Sheen, who had a national television program, ranked ahead of the pope in three of those six years. Mother Teresa has appeared on the most admired women list since 1979, when she won the Nobel Peace Prize. Before she appeared on the list, the only religious figure to appear was singer and Evangelical activist Anita Bryant, who was named in 1977, 1978 and 1979.

ISRAEL AND THE MIDDLE EAST

After American Jews, the strongest supporters of Israel in the United States are white Evangelical Protestants. And while blacks are the least likely group to describe themselves as "pro-Israel," Black Protestants who are Evangelicals hold a more positive view of Israel than those who are not[26].

In general, support for Israel increases with age and education. Overall, 22 percent of Americans are weak supporters of Israel and 26 percent are strong supporters. These findings are drawn from the Times Mirror Corporation's study, "The People, Press and Politics." This survey was conducted before the outbreak of violence on the West Bank in December 1987.

The study asked respondents to indicate on a scale of 1 to 10 how well the term "pro-Israel" described them, with 1 indicating that the description was "totally wrong" and 10 indicating that the description was "perfect."

Scores of 1–3 are combined as "weak" identification with the description, and scores of 8–10 are combined as "strong" identification. Within the context of the survey, weak identification with the label "pro-Israel" does not necessarily translate into opposition to Israel.

It's no surprise that identification with the self-description "pro-Israel" was strongest among Jews—86 percent strongly identified with this description, while only 4 percent were weak in their identification with it.

But among white Evangelical Protestants, 13 percent were weak supporters of Israel, while 37 percent were strong supporters. In contrast, white non-Evangelical Protestants were more evenly divided, with 23 percent indicating weak support and 20 percent indicating strong support.

Among black Evangelical Protestants, 27 percent were weak supporters of Israel and 20 percent were strong supporters. Among black non-Evangelical Protestants, however, 30 percent were weak supporters and only 13 percent were strong supporters.

The importance of Israel in Evangelical theology appears to be responsible for these differences in views. At one level, Evangelicals believe that God's promise to Abraham in the Book of Genesis—"I will bless those who bless you and curse those who curse you"—is still in effect. At another level, many believe that events leading to the Second Coming of Christ—the battle of Armageddon—will take place in the Middle East and that the creation of the State of Israel in 1948 is the clearest signal that the thousand-year earthly reign of Christ is imminent.

The views of Catholics are virtually identical to those of white non-Evangelical Protestants—24 percent are weak supporters of Israel, while 22 percent are strong supporters. Among those with no religious preference, 22 percent are weak supporters of Israel and 19 percent are strong supporters.

Support for Israel is weakest among blacks and Hispanics: 30 percent and 29 percent, respectively, are weak supporters of Israel, and 18 percent and 20 percent, respectively, are strong supporters. Among whites, strong supporters outnumber weak supporters by 30 to 20 percent.

Americans over 30 are more likely than those under 30 to be strong supporters of Israel. Twenty-seven percent of those under 30 are weak supporters, while 19 percent are strong supporters. But 27 percent of those over 30 are strong supporters of Israel; 22 percent of those 30–49 and 19 percent of those over 50 are weak supporters.

Table 6.21 shows that support for Israel increases with education.

Table 6.22 shows that, regionally, support for Israel is strongest in the South, where white Evangelical Protestants are concentrated.

Support for Israel is weaker among Democrats than among Republicans. This largely reflects the fact that blacks are overwhelmingly Democratic. Among Republicans and those who lean Republican, 18 percent are weak supporters of Israel and 29 percent are strong supporters. Among Democrats, 24 percent fall into each group.

A similar pattern holds up along ideological lines. Self-described conser-

Table 6.21
SUPPORT FOR ISRAEL, BY EDUCATION

	Weak Supporters	Strong Supporters
College Grad.	19%	27%
Some College	21	26
High School Grad.	22	25
Less Than High School	25	22

vatives are stronger supporters of Israel—29 percent are strong supporters and 19 percent are weak supporters. Among self-described liberals, 24 percent are weak supporters and 22 percent are strong supporters.

In a separate question, 37 percent of Americans said their sympathies in the Middle East were more with Israel and 15 percent said they were more with the Palestinian Arabs; 22 percent volunteered the responses "neither" or "both." There were no significant differences along religious lines: Protestants sided with Israel by 38 to 16 percent; Catholics by 34 to 15 percent; all Evangelicals by 38 to 13 percent; white Evangelicals by 39 to 13 percent; and non-Evangelicals by 37 to 17 percent.

ANTICOMMUNISM

White Evangelical Protestants are the most suspicious religious group when it comes to dealing with the Soviets, while Catholics, Jews and those with no

Table 6.22
SUPPORT FOR ISRAEL, BY REGION

	Weak Supporters	Strong Supporters
East	22%	25%
Midwest	23	23
South	19	26
West	26	25

religious preference are the least suspicious. Particular opposition to the athe-
istic nature of communism among Evangelicals appears to make them more
suspicious of the Soviet Union[27].

Despite these differences, however, white Evangelical Protestants are only
somewhat less likely than other groups to support the U.S.-Soviet treaty on
Intermediate Range Nuclear Forces, the INF treaty. These findings are based
on Gallup surveys conducted for the Times Mirror Corporation's study, "The
People, Press and Politics."

In the responses to questions asked before the INF treaty-signing, there
were major differences along religious lines on the issue of whether the United
States is too willing or not willing enough to compromise with the Soviet Union.
Among white Evangelicals, 29 percent believe the United States is too willing
to compromise, while 14 percent believe it is not willing enough; 50 percent
were satisfied with the level of compromise.

White non-Evangelical Protestants were more evenly divided, with 22 percent saying the United States was too willing to compromise, 20 percent saying
it was not willing enough and 50 percent satisfied.

Among black Protestants, 24 percent of Evangelicals said the United States
was too willing to compromise, 19 percent said it was not willing enough and
45 percent were satisfied. Non-Evangelical black Protestants, however, felt,
by 28 to 20 percent, that the United States was not willing enough to compromise; 37 percent were satisfied.

The views of Catholics were almost identical to those of black non-Evangelical Protestants: 21 percent said the United States was too willing to compromise, 27 percent said it was not willing enough and 44 percent were satisfied.

Jews and those with no religious affiliation were more likely to support
greater compromise. Among Jews, 19 percent said the United States was too
willing to compromise, 32 percent said it was not willing enough and 44 percent
were satisfied. Among those with no affiliation, the responses were 17 percent,
34 percent and 41 percent, respectively.

White Evangelical Protestants, Jews and those with no affiliation stood out
on the question of whether there was a greater risk for the United States in
trusting the Soviet Union or being too suspicious. While the other groups were
evenly divided, a majority of white Evangelical Protestants said trusting the
Russians was the greater risk, while a majority of Jews and the unaffiliated
said being too suspicious was the greater risk. Table 6.23 shows specific findings.

A similar pattern emerged on the question of whether there was a greater
risk to the United States in an arms buildup or in falling behind the Russians.
Table 6.24 shows this pattern.

Despite their greater distrust of the Soviet Union, white Evangelical Protestants still indicated strong support for the INF treaty in a January 1988
survey. The survey asked if respondents would be more or less likely to vote
for a candidate who opposed ratifying the treaty. Among white Evangelical
Protestants, 49 percent said they would be less likely to vote for such a can-

Table 6.23

TRUST OR SUSPICION OF USSR GREATER RISK FOR PEACE?

	Trusting Greater Risk	Being Too Suspicious Greater Risk
White Evangelicals	54%	33%
White Non-Evangelicals	43	43
Black Evangelicals	35	38
Black Non-Evangelicals	39	34
Catholics	42	43
Jews	33	56
No Affiliation	32	54

didate, while 30 percent said they would be more likely; the rest had no opinion or said the issue would have no effect on their vote. (These figures will be dropped for other groups.)

White non-Evangelical Protestants were less likely to vote for an anti-INF candidate by 61 to 24 percent. Black Protestants were less likely to vote for

Table 6.24

ARMS BUILDUP OR FALLING BEHIND GREATER RISK?

	Buildup Greater Risk	Falling Behind Greater Risk
White Evangelicals	32%	53%
White Non-Evangelicals	43	42
Black Evangelicals	39	40
Black Non-Evangelicals	46	37
Catholics	45	38
Jews	53	28
No Affiliation	47	37

such a candidate by 48 to 26 percent. (Figures for Evangelicals and non-Evangelicals were not available in this survey.)

Catholics were opposed to an anti-INF candidate by a 55 to 26 percent margin; those with no religious affiliation were opposed by a 56 to 20 percent margin. The sample size for Jews was too small to be accurate in this survey, but it indicated overwhelming opposition to an anti-INF candidate.

SOCIAL MOVEMENTS

There are important differences among religious groups in their level of identification with leading social movements. For example, Jews and black Protestants are most likely to support the women's movement, while white Evangelical Protestants are most likely to support the antiabortion movement. At the same time, white Catholics were more likely than white Protestants to support the civil rights movement[28].

These patterns emerge from a Gallup survey conducted for the Times Mirror Corporation's study, "The People, Press and Politics." The survey asked respondents to indicate their level of agreement with a description of themselves, with 1 on a scale of 1 to 10 signifying that the description was "totally wrong," and 10 signifying that it was "perfect." We have grouped responses of 8, 9 and 10 together to indicate strong identification with a label.

The survey asked respondents their level of identification with the women's movement, the antiabortion movement, the peace movement, the civil rights movement and the gay rights movement. It also asked their level of identification with the labels "an environmentalist," "pro-Israel," "anticommunist," "a supporter of business interests," "a union supporter" and "a supporter of the NRA" (National Rifle Association), a major opponent of gun control.

The degree of identification with these labels is important because, in addition to eliciting a personal statement, it reveals attitudes toward various movements. For example, Americans are more likely to support the Equal Rights Amendment than they are to strongly identify with the women's movement.

For purposes of this analysis, we have studied responses from these groups: white Evangelical Protestants; white non-Evangelical Protestants; white Catholics; Hispanics (who are 70 percent Catholic); black Protestants (80 percent of blacks are Protestant); Jews; and those with no religious affiliation.

Most groups were strongest in their identification as anticommunist, but two groups had stronger identifications with other labels. Among Jews, 73 percent identified strongly as anticommunist, while 86 percent identified strongly as pro-Israel. Among black Protestants, 84 percent identified strongly with the civil rights movement, 62 percent identified strongly with the peace movement and 55 percent identified strongly as anticommunist.

There were greater differences in priorities among the different Protestant groups than there were between white Catholics and Hispanics. Table 6.25

Table 6.25

SOCIAL MOVEMENT SUPPORT BY PROTESTANTS

White Evangelical		White Non-Evangelical		Black	
Anticommunist	80%	Anticommunist	71%	Civil Rights	84%
Antiabortion	45	Environmentalist	40	Peace	62
Peace	40	Peace	39	Anticommunist	55
NRA	39	Civil Rights	37	Union	42
Environmentalist	39	NRA	30	Women's	41
Pro-Israel	36	Business	28	Environmentalist	31
Civil Rights	33	Women's	26	Antiabortion	31
Business	29	Union	24	Business	28
Union	21	Antiabortion	21	Pro-Israel	17
Women's	20	Pro-Israel	20	NRA	16
Gay Rights	3	Gay Rights	8	Gay Rights	11

shows the priorities of each Protestant group and the percentage identifying strongly with each label.

Table 6.26 shows the similarities in attitudes between white Catholics and Hispanics.

Jews, who have traditionally been involved in a variety of social movements, had the highest rates of identification of those surveyed. Those with no religious affiliation, who traditionally are not "joiners" in any sense, had the lowest rates of identification. Table 6.27 shows the priorities of these two groups.

CONCLUSIONS

A review of this lengthy chapter produces two contradictory impressions. On the one hand, the many and often sharp differences in views held by different religious groups are dramatic. On the other hand, so are the many areas of agreement. Before looking at the differences more closely, it's important to say a few words about the consensus that has emerged within the various religious groups that make up American society.

Many of the differences we have found are of degree, not of kind. It is significant, for example, that 78 percent of white Catholics and 67 percent of white Evangelicals support the Equal Rights Amendment; these figures indicate that

Table 6.26
SOCIAL MOVEMENT SUPPORT BY CATHOLICS

White Catholics		Hispanics	
Anticommunist	74%	Anticommunist	62%
Peace	47	Civil Rights	55
Civil Rights	44	Peace	52
Environmentalist	41	Environmentalist	33
Antiabortion	39	Antiabortion	33
Business	33	Women's	28
Union	31	Union	27
Women's	28	Business	20
NRA	27	Pro-Israel	20
Pro-Israel	23	NRA	15
Gay Rights	8	Gay Rights	8

Table 6.27
SOCIAL MOVEMENT SUPPORT BY JEWS, UNAFFILIATED

Jews		No Affiliation	
Pro-Israel	86%	Peace	55%
Anticommunist	73	Anticommunist	54
Civil Rights	61	Civil Rights	51
Peace	57	Environmentalist	48
Environmentalist	50	Women's	30
Women's	47	Pro-Israel	27
Business	29	Business	26
Gay Rights	28	Union	24
Union	21	NRA	24
Antiabortion	18	Gay Rights	17
NRA	4	Antiabortion	15

Catholics are more enthusiastic than Evangelicals in their support for equal rights for women. But it would be a terrible mistake to suggest that the fact that "only" 67 percent of white Evangelicals support the ERA means that they are opposed to women's rights; the fact that more than two-thirds of both white Catholics and white Evangelicals support the ERA is a sign of significant consensus.

Viewed in this light, the amount of consensus across religious lines is almost staggering. Similar majorities or pluralities of virtually all religious groups support more government aid for education; they want AIDS education and values education in the public schools; they support the civil rights movement and say they would vote for a qualified black, Jew or woman for president; they support stronger gun control measures; they support the existence of labor unions and an increase in the minimum wage; they support the INF treaty and oppose aid to the Contras; they sympathize with Israel; they support increased government spending for social programs.

Some differences in views among religious groups stem from the unique situation of a particular group: Catholics have a well-established network of parochial schools and are more likely to support government aid for church-run schools than those who do not have such a network; Jews are the most likely to support Israel; black Protestants, like blacks with other backgrounds, are the most likely to support the civil rights movement.

But strong differences persist among major religious groups that appear to be linked to a general worldview rather than a particular situation. Members of different religious groups often live in very different mental worlds—they hold different views on key issues, have different priorities, different heroes, different values. The following offers a profile of key religious groups on major public issues:

- White Evangelical Protestants. This is the most conservative group in the country on social issues—abortion, the women's movement, gun control, race relations, homosexuality, tolerance of atheists. Yet this conservative orientation does not always translate into conservative positions—a majority of white Evangelicals believe abortion should be legal in many instances; they support the Equal Rights Amendment; they support many gun control measures; they support the INF treaty; they oppose Contra aid; they support government social programs. White Evangelical Protestants may well be closer to the mainstream than they or others realize.
- White Non-Evangelical Protestants. This group, mostly members of mainline churches, often find themselves in the middle—not as conservative as white Evangelical Protestants, not as liberal as non-Protestants. They are distinguished primarily by their strong support for legal abortion and their lukewarm support for government social programs. They are generally more tolerant, more supportive of civil and women's rights and more dovish than are white Evangelical Protestants. On many issues, white non-Evangelical Protestants hold views more similar to Catholics than to white Evangelical Protestants.

- Black Protestants. On public issues, as we noted earlier, race is a far stronger influence than religion on American blacks. Blacks tend to be among the most liberal on government social programs and among the most dovish on foreign policy. They tend to be somewhat more conservative than non-Protestants on social issues.
- Catholics. With the exception of abortion, Catholics are more liberal than white Protestants on almost every public issue—government spending, civil and women's rights, tolerance, gun control, foreign policy.
- Jews. On most measures, Jews are the most liberal whites in America. They are the most liberal on social issues like abortion and homosexuality.
- The Religiously Unaffiliated. This growing group is also quite liberal, particularly on foreign policy, social issues and civil and women's rights; it is slightly less liberal on economic matters.

White Protestants make up approximately half of the general population; everyone else—blacks, Catholics, non-Catholic Hispanics, Jews, members of "other" religious and those with no affiliation make up the other half. It seems accurate to say that the pressure for social change in a liberal—or "progressive"—direction in the United States comes primarily from those who are not white Protestants; pressure for social change in a conservative direction comes from white Evangelical Protestants. White non-Evangelical Protestants are often pulled between the two; when it comes to specific issues, they most often seem to be influenced in the liberal direction.

CHAPTER

7

Religion and Politics

ONE of the standard clichés in America is that you're likely to get into trouble if you talk about either religion or politics. It follows, then, that talking about the mixture of religion and politics is even more controversial. That may be the reason that both political experts and religious leaders fail to pay adequate attention to religious voting patterns, attitudes toward church involvement in politics and different approaches to political issues by various religious groups. The preceding chapter spelled out many key differences by religion in attitudes toward specific social and political issues. This chapter will examine how those differences play out in terms of political affiliation and voting patterns. We include an in-depth tracking of religious attitudes toward political parties and candidates during the 1988 presidential election as a case study.

DENOMINATIONAL POLITICAL AFFILIATIONS
STABLE SINCE 1984

Even though the Democratic Party lost the presidency in 1988, it has registered gains since 1984 among most religious groups. Despite those Democratic gains, however, support for the Republican Party was higher across almost all religious groups than it was a generation ago[1].

When there is a national political trend, it generally moves in the same direction, if not in the same degree, in all groups. So, for example, a Democratic trend is likely to be stronger among normally Democratic Catholics than among normally Republican Presbyterians, but the Democrats will make some gains in both groups.

Generally, Catholics, Jews and Baptists are the most Democratic denominations, while mainline Protestant denominations are the most Republican.

In more than 15,000 interviews conducted throughout 1988, 29 percent of Americans identified themselves as Republicans and 40 percent identified themselves as Democrats.

In 1988, 44 percent of Catholics identified themselves as Democrats and 25 percent as Republicans. This was virtually identical to the 1984 figures of 41 percent Democratic and 25 percent Republican. These figures represent significant Republican longterm gains, however; only 16 percent of Catholics in 1966 and 17 percent in 1976 said they were Republicans while 56 and 53 percent, respectively, said they were Democrats. Protestant figures were almost identical to those in 1984: 33 percent said they were Republicans and 39 percent said they were Democrats. In 1984, Democrats led by 37 to 32 percent. In 1976, 44 percent of Protestants were Democrats and 27 percent were Republicans; in 1966, it was 42 percent Democratic, 31 percent Republican.

The most Democratic Protestant group is Baptists. In 1988, Democrats outnumbered Republicans in this group by 50 to 24 percent. The percentage of Baptists identifying themselves as Democrats was 55 in 1966, 57 in 1976 and 49 in 1984. The percentage identifying themselves as Republicans was 20 percent in 1966, 17 percent in 1976 and 24 percent in 1984.

Methodists are fairly evenly divided, with 38 percent saying they are Republicans and 36 percent saying they are Democrats. The figures for Republicans were 34 percent in 1966, 30 percent in 1976 and 36 percent in 1984; for Democrats, it was 40 percent in 1966, 45 percent in 1976 and 35 percent in 1984.

Among Lutherans, 40 percent are Republicans and 27 percent Democrats. In 1984, 37 percent were Republicans and 28 percent Democrats; in 1976, 35 percent identified with each party, and in 1966, 38 percent were Republicans and 34 percent Democrats.

Presbyterians are the most heavily Republican denomination. In 1988, Republicans outnumbered Democrats by 47 to 22 percent, about the same as the 47 to 24 percent margin in 1984. In 1976, the margin was closer, with 39 percent Republican and 32 percent Democratic. In 1966, the pattern was closer to what it is today, with 44 percent Republican and 28 percent Democratic.

Democrats registered surprising gains among normally Republican Episcopalians in 1988. In 1988, 37 percent said they were Republicans and 34 percent said they were Democrats. This contrasts with 1984, when the figures were 43 percent Republican and 25 percent Democratic. In 1976, Republicans led by 38 to 27 percent; in 1966, it was 42 percent Republican, 27 percent Democratic.

Members of the United Church of Christ are heavily Republican, with 44 percent Republican and 32 percent Democratic. Among members of the Christian Church (Disciples of Christ), 38 percent are Democratic and 34 percent Republican.

Those Americans who belong to other Protestant denominations too small to register separately on surveys are evenly divided: 35 percent are Republican, 36 percent are Democratic. Those Americans who say they are Protestant, but do not specify a denomination, are also evenly split, with 31 percent Republican and 32 percent Democratic.

American Jews remain the most strongly Democratic denomination; in 1988, 56 percent were Democratic and 13 percent were Republican, about the same as the 55 to 14 percent Democratic margin in 1984. In 1976, Democrats outnumbered Republicans among Jews by 56 to 8 percent; in 1966, they led by 64 to 9 percent.

Mormons are a heavily Republican group; 43 percent are Republican and 22 percent are Democratic.

Those with no religious affiliation are heavily Democratic; in 1988, 37 percent were Democrats and 20 percent were Republicans.

Figures for some groups listed above are not available in all previous surveys.

When we move beyond the question of denominational affiliation to broad religious families, we find new patterns. White Evangelical Protestants tilt Republican, white Catholics tilt Democratic and white non-Evangelical Protestants are evenly divided between the two parties. These patterns apply to both party identification and intensity of support for the parties[2].

All three groups are more Republican than in their parents' generation, in contrast to black Protestants and Jews, who remain strongly Democratic. But the Republican shift has not been uniform—it is strongest among white Evangelical Protestants and weakest among white Catholics.

Among white Evangelical Protestants, 47 percent said their parents were Democrats and 27 percent said their parents were Republicans. Today, however, 35 percent identify themselves as Republicans and 29 percent as Democrats. When Independents who lean toward one party or the other are included, 51 percent are Republicans and 40 percent are Democrats.

The Republican shift has not been as great among white Protestants who are not Evangelicals. Among this group, 41 percent said their parents were Democrats and 31 percent said their parents were Republicans. Today, 31 percent of white non-Evangelical Protestants are Republicans and 29 percent are Democrats. When leaners are included, 46 percent are Republicans and 42 percent are Democrats.

Among white Catholics (excluding Hispanic and Asian Catholics as well as blacks), 53 percent said their parents were Democrats and 21 percent said their parents were Republicans. Today, 38 percent of white Catholics say they are Democrats and 25 percent say they are Republicans. When leaners are included, 52 percent are Democrats and 36 percent are Republicans.

One surprising finding is that there is very little difference in attitude between white Catholics and minority Catholics, primarily Hispanics. For example, among all Catholics, 53 percent are Democrats or lean Democratic and 33 percent are Republicans or lean Republican.

The gap between white and nonwhite Catholics is far less than the gap between white and nonwhite Protestants. One reason for this is that most nonwhite Protestants are blacks and most nonwhite Catholics are Hispanics; a much higher percentage of blacks than Hispanics are Democrats. At the same time, white Catholics have been more resistant to the Republican trend in the past decade.

White Evangelical Protestants are more likely to say they like Republican policies and candidates and that it is hard for them to vote against a Republican. White Catholics are more likely to say they like Democratic policies and candidates and that it is hard for them to vote against a Democrat. White non-Evangelical Protestants are again evenly divided. Table 7.1 shows these findings in detail.

Among black Protestants, Evangelicals are somewhat more likely to identify as Democrats, although the difference disappears when leaners are included. Seventy-six percent of black Evangelical Protestants say they are Democrats and 9 percent say they are Republicans; 66 percent of black non-Evangelical Protestants say they are Democrats and 9 percent say they are Republicans. When leaners are included, 85 percent of black Evangelicals and 83 percent of black non-Evangelicals are Democrats and 11 and 10 percent, respectively, are Republicans.

Table 7.1

ATTITUDES TOWARD POLITICAL PARTIES, BY RELIGION

	White Evan. Protestants	White Non-Evan. Protestants	White Catholics
Generally Like Policies of:			
Republicans	45%	39%	30%
Democrats	33	37	44
Generally Like Candidates of:			
Republican	43%	36%	31%
Democrats	27	32	37
Find It Hard to Vote Against:			
Republican	26%	21%	17%
Democrats	20	22	28

Among Jews, 48 percent are Democrats and 16 percent are Republicans. When leaners are included, 69 percent are Democrats and 22 percent are Republicans.

The political conventional wisdom holds that American Jews are both considerably more liberal and considerably more politically active than the rest of the population; and, in fact, they are[3].

Because Jews make up only 2 percent of the total population, there are not enough interviews with Jews in most surveys to provide a meaningful sample. The large sample used for the Gallup Poll for the Times Mirror Corporation's study, "The People, Press and Politics," however, included interviews with ninety-two Jews. While the margin of error for a group this size is large—10 percentage points in either direction—the results are still meaningful. And, in fact, many of the differences are larger than the margin of error.

For example, while 78 percent of all Americans say they are registered to vote, 89 percent of Jews say they are registered. There is an even larger difference on another important indicator of political activity: while only 9 percent of all Americans say they contribute money to Political Action Committees that support candidates or parties, 26 percent of Jews say they contribute to PACS.

On most other measures of political involvement, Jews are more active than the general population, but by much smaller margins:

- 17 percent of all Americans and 19 percent of Jews say they have attended a political meeting or rally.
- 11 percent of all Americans and 15 percent of Jews say they are active in party politics.
- 15 percent of all Americans and 17 percent of Jews have contributed money to a candidate.
- 12 percent of all Americans and 13 percent of Jews have contributed to a party.
- 30 percent of all Americans and 35 percent of Jews check off the option on their tax returns allowing the use of one dollar of their taxes for funding presidential races.

There was only one measure in which Jews were less involved than other Americans—wearing campaign buttons; 27 percent of all Americans and 21 percent of Jews wear buttons.

One reflection of the liberalism of American Jews is found in their self-description; they are more than twice as likely as the general population to describe themselves as liberals.

The survey asked respondents to indicate how well the terms "liberal" and "conservative" described them, on a scale of 1 to 10, with 1 meaning that the description is "completely wrong" and 10 meaning that the description is "perfect." Scores of 1–3 are defined as weak identification and scores of 8–10 are identified as strong identification.

Nationally, 38 percent of Americans were weak in their identification as liberals, while only 19 percent were strong in that identification. In contrast, 24 percent of Jews were weak in their identification, while 42 percent strongly identified as liberals.

The same pattern held up in self-identification as conservatives. The general population was evenly divided, with 28 percent each showing weak and strong identification with the label. Among Jews, however, 47 percent were weak in their identification as conservatives, while only 18 percent were strong in that identification.

This pattern is reflected again in identification with various social movements. Jews were consistently more likely to identify strongly with more liberal movements and less likely to identify with more conservative ones. Table 7.2 shows this pattern.

The high support for the civil rights movement and the relatively high support for the gay rights movement among Jews reflect the fact that, as a group very conscious of their minority status in America, Jews have traditionally believed that they are more secure when all minorities are secure.

THE NEW POLITICAL TYPOLOGIES

One of the most exhaustive studies of the American electorate ever undertaken shows that religion is a major factor in determining political attitudes, often in surprising ways. The Gallup survey conducted for the Times Mirror Corporation as part of its ongoing study of "The People, Press and Politics" also found that the most politically active Americans—both Republicans and Democrats—are more likely to be highly religious than other Americans. The

Table 7.2
COMPARISON OF U.S., JEWS, ON SOCIAL MOVEMENTS

	U.S.		Jews	
	Weak	Strong	Weak	Strong
Women's Movement	22%	29%	11%	47%
Environmental	9	39	6	50
National Rifle Association (NRA)	37	28	69	4
Peace Movement	13	46	10	57
Civil Rights Movement	12	47	4	61
Antiabortion Movement	36	33	60	18
Gay Rights Movement	66	9	30	28

religious commitment scale was based on responses to questions such as importance of prayer and consciousness of God's existence.

For example, 44 percent of those who said they were very likely to vote in 1988 were highly religious, compared to 33 percent of those who said they were not very likely to vote. There was no significant difference between parties, with 45 percent of Democrats and 44 percent of Republicans saying they were very likely to vote also expressing strong religious convictions.

The study analyzed responses to some one hundred questions and divided Americans into eleven political groups. Religion was a significant factor in determining the identity of six of the groups[4].

The most clearly defined group in terms of religion was the "Moralists," who make up 11 percent of the adult population. The Moralists are primarily middle-age and middle-income, with a heavy concentration of southerners. Ninety-four percent are white, and they tend to live in suburbs, small cities and rural areas, are regular churchgoers and include a large number of Evangelicals.

Moralists are strongly antiabortion and pro-school prayer; they favor the death penalty and a quarantine on AIDS victims; they are strongly anticommunist and prodefense; they support social spending except when it is targeted at minorities. They make up one of the two strongest Republican blocs in the country; 97 percent voted for President Reagan in 1984, 95 percent voted for Republican congressional candidates in 1986 and 99 percent identify themselves as Republicans or lean Republican.

White Evangelical Protestants make up the largest segment of this group (37 percent), followed by white non-Evangelical Protestants (26 percent), Catholics (19 percent), those with no religious affiliation (4 percent), black Evangelical Protestants (2 percent) and black non-Evangelical Protestants and Jews (1 percent each).

But Republicans do not have a monopoly on religious commitment. Four groups that are heavily Democratic express deep religious views, equal to those of the Moralists:

- 1960s Democrats (8 percent of the population). This group—60 percent female and 16 percent black—is well educated and upper middle class; members strongly identify with the peace and civil rights movements and environmental groups that grew out of the sixties. They combine churchgoing and religious beliefs with a very high degree of tolerance for beliefs and lifestyles they do not share. Seventy-five percent voted for Walter Mondale in 1984, 85 percent voted Democratic in 1986 and 90 percent identify themselves as Democrats or lean Democratic. Catholics make up the largest segment of this group (28 percent), followed by white non-Evangelical Protestants (24 percent), white Evangelical Protestants (13 percent), black Evangelical and non-Evangelical Protestants (6 percent each), and Jews and the unaffiliated (2 percent each).
- New Deal Democrats (11 percent of the population). This group is older

and more blue collar in membership, and intolerant on questions of personal freedom, but very supportive of social spending. Seventy percent voted for Mondale, 92 percent voted Democratic in 1988 and 99 percent identify themselves as Democrats or lean Democratic. Catholics make up the largest segment of this group (29 percent), followed closely by white Evangelical Protestants (27 percent) and white non-Evangelical Protestants (25 percent), black Evangelical and non-Evangelical Protestants (4 percent each), Jews and the unaffiliated (1 percent each).

- The Partisan Poor (9 percent of the population). This is a low-income group, 37 percent black, heavily southern, urban and poorly educated, with primarily economic concerns and a high degree of faith in the Democratic Party. Eighty-one percent voted for Mondale, 95 percent voted Democratic in 1986 and 98 percent identify themselves as Democrats or lean Democratic. Catholics make up the largest segment in this group (31 percent), followed by black Evangelical Protestants (17 percent), white non-Evangelical Protestants (15 percent), black non-Evangelical Protestants (12 percent), White Evangelical Protestants (11 percent), the unaffiliated (3 percent) and Jews (1 percent).

- The God-and-Country Democrats (7 percent of the population). This group is similar to the partisan poor, but feels only moderate economic pressure, 87 percent Democratic. Catholics make up the largest segment within this group (29 percent), followed by white non-Evangelical Protestants (16 percent), black Evangelical Protestants (14 percent), white Evangelical Protestants (13 percent) and black non-Evangelical Protestants (12 percent), the unaffiliated (4 percent) and Jews (1 percent).

Two groups that lean Democratic are notable for their lack of religious convictions:

- Followers (7 percent of the population, 4 percent of the electorate). This group is young, poorly educated, 25 percent black and 18 percent Hispanic and is concentrated in the East and South; it is low in religious commitment. Forty-six percent voted for Mondale, 65 percent voted Democratic in 1986 and 55 percent identify themselves as Democrats or lean Democratic.

- The Seculars (8 percent of the population, 9 percent of the electorate). This white, educated, middle-aged group is the only group in the country that professes no religious belief. They are professional, concentrated on the East and West coasts and 11 percent are Jewish. While they agree with the Democrats on many issues, they are not actively involved in party politics in general. Sixty-six percent voted for Mondale, 72 percent voted Democratic in 1986 and 77 percent identify themselves as Democrats or lean Democratic.

The other overwhelmingly Republican group is the Enterprisers (10 percent of the population). This group, 99 percent Republican, is strongly probusiness and antigovernment. Thirty-nine percent of the Enterprisers are white non-

Evangelical Protestants, followed by white Evangelical Protestants and Catholics (22 percent each), the unaffiliated (6 percent) and Jews (1 percent).

Two other groups are key swing voters:

- The Upbeats (9 percent of the population) are young, optimistic, pro-business but not antigovernment, 66 percent Republican.
- The Disaffecteds (9 percent of the population) are alienated, pessimistic, skeptical of both government and business; they lean Republican (44 percent) but have strong historic ties to the Democrats.

The final group is known as the Bystanders (11 percent of the population) because they are chronic nonvoters. They are young, poorly educated and often single; they have little involvement in politics and are evenly split, with 29 percent Republicans and 33 percent Democrats.

Table 7.3 shows the religious makeup of those groups not overwhelmingly Democratic or Republican.

RELIGION AND THE PRESIDENCY

Americans express a great deal of ambivalence about religion when it comes to the presidency:

- They are less likely to vote for a candidate who describes himself as a Born-Again or Evangelical Christian.
- But they are more likely to vote for a candidate who says that Jesus is his "personal savior."
- An overwhelming majority would vote for a Catholic or Jew for president, but most reject an atheist.

Table 7.3
RELIGIOUS PROFILES OF "TYPOLOGY" GROUPS

	Upbeats	Disaffected	Followers	Seculars	Bystanders
White Evan.	21%	23%	9%	3%	13%
White Non-Evan.	29	32	16	28	27
Black Evan.	2	1	7	–	3
Black Non-Evan.	2	2	13	2	5
Catholic	33	22	36	19	24
Jewish	2	2	2	11	1
None	3	7	9	33	12

- Despite this, when Americans were asked to name the characteristics they look for in a president, only 4 percent volunteered the description "religious."
- A large number of Americans reject the idea of a minister running for president and held highly negative views of the two ministers—Jesse Jackson and Pat Robertson—who ran in the 1988 primaries[5].

A survey conducted in April 1987 asked, "Aside from how you feel about a presidential candidate in other respects, would you be more likely to vote for a candidate who considers himself a 'Born-Again' Evangelical Christian, less likely to do so, or wouldn't it make any difference either way?"

Twenty-nine percent of Americans said they would be less likely to vote for an Evangelical, twice the figure (15 percent) who said they would be more likely to vote for an Evangelical; 52 percent said it would make no difference. This represented a sharp change from 1980, when 19 percent of Americans said they would be more likely to vote for an Evangelical, 9 percent said they would be less likely and 66 percent said it would make no difference. It is likely that the timing of this poll—in the wake of the scandal involving Jim and Tammy Bakker and the PTL Club—increased negative attitudes toward self-described Born-Again Christians.

Forty-one percent of Evangelicals said they would be more likely to vote for an Evangelical, while only 6 percent said they would be less likely. On the other hand, 39 percent of non-Evangelicals said they would be less likely to vote for an Evangelical, while only 5 percent said they would be more likely.

Catholics were less likely to vote for an Evangelical by a 34 to 6 percent margin; Protestants were evenly divided, with 22 percent saying they would be more likely and 22 percent saying they would be less likely to vote for an Evangelical. Among mainline Protestants, 33 percent said they would be less likely to vote for an Evangelical while 12 percent said they would be more likely.

Those showing the highest support for an Evangelical candidate were women (18 percent), blacks (26 percent), southerners (22 percent) and those with less than a high school education (26 percent).

Overall, 37 percent of Americans say they would be more likely to vote for a candidate who said Jesus was his savior, 24 percent said they would be less likely and 33 percent said it would make no difference.

There are important differences among religious groups on these issues. In general, white Evangelical Protestants and black Protestants are more supportive than other groups of minister-candidates and candidates who announce Jesus as their savior. This finding apparently reflects the fact that the Rev. Jesse Jackson, a black Baptist minister, and Pat Robertson, a former Southern Baptist minister and a white Evangelical, were running for president.

Among white Evangelical Protestants, 65 percent said such a declaration would make them more likely to vote for a candidate and only 7 percent said it would make them less likely; 25 percent said it would make no difference. The responses among black Protestants were similar—59 percent said they would be more likely to vote for such a candidate, 15 percent said they would be less likely and 21 percent said it would make no difference.

But white non-Evangelical Protestants were evenly divided: 28 percent said they would be more likely to vote for a candidate who said Jesus was his savior, 26 percent said they would be less likely and 41 percent said it would make no difference.

And a plurality of Catholics—31 percent—said they would be less likely to vote for such a candidate; 26 percent said they would be more likely and 37 percent said it would make no difference.

Among those with no religious preference, only 12 percent said they would be more likely to vote for a candidate who said Jesus was his savior; 44 percent said they were less likely and 35 percent said it made no difference.

A large plurality of Americans—39 percent—believe that it would be "a bad thing" for a clergyman or minister to run for president of the United States. Only 16 percent said it would be a "good thing," while 41 percent said it would make no difference. The strongest support for a minister running for president comes from black Protestants: 33 percent said it would be a good thing, while 21 percent said it would not and 35 percent said it would make no difference.

A slight plurality of white Evangelical Protestants—by 28 to 24 percent— said a minister running for president was a good thing, while 44 percent said it would make no difference.

But white non-Evangelical Protestants, Catholics and those with no religious preference were strongly opposed to a minister running for president: only 9 percent of white non-Evangelical Protestants, 10 percent of Catholics and 12 percent of those with no religious preference said such a candidacy was a good thing; 45, 47 and 38 percent, respectively, said it was a bad thing.

The negative attitudes toward a ·minister running for president seem to stem from the belief that ministers are not well prepared for public office and, as president, would create religious tensions within society:

· By 50 to 44 percent, Americans reject the idea that a minister will be more honest than the typical politician.
· They do say, by 55 to 38 percent, that a minister will have higher moral standards than the typical politician.
· 64 percent disagree that a minister's training and background would make him more able to deal with the nation's problems; 29 percent agree.
· Americans agree by 69 to 25 percent that a minister would press his religious position on moral issues.
· They agree by 67 to 27 percent that a minister-candidate would create tension between religious groups in society.

Among Americans who said in the spring of 1988 that they knew something about Jesse Jackson, only 5 percent believed he would make an "excellent" president and only 18 percent believed he would make a "good" president. Twenty-four percent believed he would make a "fair" president, while 41 percent believed he would be a "poor" one.

The strongest gap in attitudes toward Jackson involved race. Twenty-four percent of blacks and only 2 percent of whites said he would make an excellent president; 50 percent of blacks and 13 percent of whites said he would make a good president. At the other extreme, 46 percent of whites and only 5 percent of blacks said Jackson would make a poor president.

There was no significant gap between Evangelicals and non-Evangelicals in attitudes toward Jackson. Twenty-two percent of non-Evangelicals, 23 percent of all Evangelicals and 15 percent of white Evangelicals said he would be an excellent or good president.

Those more likely to give Jackson a "good" or "excellent" rating were women (26 percent), those 18–29 (31 percent), those with less than a high school education (32 percent), those with family incomes below $15,000 a year (31 percent) and Democrats (34 percent).

Among those Americans who said they knew something about Robertson, 3 percent said he would make an excellent president, 9 percent said he would do a good job, 15 percent said he would be fair and 56 percent said he would be a poor president.

Evangelicals and non-Evangelicals split sharply over Robertson. Twenty-four percent of Evangelicals and 25 percent of white Evangelicals, but only 7 percent of non-Evangelicals, said he would make a good or excellent president. Sixteen percent of Protestants but only 7 percent of Catholics said he would make a good or excellent president.

Robertson was more likely to receive a good or excellent rating from women (15 percent), those 18–29 (16 percent), those with less than a high school education (23 percent), blacks (18 percent), those with incomes below $15,000 a year and Republicans (17 percent each).

THE CHURCHES AND POLITICS

Americans not only do not want ministers to run for president; by a 3-to-2 margin, they reject clergy involvement in politics at all. At the same time, however, about one American in five reports voting for a candidate largely because of their own religious beliefs[6].

Attitudes toward clergy involvement in politics emerged in response to two questions. The first question asked, "Should churches keep out of political matters, or should they express their views on day-to-day social and political questions?"; 56 percent of Americans said the churches should keep out of politics and 37 percent said they should express their views.

The second question asked respondents to agree or disagree with this statement: "Religious organizations should persuade senators and representatives to enact legislation on ethical and moral issues they would like to see become law"; 35 percent of Americans agreed with this statement, while 52 percent disagreed.

These responses suggest that a decade of increased visibility of religious leaders speaking out on political and social issues and the Jackson and Robertson campaigns have left most Americans turned off by such activity. There are some important exceptions, however.

Evangelicals were about evenly divided on the question of church involvement in day-to-day politics: 44 percent said the churches should keep out, but 49 percent said they should express their views. In response to the second question, 53 percent of Evangelicals said religious organizations should persuade members of Congress to enact laws, while 36 percent disagreed. Non-Evangelicals held sharply different positions: they said by a 2-to-1 margin (63 to 32 percent) that churches should keep out of politics, and rejected lobbying by religious organizations by a similar margin (61 to 27 percent).

Those who said they had attended church within the past seven days, regardless of their denomination, were also far better disposed to church involvement in political activity: 45 percent said the churches should keep out of politics, while 50 percent said they should not. At the same time, 52 percent said religious organizations should lobby members of Congress, while 36 percent said they should not. Those who had not attended church in the past seven days strongly felt the opposite: 64 percent said the churches should keep out of politics, while 29 percent disagreed; similarly, 64 percent opposed lobbying by religious organizations, while 24 percent approved.

Opposition to church involvement in politics tended to increase with age and decrease with education; blacks and Hispanics were less likely to support church political activity. Opposition was highest in the West, and lowest in the Midwest, where residents were split about evenly. Table 7.4 shows responses to both questions.

In terms of their personal activities, four Americans in ten (42 percent) said they had done the following largely because of their religious beliefs during the past three years:

- 17 percent of Americans said they had voted for a candidate.
- 21 percent said they had prayed in support of a particular candidate or issue.
- 12 percent said they had talked to others about why they should support a candidate.
- 6 percent said they had written a letter to the editor about a national problem.
- 6 percent said they had contributed money to a candidate or a political organization.
- 5 percent said they had attended a political event or rally.
- 4 percent said they had worked for a candidate.
- 3 percent said they had demonstrated or protested about a national problem.

Table 7.4

ATTITUDES TOWARD CHURCH INVOLVEMENT IN POLITICS

	Churches Should Keep Out of Politics		Religious Groups Should Persuade Legislators	
	Yes	No	Yes	No
U.S.	56%	37%	36%	52%
Men	58	36	36	53
Women	54	38	35	51
18–29	52	41	39	52
30–49	57	38	34	57
50+	58	34	34	48
College Grad.	51	47	33	61
Some College	57	37	38	55
High School Grad.	55	37	37	47
Less Than High School	62	29	33	49
White	57	37	37	52
Black	54	33	24	54
Hispanic	54	33	23	57
East	56	36	29	56
Midwest	48	46	43	48
South	57	33	38	46
West	64	33	30	65
$40,000+/Year	55	42	38	55
$25,000–40,000	56	38	38	54
$15,000–25,000	56	37	36	52
Less Than $15,000	57	34	30	50

Table 7.4 (CONT.)

ATTITUDES TOWARD CHURCH INVOLVEMENT IN POLITICS

	Churches Should Keep Out of Politics		Religious Groups Should Persuade Legislators	
	Yes	No	Yes	No
Republican	55	40	38	52
Democrat	58	33	33	53
Independent	54	42	36	52
Evangelical	44	49	53	36
Non-Evangelical	63	32	27	61
Catholic	54	40	33	53
Protestant	54	39	41	48
Baptist	50	42	44	42
Mainline Protestant	56	37	37	54
Church Attenders	45	50	52	36
Nonattenders	64	29	24	64

· 3 percent said they had joined an organization to deal with a national problem.

As might be expected, Evangelicals (23 percent) were more likely than non-Evangelicals (14 percent) to say they had voted for a candidate because of their own religious beliefs. Protestants (27 percent) were more likely than Catholics (19 percent) to say they had done so. Blacks (24 percent) were more likely than whites (17 percent) or Hispanics (11 percent) to cite their own religious beliefs as reason for voting for a candidate.

Age and education were also factors. Only 10 percent of those under 30 and 15 percent of those 30–49 said they had voted for a candidate because of their own religious beliefs, but one in four (25 percent) of those over 50 said they had done so. Somewhat surprisingly, college graduates (22 percent) were somewhat more likely than those with less education to cite their religious beliefs as reason for voting for a candidate. They were also the most likely to say they had joined a national organization to work on a national problem; 8 percent had done so.

Finally, members of one political party were no more likely than those of the other to say their religious beliefs had influenced their vote—21 percent of Republicans and 20 percent of Democrats said they had voted for a candidate because of their own religious beliefs.

THE 1988 ELECTION

The 1988 presidential election was the first since 1960 in which a new president would be chosen after the previous president had completed two four-year terms. But given the political dominance and personal popularity of Ronald Reagan, there was little doubt that the 1988 elections would reflect the state of his popularity at the time. This did not make the election any easier to predict; even at the height of the president's popularity, the public was always far more favorably disposed toward Reagan personally than it was toward his policies or his handling of the major issues of the day. A key question about the 1988 race would be the action of two religious groups who were key swing voters—Catholics and white Evangelicals.

Reagan's popularity—and that of his party—plummeted in early 1987 in the wake of revelations in November 1986 that his administration had sold arms to Iran in an effort to free American hostages there and that some of the proceeds had been used to buy arms for the Nicaraguan Contras after Congress had rejected further U.S. aid to them. Reagan's standing fell dramatically among both Catholics and Evangelicals. At the same time, both groups showed a strong preference for former Democratic Sen. Gary Hart of Colorado over both Vice President George Bush and Senate Majority Leader Robert Dole of Kansas in a January 1987 trial heat for the 1988 presidential election.

In July 1986, 66 percent of Catholics approved of Reagan's handling of the presidency and only 26 percent disapproved. In January 1987, however, Catholics were evenly divided, with 46 percent approving of Reagan's job performance and 45 percent disapproving[7].

Evangelicals, who approved of Reagan's handling of the presidency by a 68 to 26 percent margin in July, approved by 54 to 40 percent in January. Reagan's approval rating among all Protestants fell from a 64 to 27 percent margin to a 51 to 41 percent margin. Non-Evangelicals shifted from approval by a 62 to 28 percent margin to a virtual even split, with 46 percent approving and 44 percent disapproving.

In a trial heat poll in July 1986, Bush and Hart were tied, with 45 percent of registered voters favoring each candidate and the rest undecided. In January, however, 51 percent of registered voters favored Hart, while 38 percent favored Bush. In the July poll, Bush had a strong 53 to 39 percent lead among Evangelicals, which offset Hart's lead of 47 to 42 percent among non-Evangelicals.

In a January poll, Hart increased his lead among non-Evangelicals to 52 to 37 percent.

But Hart's most dramatic turnaround came among Evangelical voters, who now favored him by a 48 to 41 percent margin over Bush. Hart also gained dramatically among all Protestants: in July, he trailed by 48 to 43 percent among Protestants, but in January, he led by 50 to 41 percent in this group.

Hart's gains among Catholics were actually more modest, but only because a majority of Catholics already supported him. Hart led by 51 to 41 percent among Catholics in July and by 52 to 36 percent in January.

Nationally, Sen. Dole did no better than Bush against Hart, trailing by 50 to 37 percent. Dole ran slightly worse than Bush among Evangelicals, trailing Hart by 50 to 38 percent.

There was no difference along religious lines on the question of whether Reagan had told all he knew about the Iran arms sale. Three in four Protestants, Catholics, Evangelicals and non-Evangelicals believed the president had not told all he knew. Six in ten in each of those groups believed the scandal had made it very difficult for Reagan to be an effective president over the next two years.

But Catholics were more strongly opposed than most other Americans to Reagan's handling of the Iran arms deal and to aid to the Contras. They disapproved of Reagan's handling of the arms deal by 81 to 12 percent: this was stronger than the opposition of non-Evangelicals (77 to 14 percent), Protestants (72 to 18 percent) and Evangelicals (71 to 19 percent).

Similarly, 73 percent of Catholics opposed an additional $40 million in U.S. military aid to the Contras, while 18 percent supported the aid. Protestants opposed the aid by 66 to 25 percent, Evangelicals by 65 to 26 percent, non-Evangelicals by 71 to 20 percent.

By July 1987, the Democratic Party had grown in support and esteem across major American religious groups since the 1984 presidential election. In a July survey, 42 percent of all Americans said they were more likely to vote for the Democratic candidate in 1988, while 33 percent said they were more likely to vote for the Republican candidate. Eighteen percent were undecided and 1 percent favored a candidate from another party[8]. In 1984, 59 percent of Americans voted for Ronald Reagan and 41 percent voted for former Vice President Walter Mondale.

In July, 45 percent of Catholics said they were more likely to vote for a Democrat, while 31 percent said they were more likely to vote for a Republican. If we disallow the percentage who were undecided, this works out to a proportion of 59 percent of those with a preference favoring a Democrat and 41 percent favoring a Republican. In 1984, Gallup surveys taken on the eve of the election—a reliable indicator—showed that 61 percent of Catholics planned to vote for President Reagan and 39 percent planned to vote for Walter Mondale.

In the July survey, 40 percent of all Protestants said they were more likely to vote for a Democrat in 1988 and 34 percent said they were more likely to vote for a Republican. Again disallowing the undecided, this works out to a 54 to 46 percent edge for the Democrats. In 1984, 61 percent of Protestants said they planned to vote for Reagan and 39 percent for Mondale.

White Evangelicals were strong Republican supporters, with 42 percent saying they were more likely to vote for a Republican in 1988 and 29 percent saying they were more likely to vote for a Democrat. Again, if we disallow the undecided, this leaves 59 percent preferring a Republican and 41 percent preferring a Democrat. But this was down substantially from 1984, when 79 percent of white Evangelicals said they would vote for Reagan and only 21 percent said they would vote for Mondale.

In the July survey, 43 percent of non-Evangelicals said they were more likely to vote for a Democrat and 32 percent said they were more likely to vote for a Republican. This means that 57 percent of non-Evangelicals with a preference favored the Democrats, in contrast to the 41 percent of non-Evangelicals who voted for Mondale.

The degree to which Americans intended to vote for the Republican candidate for president in 1988 was directly linked to their level of approval of President Reagan's handling of the presidency, with two important exceptions: non-Evangelicals and Catholics were less likely to say they would vote for a Republican for president than they were to approve of Reagan's job performance.

Fifty-two percent of Catholics approved of Reagan's job performance, but only 41 percent of those with a preference expected to vote for a Republican. Forty-nine percent of non-Evangelicals approved of Reagan and 43 percent expected to vote for a Republican. Table 7.5 compares the percentage approving of Reagan's job performance and the percentage of those with a preference planning to vote for a Republican for other religious groups.

An August 1987 survey asked if the next president should continue in the same direction as Reagan or go in a different direction. Sixty percent of Catholics said he should go in a different direction, while only 33 percent said he should go in the same direction as Reagan. Protestants preferred that the next president go in a different direction by a smaller, 53 to 40 percent, margin. Among all Evangelicals, 53 percent preferred a new direction, while 43 percent wanted the next president to go in the same direction as Reagan. Non-Evangelicals preferred a new direction by 60 to 33 percent[9].

As Americans examined the various presidential candidates within each party, religious differences were again a factor. The race was complicated in the spring of 1987, when Gary Hart, the Democratic front-runner, withdrew from the race following the scandal about his involvement with model Donna Rice, and there was no clear party front-runner for some time after that. There were some important shifts in support among religious groups between July and October 1987. For example, Bush and Dole, on the Republican side, and the Rev. Jesse Jackson, Massachusetts Gov. Michael Dukakis and Rep. Richard Gephardt of Missouri, on the Democratic side, all registered at least small gains across major religious groups between July and October[10].

Table 7.5

COMPARISON OF REAGAN APPROVAL AND PLANS TO VOTE REPUBLICAN

	Percentage Approving of Reagan's Performance	Percentage Expecting to Vote Republican
Catholics	52%	41%
White Evangelicals	60	59
Evangelicals	51	47
Non-Evangelicals	49	43
Protestants	48	46
All Baptists	36	33
Southern Baptists	49	51
Mainline Protestants	53	56

On the other hand, Republicans Jack Kemp, a New York representative, and Alexander Haig lost support among key religious groups. Pat Robertson failed to make any gains among Republicans who were not Evangelicals. On the Democratic side, Sen. Paul Simon of Illinois showed slight gains among Catholics and slight losses among Protestants, while Sen. Albert Gore of Tennessee showed losses among Catholics and non-Evangelicals.

The late October survey did not include Hart, who had since re-entered the race. Some of the increased support for other candidates was due to the fact that several candidates listed on the July survey—Democrats Sen. Joseph Biden of Delaware and Gov. Bill Clinton of Arkansas and Republican Paul Laxalt, former senator from Nevada—had ruled themselves out of the race.

Knowing a presidential candidate's support from different religious groups is important for a variety of reasons. First, a candidate is most likely to be successful if he has balanced support across all groups. Second, strong support from one group, such as Catholics or Evangelicals, can offset weakness among other groups or account for a strong showing in a region of the country where that group is highly represented. At the same time, a candidate who shows particular strength with a group that usually votes for the other party has an electoral advantage; for example, a Republican with particular appeal to Catholics in his own party may do particularly well with Catholics who normally vote Democratic.

Table 7.6 compares support for the Republican candidates by religious group in July and October 1987. Table 7.7 compares support for the Democratic candidates by religious group in July and October 1987.

In January 1987, 43 percent of all Protestants said they were Republicans or Independents who lean Republican; 44 percent said they were Democrats or leaned Democratic. In October, the percentages were virtually identical, with 45 percent identifying as Republicans or Republican leaners and 46 percent saying they were Democrats or Democratic leaners.

Catholic sympathies shifted only slightly, from a 55 to 36 percent Democratic majority to a 52 to 39 percent Democratic lead.

Evangelicals were split, with 43 percent Republicans and 46 percent Democrats in January and 45 percent Republicans and 44 percent Democrats in October.

Non-Evangelicals backed the Democrats by a 49 to 39 percent margin in January and a 50 to 42 percent margin in October[11].

A survey for the Times Mirror Corporation's study, "The People, Press and Politics," conducted in January 1988, asked respondents if they would be more or less likely to vote for a presidential candidate who took specific stands. The survey found some important differences by religious group. A presidential candidate who favors changing the law to make it more difficult for a woman to get an abortion would pick up considerable support from white Evangelical Protestants, but would lose support among other major U.S. religious groups —including Catholics[12]. In general, however, those religious groups differ only in degree, not in basic attitude, on a number of other issues raised in the 1988 presidential campaign.

Table 7.6

SHIFTS IN REPUBLICAN PRIMARY PREFERENCES, BY RELIGION

	Protestant		Catholic		Evangelical		Non-Evangelical	
	July	Oct.	July	Oct.	July	Oct.	July	Oct.
Bush	39%	46%	47%	50%	36%	45%	42%	49%
Dole	20	24	13	20	19	21	17	24
Du Pont	3	1	3	1	1	1	1	1
Haig	3	4	15	4	4	3	4	3
Kemp	9	4	9	5	8	4	8	4
Robertson	7	10	1	3	15	17	1	1

Table 7.7

SHIFTS IN DEMOCRATIC PRIMARY PREFERENCES, BY RELIGION

	Protestant		Catholic		Evangelical		Non-Evangelical	
	July	Oct.	July	Oct.	July	Oct.	July	Oct.
Babbitt	2%	1%	2%	2%	–	1%	3%	2%
Dukakis	8	12	15	16	5	9	15	17
Gore	11	10	7	3	11	10	8	6
Gephardt	3	7	3	6	4	6	3	5
Jackson	20	25	13	19	28	28	13	19
Simon	9	6	7	11	7	8	8	8

On abortion, 31 percent of white Evangelical Protestants said they would be less likely to vote for a presidential candidate who wanted to make it more difficult to get an abortion, but 47 percent said they would be more likely to vote for such a candidate.

The situation was radically different for white non-Evangelical Protestants, however: only 21 percent said they would be more likely to vote for a candidate who backed abortion restrictions, while 56 percent said they would be less likely to vote for such a candidate. Black Protestants said they would be less likely to vote for such a candidate by a 48 to 29 percent margin. Among those with no religious preference, only 13 percent said they would be more likely to vote for such a candidate, while 65 percent said they would be less likely.

The results for Catholics, whose church condemns abortion, were a particular surprise. While 33 percent said they would be less likely to vote for an antiabortion candidate, 37 percent said they would be more likely to vote for such a candidate. While these findings are within the margin of error, even a standoff among Catholics on this issue challenges the conventional wisdom that Catholics are heavily influenced by the abortion issue when they vote.

There were differences along religious lines on three other issues:

· White Evangelical Protestants and black Protestants said by small margins that they would be more likely to vote for a candidate who supported limiting public access for AIDS victims, but the other groups were more likely to oppose such a candidate by wide margins.
· White Protestants, both Evangelical and non-Evangelical, and those with no religious preference were evenly divided on voting for a candidate who

supported reducing Social Security payments for those earning more than
$25,000 a year. But black Protestants and Catholics were sharply opposed.
· On another Social Security question, Catholics and white Evangelical Protestants were evenly divided over eventually replacing the system with a
private insurance program; black Protestants and white non-Evangelical
Protestants were less likely to vote for a candidate who supported change
to a private system, and those with no religious preference were more likely
to vote for such a candidate.

On other issues, all five religious groups were more likely to vote for candidates who:

· Oppose military aid to the Contras in Nicaragua.
· Support development of a space-based missile defense system.
· Support a constitutional amendment on school prayer.
· Support mandatory drug testing for people applying for a driver's license.
· Support increased taxes on foreign imports to protect American jobs in
certain industries.
· Support ratification of the U.S.-Soviet treaty to eliminate intermediate range
nuclear weapons.
· Oppose an increase in income taxes to reduce the federal deficit.
· Support automatic cost-of-living increases in Social Security and federal
pensions.
· Support a government public works program for the unemployed.
· Support a voucher plan giving parents more choice in which public or private
school their children attend.

As the primaries progressed and candidates with the least support dropped
out, basic religious patterns of support hardened. On the Republican side,
Bush knocked out Dole early and won the nomination virtually uncontested.
On the Democratic side, the race came down to three, and then two
candidates—Dukakis, Jackson and Gore. Jackson had the black vote virtually
to himself; white Evangelicals backed Gore and Catholics preferred Dukakis.

By May, it was clear that the fall election would be between Bush and
Dukakis. At that point, white Evangelicals were the only major group who
believed that Bush would do a better job than Dukakis of handling eight major
issues facing the nation[13]. Overall, white Evangelicals gave Bush the edge on
six of the eight issues. Other groups—white non-Evangelicals, all Evangelicals,
all non-Evangelicals, Catholics and Protestants—gave Democrat Dukakis the
edge on five issues.

Bush's strong support among white Evangelicals was partly due to his
identification with President Reagan. At the time of the survey, white Evangelicals approved of Reagan's handling of the presidency by a 2-to-1 margin,
compared to a 5-to-4 margin among the total population.

The difference in views between white Evangelicals and white non-Evangelicals was greater than the difference in views between all Evangelicals and all non-Evangelicals. This reflects the fact that there is little difference in opinion between Evangelical and non-Evangelical blacks, both of whom are overwhelmingly Democratic.

When responses on all eight issues are averaged, 40 percent of white Evangelicals believed Bush could handle the issues better, while 34 percent believed Dukakis could do a better job. The response was reversed among white non-Evangelicals: 40 percent believed Dukakis could do a better job, while 35 percent believed Bush could.

The gap between all Evangelicals and non-Evangelicals was smaller: A plurality of Evangelicals (by 39 to 36 percent) and non-Evangelicals (42 to 34 percent) gave the edge to Dukakis. Catholics (by 41 to 35 percent) and Protestants (by 39 to 36 percent) also believed Dukakis could best handle the important issues.

Nationally, Bush led on three issues—keeping the country prosperous, dealing with the Soviet Union and making people proud to be Americans. Dukakis led on five issues—keeping the country out of another war, reducing the federal budget deficit, eliminating corruption in government, helping the poor and needy and protecting the civil rights of minorities.

Following are findings on specific issues:

- *Keeping the country prosperous.* Bush led among all religious groups on this issue, although in some groups there was a virtual tie. Nationally, 41 percent of Americans said Bush could do a better job, while 37 percent said Dukakis could.
  Forty percent of Protestants and 42 percent of Catholics gave the edge to Bush; 38 and 36 percent, respectively, gave the edge to Dukakis. Bush led among Evangelicals by 41 to 35 percent, but had only an insignificant 1-point lead—40 to 39 percent—among non-Evangelicals. He had a 16-point lead (46 to 30 percent) among white non-Evangelicals, and only a 6-point lead (41 to 35 percent) among white non-Evangelicals.
- *Keeping the country out of another war.* While Protestants were evenly divided, with 39 percent picking each candidate, Catholics chose Dukakis by a 45 to 32 percent margin. Evangelicals (by 40 to 37 percent) and non-Evangelicals (by 43 to 36 percent) chose Dukakis. The split between Evangelical and non-Evangelical whites appeared on this issue, with Evangelicals picking Bush by 40 to 34 percent, and non-Evangelicals picking Dukakis by 40 to 37 percent.
- *Dealing with the Soviet Union.* Bush led by a 5-to-3 margin among all groups.
- *Reducing the deficit.* White Evangelicals picked Bush as best on this issue by a slight plurality, 37 to 34 percent, while other groups chose Dukakis by slightly larger margins. For example, non-Evangelicals picked Dukakis by 41 to 33 percent.
- *Eliminating corruption in government.* Here again, white Evangelicals bucked

the trend and chose Bush (by 38 to 32 percent) while other groups picked Dukakis, who led, for example, by 40 to 29 percent among white non-Evangelicals.

- *Helping the poor and needy.* All groups picked Dukakis on this issue, although his margin among white Evangelicals (46 to 33 percent) was lower than among other groups.
- *Making people proud to be Americans.* Bush led by only 37 to 34 percent nationally, and was virtually tied among all groups, except white Evangelicals, who gave him a 42 to 31 percent lead.
- *Protecting the civil rights of minorities.* Dukakis led by a wide margin among all groups, except white Evangelicals, where he led by 41 to 33 percent.

After the primaries, attention centered on the parties' conventions. The past pattern has been that candidates get a temporary "bump" in the polls immediately after their conventions; the second convention provides a smaller boost than the first, and polls generally settle back to preconvention levels in about a month. The 1988 election did not follow this pattern.

Michael Dukakis did get a significant "bump" in a postconvention Gallup Poll; it was largely due to an increase in support among white Protestants, normally a strong Republican group. At the same time, Dukakis held on to a strong lead among white Catholics.

In a survey conducted July 1–7, on the eve of the Democratic convention, Dukakis led by 47 to 41 percent nationally. He trailed by 54 to 34 percent among white Protestants, but led 57 to 37 percent among white Catholics (excluding Hispanics as well as blacks). In a similar poll conducted the weekend after the convention, Dukakis led nationally by 54 to 37 percent. He held steady among white Catholics, with a 57 to 36 percent lead. But he moved to a statistical tie with Bush among white Protestants, trailing by only 1 point, 46 to 45 percent[14].

Dukakis held a wide lead among Catholics even when his overall lead was much smaller on the eve of the Democratic convention. For example, in a June survey, Dukakis led by 45 to 41 percent nationally; he led by 50 to 39 percent among white Catholics and trailed by a similar margin—50 to 38 percent—among white Protestants.

In a May poll, Dukakis led nationally by 53 to 40 percent. In that survey, he led by 58 to 38 percent among white Catholics and trailed by 49 to 44 percent among white Protestants.

By the eve of the Republican convention, Dukakis' lead had fallen back to the pre-Democratic convention level; he led Bush nationally by 49 to 42 percent. As expected, Bush got a "bump" from his convention, taking a 48 to 44 percent lead. What was surprising was that his bump was not temporary—it held steady and actually grew as the campaign progressed.

In early July, Dukakis led by 6 points nationally. In a survey conducted October 6–8, just before the second presidential debate of the campaign, Bush held a 6-point lead. The difference was almost entirely attributable to a dramatic shift toward the Republican Bush among normally Democratic white Catholics. But, despite this dramatic shift, the Catholic vote was still soft; in the same survey, they gave Dukakis better ratings than Bush on a variety of issues.

At this point in early October, Dukakis was running far better among white Evangelicals than Walter Mondale did in 1984. While Dukakis trailed Bush by 56 to 36 percent among this group, only 20 percent of white Evangelicals had voted for Mondale.

In early July, Dukakis led Bush by 47 to 41 percent. At that time, Bush led among all white Protestants by 54 to 34 percent. But Dukakis led among white Catholics by 57 to 37 percent. In the October poll, Bush led by 49 to 43 percent. His support among white Protestants was virtually the same as it was in July—he led Dukakis by 58 to 35 percent in this group. But in early October, Bush led Dukakis by 46 to 43 percent among white Catholics.

Despite the shift toward Bush, Catholics remained favorably disposed toward Dukakis. In an early September survey that asked respondents to rate the candidates on fourteen issues, white Catholics gave Dukakis a better rating than did white Protestants on all fourteen. While white Protestants gave the edge to Dukakis on only one issue—avoiding another Iran-Contra affair—Catholics gave Dukakis the advantage on six of the fourteen issues.

In particular, Catholics gave Dukakis a 53 to 33 percent margin on the question of which candidate "cares about people like me." White Protestants gave Bush a 47 to 34 percent edge on this question.

At this point in the campaign, there was no significant difference between Bush's support among white Evangelical Protestants and white non-Evangelical Protestants. In contrast, Reagan ran considerably better among white Evangelical than white non-Evangelical Protestants in 1984. The early July survey cited above was the only one in which there was more than 2 points' difference in Bush's support among white Evangelical Protestants and white non-Evangelical Protestants.

Throughout the rest of the campaign, three significant things happened in terms of religious patterns. First, Bush maintained an even split among white Catholics. Second, he increased his lead among all white Protestants. Third, he finally opened up a differential between white Evangelical and white non-Evangelical Protestants, with the former giving him a wider margin.

The final pre-election Gallup Poll showed 56 percent of Americans favoring Bush and 44 percent favoring Dukakis[15]. This was within the margin of error of the actual results, 54 to 46 percent for Bush. This survey showed that George Bush built his winning presidential coalition on the support of two out of every three white Protestants who voted. Michael Dukakis did, however, improve over Walter Mondale's 1984 standing with key groups distinguished by both high and low degrees of religious activity.

The pre-election survey showed White Protestants preferring Bush by 64 to 32 percent. White Catholics were evenly divided in the Election Eve poll, with 48 percent supporting Bush and 47 percent supporting Dukakis.

White Evangelicals supported Bush by better than a 2-to-1 margin, 68 percent to 27 percent. Non-Evangelicals favored Bush by 53 percent to 42 percent.

Blacks, who are predominantly Protestant, preferred Dukakis by 82 to 11 percent. A majority of Hispanics, who are predominantly Catholic, supported Dukakis. Figures from pre-election polls suggest that 70 percent of Jews voted for Dukakis.

Table 7.8 shows the pattern of shifts among major religious groups in candidate preference from early July through Election Eve.

We can gain further insight into the religious dimensions of the election results from a postelection survey for the Times Mirror Corporation's study, examining the way the new "typologies" voted. Following are findings for key groups:

· Moralists (12 percent of the 1988 electorate): 98 percent voted for President Reagan in 1984, and 96 percent voted for Bush in 1988.
· 1960s Democrats (11 percent of the electorate): 25 percent voted for Reagan in 1984, and 12 percent voted for Bush in 1988.
· New Deal Democrats (10 percent of the 1988 electorate): 30 percent voted for Reagan and 27 percent voted for Bush. But turnout among this traditionally Democratic group was low—they make up a potential 15 percent of the electorate—and Dukakis had an even bigger lead among New Deal Democrats earlier in the campaign.
· The Partisan Poor (9 percent of the electorate): Reagan and Bush each won 19 percent of their votes.
· God and Country Democrats (7 percent of the electorate): 31 percent voted for Reagan, but 38 percent voted for Bush, a significant gain.
· Followers (6 percent of the electorate): 54 percent voted for Reagan, but 46 percent voted for Bush.
· Seculars (8 percent of the electorate): 34 percent voted for Reagan, but only 24 percent voted for Bush.

The other groups are:

· Enterprisers (12 percent of the electorate): 96 percent voted for Reagan, 98 percent voted for Bush.
· Upbeats (12 percent of the electorate): 86 percent voted for Reagan, 83 percent voted for Bush.
· Disaffecteds (11 percent of the electorate): 81 percent voted for Reagan, 68 percent voted for Bush.

The 1988 election reflected, to a considerable degree, the candidates' ideological images and the way they matched up with the voters' ideological self-perception. Members of most religious groups view themselves as more liberal than George Bush and more conservative than Michael Dukakis; the presidential candidates did best with those groups to whom they were the closest ideologically, and most were closer to white Protestants. White Evangelicals —those who describe themselves as Born-Again Christians—are the most po-

Table 7.8

TRIAL HEATS, BY RELIGION

	U.S.	White Protestant	White Catholic	White Evangelical	Non-Evangelical
Early July					
Bush	41%	54%	37%	59%	41%
Dukakis	47	34	57	31	48
Late July					
Bush	37	46	36	46	37
Dukakis	54	45	58	44	55
Early Aug.					
Bush	42	52	42	53	44
Dukakis	49	40	51	39	47
Late Aug.					
Bush	48	57	46	57	49
Dukakis	44	36	44	34	44
Early Sept.					
Bush	49	58	47	59	50
Dukakis	41	32	45	31	40
Late Sept.					
Bush	47	59	44	59	47
Dukakis	42	33	42	34	42
Early Oct.					
Bush	49	58	46	56	52
Dukakis	43	35	43	36	40
Late Oct.					
Bush	50	61	45	60	52
Dukakis	40	29	45	30	38
November					
Bush	56	64	48	68	53
Dukakis	44	32	47	27	42

litically conservative major religious group in the United States, while Jews and black Protestants are the most liberal.

The survey asked respondents to rate themselves and each of the candidates on a 6-point scale, with 1 representing "very conservative" and 6 representing "very liberal." Separate questions asked them to indicate whether they considered themselves "much more conservative" than the candidates, "somewhat more conservative," "the same," "somewhat more liberal" or "much more liberal."

We dropped the 3 and 4 responses as moderate and grouped the 1 and 2 responses as "conservative" and the 5 and 6 responses as "liberal." Using this system, 28 percent of white Protestants were conservative and 19 percent were liberal; 32 percent of white Evangelicals were conservative and 19 percent were liberal. About 90 percent of white Evangelicals are Protestant.

The pattern for Jews and blacks was almost the reverse: 13 percent of Jews were conservative, and 35 percent were liberal. Among blacks—80 percent of whom are Protestant—19 percent were conservative and 43 percent were liberal.

White Catholics were more evenly divided, with 19 percent conservative and 22 percent liberal. Among Hispanics—70 percent of whom are Catholic—26 percent were conservative, while 32 percent were liberal.

Among all non-Evangelicals, 20 percent were conservative and 23 percent were liberal.

All groups saw Bush as conservative and Dukakis as liberal. Table 7.9 shows the perceptions of the candidates among each group.

No religious group felt completely comfortable with either candidate; no more than one-third of any group said they felt "the same" ideologically as either candidate. For the most part, however, the groups supported the candidate to whom they felt closest ideologically. For example, about two in three white Protestants supported Bush. While 40 percent of white Protestants described themselves as more liberal than Bush, 56 percent described themselves as more conservative than Dukakis, including 44 percent who described themselves as "much more conservative." Table 7.10 shows how each group compared themselves to Bush.

Table 7.11 shows how each group compared themselves to Dukakis.

The election's ideological component is emphasized by the fact that the issues most likely cited by Bush voters were Dukakis' liberalism and Bush's conservatism, Dukakis' veto of a Massachusetts bill to require teachers to lead the Pledge of Allegiance and the Massachusetts prison furlough program. Bush had made all these issues a campaign priority in order to portray Dukakis as outside the political mainstream. Dukakis voters said the main issues were allegations about Bush's role in the Iran-Contra affair, the Reagan administration's dealing with Gen. Noriega of Panama and Bush's selection of Sen. Dan Quayle as his running mate.

In effect, Dukakis was hurt by his inability to define "liberal" and by the reaction of different audiences to the label. Traditional Democrats—Catholics, Jews, blacks—view "liberal" in economic terms and relate it to New Deal and Great Society social programs they favor. White Protestants, particularly Evangelicals, view "liberal" in social terms and relate it to softness on crime and family values.

Dukakis was also hurt by his inexperience in foreign affairs and the per-

Table 7.9

VIEWS OF BUSH AND DUKAKIS, BY RELIGION

	Conservative	Liberal
White Protestant		
Bush	49%	11%
Dukakis	10	55
White Catholic		
Bush	45	16
Dukakis	10	50
Jewish		
Bush	63	5
Dukakis	5	52
Black		
Bush	40	20
Dukakis	12	52
Hispanic		
Bush	42	19
Dukakis	13	52
White Evangelical		
Bush	44	14
Dukakis	13	54
Non-Evangelical		
Bush	49	13
Dukakis	9	52

ception that defense issues were not a priority for him; twice as many Bush voters (72 percent) as Dukakis voters (37 percent) said "strengthening our country's defenses" was "very important" in determining their choice.

In many ways, however, Bush's victory may have been sealed at the Republican convention, when he became fixed in the public eye as both Ronald Reagan's heir and his own man. By August of 1988, the Iran-Contra affair no longer hurt Reagan, and he was helped by the success of the Intermediate Range Nuclear Forces (INF) treaty with the Soviet Union. A year earlier, there was a clear link between those who approved of Reagan's performance in office and those who said they intended to vote Republican in 1988. That link held up in November 1988—but by then Reagan had regained his former popularity: on the eve of the election, 66 percent of white Protestants, 60 percent of white Catholics, 69 percent of white Evangelicals and 59 percent of non-Evangelicals approved of his performance in office.

Table 7.10
COMPARISON OF SELF TO BUSH

	Much More Lib.	Somewhat More Lib.	Same	Somewhat More Con.	Much More Con.
White Protestants	23%	17%	30%	11%	7%
White Catholics	23	21	29	10	8
Jewish	43	27	17	9	–
Black	38	8	15	6	10
Hispanic	26	19	25	9	8
White Evangelicals	17	14	32	13	9
Non-Evangelicals	27	21	27	8	7

Table 7.11
COMPARISON OF SELF TO DUKAKIS

	Much More Lib.	Somewhat More Lib.	Same	Somewhat More Con.	Much More Con.
White Protestant	8%	7%	17%	12%	44%
White Catholic	9	9	22	14	37
Jewish	8	10	32	20	24
Black	7	8	34	10	17
Hispanic	14	8	23	9	34
White Evangelical	10	6	16	10	45
Non-Evangelical	9	9	21	15	37

CONCLUSIONS

When it comes to mixing religion and politics, Americans exhibit two contradictory sets of behavior. On one hand, they do not want churches and religious leaders involved in politics, either as candidates or lobbyists. On the other hand, religious worldviews clearly influence political affiliation, and religious affiliation remains one of the most accurate, and least appreciated, political indicators available.

In the last chapter, we saw that different religious groups had different profiles of belief on major political and social issues. Most, but not all, of those differences translate into political patterns. These patterns are clearest at the extremes. Jews and blacks are the most "liberal" groups, and they are the most reliable base of the Democratic Party, with Hispanics ranking slightly behind. White Evangelical Protestants, whose conservatism is primarily reserved for social and cultural issues, are now the most reliable base of the Republican Party.

White non-Evangelical Protestants are less enthusiastic about the Republican Party than their Evangelical counterparts; they are more liberal on social and foreign policy issues, somewhat less liberal on economic issues. They are a bit more likely to look to the Democrats as an alternative when things are not going well, but they are reliably Republican.

White Catholics are the least appreciated element of the Democratic Party base; they will bolt the party, but they do so reluctantly. No Democrat can be elected president without something approaching 60 percent of the Catholic vote. When all Catholics are considered, Dukakis won a majority in 1988, but it was not big enough.

The basic fact of political life at the presidential level, however, is that the Democrats cannot elect a president if they begin every election by conceding two of every three white Protestant votes to the Republicans. The 1988 election suggests that Democratic candidates are not hurt by, and are actually helped by, relatively liberal economic programs. The prescription for a Democratic presidential candidate to capture enough white Protestant votes (as well as other votes) to craft a majority would seem to include the following:

1. Essentially traditional Democratic policies on social programs.
2. Credibility on defense issues. This does not mean being a hawk; surveys show, for example, that even white Evangelicals oppose aid to the Contras. But a Democratic presidential candidate must show mastery of defense and foreign policy issues.
3. A moderate image on social issues, particularly crime. It is worth noting that Dukakis' running mate, Sen. Lloyd Bentsen of Texas, was considerably more popular than Dukakis and, in some polls, more popular than Bush, despite the fact that, for example, he, like Dukakis, is pro-choice on the abortion issue.

Consider these findings from a survey conducted two weeks before the election. Nationally, Bush had a 59 percent favorable rating and a 36 percent negative rating. This was better than Dukakis' 50 to 43 percent favorable rating. But Bentsen, like Bush, had a 59 percent favorable rating and only a 27 percent negative rating[16].

The major difference between Dukakis and Bentsen was that Bentsen was far more popular among white Protestants. Among all white Protestants, 41 percent had a favorable impression of Dukakis, while 53 percent had a negative impression. But the same group gave Bentsen a 56 to 31 percent favorable rating, close to the 67 to 28 percent favorable rating they gave Bush. A similar pattern held among white Evangelicals. Bentsen was even more popular than Dukakis among white Catholics; they gave Dukakis a 56 to 38 percent favorable rating, and Bentsen a 61 to 25 percent favorable rating.

These figures do not prove that the Democrats would have won in 1988 if Lloyd Bentsen had been at the top of the ticket; they do prove, however, that it is not impossible for a Democrat to be popular with white Protestants.

CHAPTER

8

America's Faith in the 1990s

T HE PRECEDING CHAPTERS have described the dimensions and implications of the "People's Religion" in the United States. Now, we will recap some major themes and make some predictions about the shape of the American faith in the 1990s and beyond. First, we will examine the nature of the American faith itself and its relationship to institutional religion; second, we will examine the factors that influence faith and religious practice; finally, we will speculate about the future religious makeup of the United States.

THE AMERICAN FAITH AND THE CHURCHES

One of the most remarkable aspects of America's faith is its durability. Despite all of the dramatic social changes of the past half century—depression, war, the civil rights movement, social unrest, technological change—the religious beliefs and practices of Americans today look very much like the beliefs and practices of the 1930s and 1940s. Church membership and attendance figures today are identical to what they were in the thirties; belief in God has held steady; the same percentage of Americans today as in the late forties believe in an afterlife. In some ways, Americans are even more "religious" today than they have been in the past. In the 1930s, 10 percent of Americans read the Bible daily; in the 1980s, it was 15 percent. In the decade between 1978 and 1988, belief in the divinity of Christ and personal commitment to Christ increased. America has been "secularized" in many ways, but it would be hard to prove it by looking at America's religious beliefs. America's faith has held steady, and there is no reason to expect that to change in the near future.

Despite this consistent orthodoxy, however, Americans remain highly independent in their religious lives; they are certainly independent of their religious institutions. While their attitudes about the institutional aspects of religion—confidence in organized religion and the clergy's ethical standards, criticism of church behavior and attitudes about the influence of religion—rise and fall with transitory events, their core beliefs remain stable. Americans, as we noted earlier, increasingly view their faith as a matter between them and God, to be aided, but not necessarily influenced, by religious institutions.

This attitude is rooted in very specific beliefs:

- The vast majority of Americans believe it is possible to be a good Christian or Jew without going to church or synagogue.
- A similar majority believe that people should arrive at their religious beliefs independently of any church or synagogue.
- A majority agree that it doesn't make any difference which church a person attends, because one is as good as another.
- Americans are evenly divided on the statement, "I don't have to belong to an organized religion because I lead a good life."
- An overwhelming majority of Americans believe that their faith is strengthened by being constantly challenged.
- Americans say they rely on themselves, not an outside power such as God, to solve their problems.
- Only a large minority of Americans agree that there are clear standards for judging good and evil that never change.

There is one other significant dimension to Americans' religious independence. Over the past decade or more, a consistent one-third of the American people have reported having had a "religious experience," or "a moment of religious insight or awakening that changed the direction of their lives." This finding, that one in three Americans has had such a breakthrough experience, is one of the most significant survey results ever uncovered. Perhaps part of the reason that experiences of this sort have not received the attention they deserve is the belief that one can reach God only through intense mental effort, through a gigantic intellectual struggle. But if that were the case, for example, Christianity would have died out in the first or second century.

All of these factors indicate that Americans have a clear sense of what they want from their churches and synagogues, because they see religious institutions as serving the people, not the people serving the institutions. One thing that millions of Americans clearly want from their churches is more influence for the laity, the people in the pews.

In a special survey conducted for this book, we asked respondents, "Who do you think should have greater influence in determining the future of religion in America: the clergy, or the people who attend services?" By a 6-to-1 margin,

Americans said the laity, the people who attend religious services, should have greater influence. Six in ten (61 percent) held this view, while one in ten (12 percent) said the clergy should have greater influence. Another two in ten (22 percent) volunteered the response that each should play an equal role in determining the future of religion.

These findings show overwhelming support for a greater lay role in church leadership in the coming decade. Support was strong across the board, but it was particularly strong among several key groups. For example, among young adults, those 18–29, 70 percent supported greater influence for the laity, while only 9 percent supported greater influence for the clergy. At the same time, 65 percent of college graduates supported greater influence for the laity, while only 10 percent supported a greater role for the clergy. Clearly, for young and well-educated Americans, increased lay influence is a key to greater involvement. Table 8.1 shows responses for demographic groups.

WHAT AMERICANS WANT FROM THEIR CHURCHES

Americans want a wide variety of services, both spiritual and practical, from their churches and synagogues. And whether Americans feel they are getting those services is, all in all, a more important factor in determining whether or not they will attend church than are larger philosophic questions. In fact, only a minority of those who are unchurched—who rarely, if ever, attend services—stay away because of differences in doctrine and philosophy.

One thing that Americans want from their churches is a sense of community. Our surveys show that as many as four in ten Americans admit to frequent or occasional feelings of intense loneliness. Americans are, in fact, the loneliest people in the world. The church is a major institution that provides a sense of fellowship and belonging.

One dimension of this need for community is the desire for a church life that supports and provides help for families. Most churches are family oriented, but there is a negative side to this—one reason many singles, especially young people, stay away from church is that' they feel they are not wanted because they are not part of a family.

A key element in whether people feel welcome in a church community is the behavior of the pastor. Almost one in five among the unchurched cites a bad experience with a pastor as a major reason for no longer attending church.

The spiritual dimension Americans want includes helping them to find meaning in their lives and, for Christians, to deepen their relationships to Jesus Christ. It also includes a strong desire for information about the Bible and its meaning. While Americans want spirituality from their churches, they also want practical help. They also want their churches to help them learn how to put their faith into practice; to shed light on the important moral issues of the day; to help them learn how to serve others better and to be better parents. Americans understand that for their faith to be meaningful, it must be real and have a real impact on their day-to-day lives.

Table 8.1

WHO SHOULD HAVE A GREATER INFLUENCE ON THE FUTURE OF RELIGION?

	Clergy	Laity	Both Equally
U.S.	12%	61%	22%
Men	14	61	20
Women	11	62	23
18–29	9	70	16
30–49	10	58	26
50+	17	59	21
Baby Boomer (22–42)	9	63	22
College Grad.	10	65	21
Some College	14	63	20
High School Grad.	12	59	25
Less Than High School	14	60	20
White	12	61	22
Black	13	60	22
Hispanic	12	48	34
East	13	54	25
Midwest	13	67	16
South	14	60	23
West	8	64	22
Catholic	15	54	28
Protestant	11	65	20
Baptist	11	64	21
Methodist	13	59	26
Mainline Protestant	13	64	21

The desire of one American in three for church help in learning how to be parents highlights the degree to which church is a family affair. Large numbers of young adults who have stayed away from the church for a number of years return to the church when their children are old enough to begin religious instruction.

The desire for practical help extends to the desire for the church to respond to social justice needs. It has become accepted in many quarters that Americans don't want their churches involved in such issues, but that is not the case. A plurality of Americans today believe organized religion is not concerned enough about social issues. Americans don't want their churches to become so involved in social justice issues that they lose sight of spirituality—but they don't want them to lose sight of the need to address justice issues either.

There is one thing that Americans clearly don't want from their churches and synagogues—an overemphasis on money. More than one American in five complains that "there is too much emphasis on money at my church or synagogue."

We asked a representative sampling of Americans, "What do you think churches and synagogues in the United States could do to build greater interest in religion in the coming years?" While some of the suggestions offered did not come as a surprise, others did. For example, the first suggestion, mentioned by 21 percent of those surveyed, was "more communication with the people." This was a finding that has not been so prominent in the past. It reflects both a greater sensitivity across the society to the importance of "communication" among individuals and between individuals and institutions; it also reflects concern for greater lay involvement in church leadership and decision-making. (Those surveyed were allowed to make more than one response[1].)

The second most frequently cited suggestion—by 19 percent of respondents—was for the churches and synagogues to "concentrate more on religion." This clearly reflects a desire for a deeper sense of spirituality and closeness to God.

The third most frequently cited suggestion was that the churches "get involved with community concerns." This response, by virtually the same percentage as those seeking greater concentration on religion, shows that Americans want both an external and internal dimension to their religion, one that seeks involvement with the greater community as well as personal piety.

Next, 14 percent of Americans cited getting young people involved in church life as a high priority for the churches. This certainly reflects a widespread concern that young people are not sufficiently active in religious life.

Other suggestions included more social activities for church members (8 percent); more personal relationships between the clergy and families, including pastoral visits (6 percent); that the churches be less money-minded (4 percent); that they advertise more (2 percent); that they be more united and work together more (2 percent); and that they stay out of politics (2 percent). Another 10 percent had miscellaneous suggestions, and 4 percent said the churches were doing just fine and didn't have to do anything new.

One surprise on this list is the small percentage citing concerns about the churches and money. In past surveys, larger percentages of people complained about the churches' emphasis on money. One explanation for this shift may be in the questions' wording—money is more likely to be mentioned when a question seeks complaints rather than suggestions for improvement.

While there was not much difference in the percentage citing the top four recommendations for the churches, some characteristic patterns emerge when we look at responses by different groups. For example, Catholics are more likely to cite improved communications, increased community involvement and attracting young people, and are considerably less likely to cite concentrating more on religion. Protestants, on the other hand, are more likely to cite concentrating on religion and less likely to cite the three other main areas; this was particularly true for Baptists.

Here are some other patterns that emerge:

- Women are more likely to cite communication, community involvement and attracting young people.
- Those 18–29, the least involved in religious activity at present, had fewer suggestions.
- Those 30–49 were more likely to call for greater community involvement, while those over 50 were more likely to call for a greater concentration on religion.
- College graduates were more likely to cite communication and community activity, while those with less than a high school degree were more likely to cite greater concentration on religion.
- Blacks and Hispanics were more likely to cite both greater concentration on religion and increased community involvement.
- Those who live in the East were more likely to cite communication, community activity and attracting young people, while those in the South were more likely to cite greater concentration on religion. Those in the West were more likely than the average to cite all four main recommendations.

FACTORS AFFECTING FAITH AND RELIGIOUS PRACTICE

While America's faith has remained stable, it is not identical for every American or every subgroup of Americans. A variety of factors affect both faith and religious practice. We believe, frankly, that one of the most significant findings in this volume is the consistency of the impact of basic "life cycle" events on religious faith and practice. We have touched on elements of the life cycle effect throughout, but when taken together, they present an impressive pattern of factors over which religious leaders have virtually no control.

Religious education begins in childhood, and there are clear patterns that affect whether parents provide such training for their children. Several groups of parents are significantly less likely than others to provide religious training—single parents, divorced parents, widowed parents and parents in marriages in which the spouses have different religious affiliations. In the last case, disagreement over how to educate the children or relative lack of interest in religion, or lack of support for mixed marriages from churches, may be factors. In the case of the variety of single parents, however, there is a large gap between those who say they want to provide religious education for their children and those who actually do provide that training. This suggests that singleness itself is a negative factor—probably because the increased demands made on single parents make it more difficult for them to meet all of their children's needs, including that for religious education.

Despite the fact that most teenagers receive some form of religious education, teens are less likely than adults to say that religion is "very important" in their lives; young people, coming to terms with so much of life, are less interested in religion. This pattern becomes clearer when we see that those 18–24 are the most likely age group to say they have no religious affiliation and are generally the least religious group in the nation. As young people leave home and begin establishing their own lives, they frequently leave religion behind.

But that does not last forever. Young people start returning to church by age 25. This is particularly true for those who get married; the married are considerably more active religiously than singles. The exception is those in religiously mixed marriages; there is no significant difference in church membership and attendance or belief that religion is "very important" between singles and those in mixed marriages. Religious involvement escalates again with parenthood; couples under 40 who have children are considerably more likely than couples the same age with no children to attend church frequently.

In general, religious interest and activity increases with age, although it increases much more for women than for men. The way a marriage ends is important to a person's religious life. If it ends in divorce, religious interest and activity decrease; if it ends in widowhood, they increase. At any point in life, a traumatic event such as abortion is associated with decreased religious activity.

Two other factors may be said to be life cycle related. One is the general distinction between people who are "joiners" and people who are not. We have seen that the unchurched are not only not involved in religious activity, they are less involved than the churched in a variety of social and charitable activities. Similarly, young people, who are less involved in church, are also less likely to be registered to vote. Church involvement, then, is part of a broader pattern of social involvement that comes with maturity, particularly with marriage.

Finally, another factor that is part of the life cycle effect is—sex. Whenever we look at some division based on religious attitudes—between the churched and unchurched, between Evangelicals and non-Evangelicals—the clearest difference in attitudes concerns sex and moral and public policy issues related to sex—abortion, pornography, homosexuality. In every instance, the more "religious" group holds considerably more conservative attitudes toward sex. To most Americans, "religion" is associated with sexual restraint. But sexual restraint is not a message that young and single people want to hear; only 15 percent of singles and 18 percent of those under 30 believe that premarital sex is always wrong. The churches' teachings on sex may be the major factor keeping young people away. As young people marry and establish their own families, however, the value of sexual fidelity and restraint becomes more important to them personally, and the churches' teachings on sex are less of a barrier to church involvement.

Religious leaders who wish to reach out to people need to understand the "Religious Life Cycle"; they can be most effective by gearing programs and responses to people at key points in the cycle. One of the most productive steps—in terms of helping retain people's church involvement—would be providing help for single parents, particularly those who are divorced or widowed.

One of the major factors affecting religious belief and practice is education, although the relationship is not simple. When we consider that college graduates are less likely than others to believe in the literal interpretation of the Bible, less likely to say they've never doubted God's existence and less likely to believe in a personal God, we might be tempted to conclude that education is related to weakened faith. But that would not be the case. College graduates are also more likely to be church members, to attend church, to take part in Bible study groups, to provide religious education for their children; they are as likely as any other educational group to describe themselves as "religious persons." College graduates treat religion with more skepticism and intellectualism, but they are far from hostile to religion. Education changes the form and focus of religious practice, but it is not an enemy of faith. Any increase in educational levels is very likely to lead to an increase in church membership and attendance.

A key indicator of church involvement is the degree of satisfaction which people feel with their local congregation. We asked respondents, "How good a job is your church or synagogue doing in meeting your own personal and family needs?" One American in four (23 percent) said their church was doing an "excellent" job of meeting their needs; 42 percent said it was doing a "good" job; 17 percent said their church was doing "only fair" at meeting their needs; and 4 percent said their church was doing a "poor" job. The 86 percent of Americans who answered the question is higher than the percentage who say they are church members, so a considerable number of nonmembers responded. Because we can fairly safely assume that nonmembers are less satisfied than members, we can conclude that satisfaction with local church performance is higher among actual members. The 65 percent of Americans saying their church does an excellent or good job of meeting their needs is about the same percentage that expresses high levels of confidence in organized religion; this suggests that attitudes toward religion in general are highly influenced by attitudes toward one's own church.

There were marked differences among key groups in the level of enthusiasm about their church. The most lukewarm support came from Hispanics: while 30 percent said their church was doing an excellent job of meeting their needs, another 31 percent—the highest among any group—said their church was doing only a fair job.

Not surprisingly, women (27 percent) were more likely than men to give their church an excellent rating; those under 30 (19 percent) were less likely than those over 50 (26 percent) to give their church an excellent rating. Blacks (18 percent) were the least likely to give their church an excellent rating.

Among religious groups, 22 percent of Catholics and 27 percent of Protestants gave their church an excellent rating. There were differences among Protestant denominations, however; 23 percent of all Baptists and 30 percent of Southern Baptists gave their church an excellent rating. While 25 percent of Methodists and 27 percent of Lutherans gave their church an excellent rating, only 18 percent of Presbyterians and 9 percent of Episcopalians did so. While the samples for Presbyterians and Episcopalians are too small to be reliable, these figures echo other indications of low satisfaction levels among members of these denominations.

There is one interesting development—an apparent increase in the percentage of Catholics giving their church high ratings. In a differently worded question in a 1986 survey that asked Catholics to rate their church's handling of the needs of a number of groups, 14 percent said the church did an excellent job of meeting their own needs, 36 percent said it did a good job, 37 percent said it did a fair job and 9 percent said it did a poor job. In the latest survey, 22 percent said their church did an excellent job of meeting their needs, 48 percent said it did a good job, 19 percent said it did a fair job and 4 percent said it did a poor job.

Table 8.2 shows responses by demographic groups.

One major indicator of future levels of religious activity is expectation of future church attendance. We asked two questions in this area. First, we asked respondents whether they expected church attendance to increase or decrease over the next fifty years. When the Gallup Organization asked the same question in late 1949, Americans predicted an increase in church attendance—one that certainly materialized in the 1950s. This time, however, Americans were clearly divided—40 percent predicted an increase in church attendance and 40 percent predicted a decrease. This seems to suggest that the stability in church attendance we have seen for the past decade is likely to continue through the next. It may also indicate that Americans are less confident in predicting long-range future developments today than they were forty years ago.

But there was a considerably different response when we asked people, "Do you, yourself, expect to attend church or synagogue more often or less often during the next five years than you do now?" Almost half of Americans said they expected to attend church more often in the coming five years; only 9 percent said they expected to attend less often. Another 44 percent volunteered

Table 8.2

RATINGS OF CHURCH ON MEETING PERSONAL
AND FAMILY NEEDS

	Excellent	Good	Only Fair	Poor
U.S.	12%	43%	17%	4%
Men	20	43	16	4
Women	27	41	17	4
18–29	19	41	19	7
30–49	23	42	17	3
50+	26	43	15	4
Baby Boomer (22–42)	21	44	17	4
College Grad.	22	40	15	5
Some College	20	40	17	5
High School Grad.	27	40	16	4
Less Than High School	23	43	18	3
White	23	41	17	4
Black	18	49	18	5
Hispanic	30	29	31	3
East	22	45	14	3
Midwest	20	46	16	5
South	26	44	17	3
West	24	31	20	5
Catholic	22	48	19	4
Protestant	27	43	16	4
Baptist	23	48	15	4
Southern Baptist	30	46	15	2
Methodist	25	45	16	5
Mainline Protestant	22	43	19	3

the response that their church attendance would stay about the same. These figures certainly suggest that church attendance could increase dramatically in the coming decade.

To some degree, these figures no doubt reflect a "New Year's Resolution"-type attitude in which people say they expect to go to church more often because they feel that is the expected response. Some groups already high in religious activity, such as blacks and southerners, may merely be indicating a desire to go to church every week instead of two or three times a month.

The most significant finding, however, is the high percentage of those under 30—59 percent—who say they expect to go to church more often in the next five years. As we have already pointed out a number of times, this is the age group that is least likely to be involved in church life today. The fact that so high a percentage expects to go to church more often in the future strongly suggests that these young adults see their absence from church or their low levels of involvement as temporary, coming during a time of their lives when they are busy going to school, building a career and socializing. Other figures show that young adults begin returning to church in their late 20s; this finding helps confirm that pattern. Overall, 49 percent of Baby Boomers say they expect to attend church more often in the next five years.

Those most likely to say they expected to attend church more often in the next five years were blacks (69 percent), southerners (58 percent), Hispanics (54 percent), Baptists (53 percent) and Southern Baptists (52 percent). Those least likely to expect to attend church more often were those over 50 and college graduates (35 percent each), mainline Protestants (38 percent), those in the Midwest (40 percent), whites, women and westerners (41 percent each). Table 8.3 shows responses by groups.

THE FUTURE RELIGIOUS MAKEUP
OF THE UNITED STATES

Over the next decade, even the next generation, America will continue to become more religiously pluralistic and less Protestant in character. The trend has clearly pointed to a growth among Mormons, those who practice non-Western religions and those who claim no religious affiliation, along with increased representation among Catholics and less representation among Protestants.

We can examine this trend more closely by looking at specific denominations and religious groups. A religious group can grow in only two ways. First, it must retain in larger numbers than before those members born into the faith. Second, it must attract converts, through individual evangelization and, as is often the case, through conversion by those who marry church members. One way to estimate the future growth of any group is to look at how well it is doing in retaining young members and how active it is in evangelizing others. Table 8.4 compares denominations on two key measures. The first is the percentage of their members who are under 30; nationally; 27 percent of the

Table 8.3

EXPECTATIONS ABOUT FUTURE CHURCH ATTENDANCE

	Expect to Attend More Often	Expect to Attend Less Often
U.S.	44%	9%
Men	41	10
Women	47	8
18–29	59	8
30–49	44	6
50+	35	12
Baby Boomer (22–42)	49	5
College Grad.	35	6
Some College	43	7
High School Grad.	47	8
Less Than High School	49	14
White	41	10
Black	69	4
Hispanic	54	7
East	34	11
Midwest	40	9
South	58	8
West	41	8
Catholic	48	8
Protestant	47	7
Baptist	53	9
Southern Baptist	52	8
Methodist	49	5
Mainline Protestant	38	8

Table 8.4

UNDER 30 MEMBERSHIP AND EVANGELISM ACTIVITY, BY DENOMINATION

	Percentage of Members Under 30	Percentage Cited by Invitees
Baptist	28%	19%
Methodist	19	4
Lutheran	17	2
Presbyterian	17	2
Episcopalian	17	–
Disciples of Christ	26	2
United Church of Christ	14	1
Other Protestant	26	44
Mormon	31	6
Catholic	31	–
Jews	19	–
No Affiliation	38	–
Evangelical	26	N/A

adult population is under 30. The second figure is the percentage for each denomination cited by those who say they were invited to join a church within the past year. (Catholics are included in the "other" category; 6 percent of those invited to join a church said they were invited by members of "other" churches.)

Groups with the largest proportion of members under 30 and the strongest track record on evangelization have the best chance of increasing their share of the population; those with the smallest proportion of members under 30 and the weakest evangelization efforts stand to decrease their share of the population. These figures suggest certain trends for each denomination:

· Catholics: While Catholics score low on evangelization, they have a significant proportion of their members under 30. Much of this is due to the fact that 41 percent of Hispanics today are under 30, and Hispanics remain overwhelmingly Catholic. This, coupled with the expected increase in immigration by Hispanics, indicates that Catholics are likely to continue increasing their proportion of the population.

- Baptists: The percentage of Baptists under 30 is one point higher than the national average, and Baptists rank high in evangelization efforts. These factors indicate that they are likely to increase their proportion of the population.
- Mormons: The proportion of Mormons under 30 is above the national average, and Mormons rank high on evangelization; they, too, are likely to increase their share of the population.
- The Unaffiliated: The proportion of those with no religious affiliation who are under 30 is substantially higher than the national average, but the unaffiliated do not "evangelize." On one hand, it is likely that some in this group will reaffiliate with a church as they grow older. As the population ages, young people, who make up the bulk of the unaffiliated, will make up a smaller proportion of all Americans. Nevertheless, the religiously unaffiliated have steadily increased as a proportion of the population and are likely to continue to do so.
- Evangelicals: Evangelicals are just about at the national average in the share of their members who are under 30; while they were not described per se in the survey question about invitations, they are, by definition, evangelizers. They are likely to increase their representation in the general population.
- Other Protestants: This group also is just about at the national average in its under-30 membership and ranks quite high in evangelization; many in this group are, in fact, Evangelicals. They are likely to increase their share of the population. This follows from the fact that when we looked at the pattern of shifts in denominational affiliation among adults, we found that the two biggest gainers were "other Protestants" and the unaffiliated.
- Disciples of Christ: The Christian Church (Disciples of Christ) is the only mainline denomination whose under-30 membership is at the national average. While church members make up 2 percent of the population, 2 percent of those invited to join a church say they were invited by Disciples. This indicates that Disciples are doing a good deal of evangelization in terms of their size. They may well be the only mainline denomination to increase their proportion in the general population over the next decade or so.
- Mainline Churches (Methodists, Lutherans, Presbyterians, Episcopalians, United Church of Christ): These mainline Protestant denominations share the same patterns; the proportion of their members under 30 is well below the national average and they are virtually invisible when it comes to evangelization. They are very likely to continue to decline as a proportion of the population. The mainline churches' best hopes of a revival is the return of young former members who now claim no religious affiliation.
- Jews: Jews do not evangelize as such, and they rank below the national average in under-30 membership; they, too, are likely to decrease their proportion in the general population.

In terms of religion, the American population that will emerge in the 1990s will be more Catholic, more non-western, more Mormon, more unaffiliated and less Protestant than it is today. Not only will it be less Protestant, but it is likely that Evangelical Protestants will outnumber non-Evangelical Protestants. Evangelicals now make up approximately 45 percent of all Protestants; if, as seems likely, Evangelicals continue to grow and non-Evangelicals continue to decline, the point will soon come when a majority of Protestants will be Evangelicals. Observers such as church historian Martin Marty and sociologists Wade Clark Roof and William McKinney have argued, in *America's Mainline Religion*, that the mainline Protestant churches are moving to the sidelines, to the margins of American religious life. Our figures support that conclusion. In fact, it is likely that tensions between Evangelical and non-Evangelical members of the same denominations will increase over the coming decade as demographic changes aggravate theological disagreements.

One other note on the future of American Protestantism; not only is it likely to be proportionately more Evangelical, it is also likely to be proportionately more black. Blacks, who now make up 15 percent of all Protestants, are younger than the general population; 32 percent are under 30. This suggests that they will make up a larger proportion of Protestants in the future.

We have seen that religious affiliation is related to political affiliation. Will America's changing religious makeup shift its political balance? Yes and no. Republicans will gain some advantage if white Evangelicals and Mormons make up a larger proportion of the population and Jews make up a smaller proportion; Democrats will gain if Catholics, black Evangelicals and the unaffiliated make up a larger proportion of the population and mainline Protestants make up a smaller proportion. These changes may have a greater impact in certain regions or states, but, all in all, neither party may gain a real advantage.

That, then, is the shape of America's faith in the 1990s: Faith will hold steady, the institutional church will be not quite so firm, and the population will be more pluralistic than it is today. And Americans will continue to be unique, with an unmatched combination of high levels of education and high levels of religious belief and activity.

NOTES

CHAPTER 2

1. Figures are based on 14,147 interviews conducted during 1987, with a 2-point margin of error.

2. Figures are based on 14,147 interviews conducted during 1987, with a 2-point margin of error.

3. Figures are based on 14,147 interviews conducted during 1987, with a 2-point margin of error.

4. Figures are based on 2,556 interviews conducted between March 11 and March 20, 1988, with a 2-point margin of error.

5. Figures are based on 4,597 interviews conducted in 1988 and 14,147 interviews conducted during 1987, each with a 2-point margin of error.

6. Figures are based on 2,041 interviews conducted in 1988 with a 2-point margin of error. Figures for church attendance on Easter are based on 1,552 interviews conducted in April 1986, with a 3-point margin of error.

7. Figures are based on 4,424 interviews conducted in April and May 1987, with a 2-point margin of error. Figures for the 1985 survey of Catholics are based on 801 telephone interviews conducted in June 1985, with a 4-point margin of error.

8. Figures are based on 14,147 interviews conducted during 1987, with a 2-point margin of error.

9. Figures are based on 2,556 interviews conducted in March and April, 1988, with a 2-point margin of error.

10. Findings for 1988 are based on 1,003 interviews conducted in March, with a 4-point margin of error. Findings for 1986 are based on 978 interviews conducted in September, with a 4-point margin of error.

11. Figures are based on 1,607 in-person interviews conducted in July 1987, with a 3-point margin of error. Figures for 1983 and 1985 are based on approximately 1,000 interviews, with a 4-point margin of error.

12. Figures are based on 1,030 interviews conducted in October 1988, with a 4-point margin of error.

13. Figures are based on 1,030 interviews conducted in October 1988, with a 4-point margin of error.

CHAPTER 3

1. Each response is based on a sample of at least 1,000 interviews conducted during the years cited, with a 4-point margin of error.

2. Figures are based on at least 1,000 interviews of adults in the years indicated, with a 4-point margin of error.

267

3. Figures are based on 1,042 telephone interviews conducted between March 18 and March 31, 1985, with a 4-point margin of error.

4. Figures are based on surveys in 1984, 1985 and 1986 of at least 1,500 adults 18 and over, each with a 3-point margin of error.

5. Figures on importance of religion, church membership and church attendance within the past seven days are based on 6,633 interviews conducted throughout 1986. The remaining figures are based on 4,424 interviews conducted in April and May 1987, with a 2-point margin of error.

6. Figures are based on 2,556 interviews conducted in April 1988, with a 2-point margin of error.

7. Figures are based on 4,424 interviews conducted in April and May 1987, with a 2-point margin of error.

8. Figures are based on 4,424 interviews conducted in April and May 1987, with a 2-point margin of error.

9. Figures are based on surveys in the years mentioned of at least 1,500 interviews, each with a 3-point margin of error.

10. Figures on commitment to Christ are based on 2,556 interviews conducted in March and April 1988, with a 2-point margin of error. The 1978 figures are based on at least 1,500 interviews, with a 3-point margin of error. The remaining figures are based on 1,509 in-person interviews conducted with adults 18 and over in January 1983, with a 3-point margin of error.

11. Figures are based on 2,556 interviews conducted in April 1988, with a 2-point margin of error.

12. Figures are based on 2,556 interviews conducted in April 1988, with a 2-point margin of error.

13. Figures are based on 2,556 interviews conducted in April 1988, with a 2-point margin of error.

14. Findings are based on 511 telephone interviews conducted in May 1987, with a 5-point margin of error.

15. Figures are based on 1,013 telephone interviews conducted February 3–20, 1986, with a 4-point margin of error.

16. Figures are based on 3,021 interviews conducted in May 1988, with a 2-point margin of error.

17. Figures are based on mail-in questionnaires gathered from 513 adults in April 1988, with a 5-point margin of error.

18. Figures are based on 2,556 interviews conducted in April 1988, with a 2-point margin of error. The 1987 survey was based on 1,607 interviews, with a 3-point margin of error.

19. Figures are based on mail-in responses from 711 religious-college graduates, with a 4-point margin of error, and from 590 secular-college graduates, with a 5-point margin of error, gathered in 1987.

20. Findings are based on 1,007 interviews conducted in October and November 1986, each with a 4-point margin of error.

21. These findings are based on 6,221 in-person interviews conducted throughout 1986, with a 2-point margin of error.

22. Findings from the surveys conducted throughout 1986 are based on 6,633 interviews, with a 2-point margin of error. The November 1986 survey is based on 1,559 interviews with a 3-point margin of error. The February 1986 survey is based on 1,013 interviews and the 1985 survey is based on 1,034 interviews, each with a 4-point margin of error.

23. Figures are based on 2,556 interviews conducted between March 11 and March 20, 1988, with a 2-point margin of error.

CHAPTER 4

1. Figures are based on 9,338 interviews with the general population, including 2,895 interviews with Evangelicals, conducted throughout 1987, with a 2-point margin of error.

2. Figures for each question are based on at least 1,000 interviews conducted during 1987, with a 4-point margin of error.

3. Figures are based on 4,424 interviews conducted in April and May 1987, with a 2-point margin of error.

4. Figures for questions on the role of conscience and increasing church contributions are based on interviews with 267 Catholics conducted in August 1987, with a 9-point margin of error. The profiles are based on 14,147 interviews, including 3,903 with Catholics, conducted in 1987, with a 2-point margin of error. Ratings of the pope in years before 1986 are based on approximately 400 interviews each, with a 6-point margin of error. All other questions are based on 476 interviews conducted in July 1986, with a 5-point margin of error.

5. Figures are based on 2,829 interviews with Baptists conducted in 1987, with a 2-point margin of error.

6. Figures are based on interviews with 990 Methodists, conducted throughout 1987, with a 4-point margin of error. Findings on church membership, attendance and importance of religion are based on 603 interviews with Methodists conducted in 1986, with a 5-point margin of error. Other questions are based on interviews conducted in 1986 and 1987 with samples of approximately 1,500 adults, including approximately 135 Methodists, with margins of error of 3 and 10 points, respectively.

7. These findings are based on 618 interviews with Lutherans conducted throughout 1987, with a 5-point margin of error. Figures on views of the Bible (based on ninety-three interviews conducted in 1983) and frequency of Bible-reading (based on ninety interviews in November 1986) have a margin of error of 11 points in either direction.

8. Figures are based on 316 interviews with Episcopalians conducted throughout 1987, with a 6-point margin of error. The Prayer Book Society survey was based on 553 mail questionnaire returns from Episcopal laity and 596 returns from Episcopal clergy, with a 5-point margin of error.

9. Figures are based on 492 interviews with Presbyterians conducted in 1987, with a 5-point margin of error.

10. Figures are based on interviews conducted in 1987: 218 with members of the United Church of Christ, with a 7-point margin of error; 296 with members of the Disciples of Christ, with a 6-point margin of error; 876 with "other Protestants," with a 4-point margin of error, and 720 with "unspecified" Protestants, with a 4-point margin of error.

11. Figures are based on 218 interviews with Mormons conducted throughout 1987, with a 7-point margin of error.

12. Figures are based on 180 interviews with American Jews conducted throughout 1986; figures for previous years are based on a similar number of interviews, with a 7-point margin of error.

13. Figures are based on 513 interviews conducted in 1986, with a 5-point margin of error. Figures for 1987 are based on 307 interviews conducted in April and May, with a 7-point margin of error.

14. Figures are based on 2,556 interviews conducted in April and May 1988, with a 2-point margin of error.

15. Figures are based on at least 1,000 interviews in the periods indicated, with a 4-point margin of error, including about a hundred blacks in each survey, with an 11-point margin of error. The 1986 figures for church membership and attendance and importance of religion were based on 6,633 in-person and telephone interviews, with a 2-point margin of error, including 571 interviews with blacks, with a 5-point margin of error.

16. Figures are based on 2,556 interviews conducted between March 11 and March 20, 1988, with a 2-point margin of error, including 363 interviews with Hispanics, with a 7-point margin of error.

17. Figures are based on interviews with 83 charismatics and Pentecostals conducted in October 1988, with an 11-point margin of error. Figures on charismatic services are based on interviews conducted in April and May 1988, of 226 people who had attended charismatic services; with a 7-point margin of error.

18. Figures for teenagers are based on 503 interviews conducted in March 1987, with a 5-point margin of error. Figures for adults are based on 1,571 interviews conducted in April 1987, with a 3-point margin of error.

19. Figures for questions on church membership, attendance and importance of religion are based on 4,760 interviews conducted throughout 1987, with a 2-point margin of error. Figures on confidence in the church, changing interest in religion over the past five years and voting for an atheist are based on 1,607 interviews conducted in July 1987 with a three-point margin of error. Figures on voting for an Evangelical are based on 1,571 interviews conducted in April 1987, with a 3-point margin of error.

CHAPTER 5

1. Figures are based on 14,147 interviews conducted in 1987, with a 2-point margin of error.

2. Figures are based on samples of at least 978 interviews conducted in 1986 and 1987, each with a 4-point margin of error.

3. Figures are based on 2,556 interviews conducted in April and May 1988, with a 2-point margin of error. Figures for 1978 are based on at least 1,500 interviews, with a 3-point margin of error.

4. Figures are based on interviews with 954 viewers and 1,054 nonviewers conducted in May 1983, with a 4-point margin of error for each group.

5. Figures are based on 1,571 in-person interviews conducted in April 1987, with a 3-point margin of error.

6. Figures are based on 1,003 interviews conducted in March 1988, with a 4-point margin of error.

CHAPTER 6

1. Figures are based on surveys in the years mentioned of at least 1,500 interviews, with a 3-point margin of error. The *Newsweek* survey was based on 757 interviews conducted in January 1985, with a 4-point margin of error.

2. Figures are based on 1,210 interviews conducted in June 1988, with a 3-point margin of error.

3. Figures are based on 4,424 interviews conducted in April and May 1987, with a 2-point margin of error.

4. Figures are based on 1,001 interviews conducted in September 1988, with a 4-point margin of error.

5. Figures are based on 1,001 interviews conducted in September 1988, with a 4-point margin of error.

6. Figures are based on 1,500 interviews conducted in 1984, with a 3-point margin of error.

7. Figures are based on at least 1,500 interviews conducted in 1986, with a 3-point margin of error.

8. Figures are based on at least 1,500 interviews conducted in 1986 and 1988, with a 3-point margin of error.

9. Figures are based on 1,571 interviews conducted in 1987, with a 3-point margin of error.

10. Figures are based on 2,118 interviews conducted in May 1988, with a 2-point margin of error.

11. Figures are based on 2,118 interviews conducted in May 1988, with a 2-point margin of error.

12. Figures are based on 1,571 interviews conducted in April 1987, with a 3-point margin of error.

13. Figures for questions on presidential candidates are based on 1,607 interviews conducted in July 1987, with a 3-point margin of error. Figures on attitudes toward neighbors are based on 1,562 interviews conducted in January 1987, with a 3-point margin of error.

14. Figures are based on 4,424 interviews conducted in April and May 1987, with a 2-point margin of error.

15. Figures for attitudes on legalization of homosexuality and hiring homosexuals are based on 1,015 interviews conducted in March 1987, with a 4-point margin of error. Figures on attitudes toward AIDS victims are based on 1,607 interviews conducted in July 1987, with a 3-point margin of error.

16. Figures are based on 1,549 interviews conducted in December 1987, with a 3-point margin of error. The sample included 789 women and 760 men, with a margin of error of 4 points in each group.

17. Figures are based on 4,424 interviews conducted in April and May 1987, with a 2-point margin of error.

18. Figures on the "Baby M" case are based on 1,472 interviews conducted in April 1987, with a 3-point margin of error. The *Newsweek* poll is based on 766 interviews conducted in January 1987, with a 4-point margin of error.

19. Figures are based on samples of at least 1,000 interviews, conducted in 1986 and 1987, with a 4-point margin of error.

20. Figures on the NRA are based on 4,244 interviews conducted in April and May 1987, with a 2-point margin of error. Figures for questions on gun ownership, regulation, licensing and registration are based on 1,001 interviews conducted in September 1988, with a 4-point margin of error. Figures on the other questions are based on 1,552 interviews conducted in April 1986, with a 3-point margin of error.

21. Figures are based on 4,424 interviews conducted in April and May 1987, with a 2-point margin of error.

22. Figures on attitudes on the importance of unions and the extent of their power are based on 3,021 interviews conducted in May 1988, with a 2-point margin of error. Figures on identification as a union supporter are based on 4,244 interviews conducted in April and May 1987, with a 2-point margin of error. Figures on the minimum wage are based on 1,011 interviews conducted in May 1988, with a 4-point margin of error.

23. Figures on Judge Bork are based on 1,009 interviews conducted in August 1987, with a 4-point margin of error. Figures for attitudes toward the Supreme Court are based on 1,607 interviews conducted in July 1987, with a 3-point margin of error.

24. Figures are based on 1,559 interviews conducted in October 1986, with a 3-point margin of error.

25. Figures are based on 1,562 in-person interviews conducted January 16–19, 1987, with a 3-point margin of error.

26. Figures for "pro-Israel" attitudes are based on 4,244 interviews conducted during April and May 1987, with a 2-point margin of error. Figures on sympathies in the Middle East are based on 1,011 interviews conducted in May 1988, with a 4-point margin of error.

27. Figures on the response to the INF treaty are based on 2,109 interviews conducted in January 1988, with a 3-point margin of error. The remaining figures are based on 4,244 interviews conducted during April and May 1987.

28. Figures are based on 4,424 interviews conducted in April and May 1987, with a 2-point margin of error.

CHAPTER 7

1. Figures are based on 15,460 interviews conducted throughout 1988, with a 2-point margin of error.

2. Figures are based on 4,244 interviews conducted in April and May 1987, with a 2-point margin of error.

3. Figures are based on 4,244 interviews conducted in April and May 1987, with a 2-point margin of error.

4. Figures are based on 4,244 interviews conducted in April and May 1987, with a 2-point margin of error.

5. Figures are based on at least 864 interviews conducted in April and June 1988, with a 5-point margin of error.

6. Figures are based on 1,030 interviews conducted in October 1988, with a 4-point margin of error.

7. Figures are based on interviews with 1,539 adults in July 1986 and 1,562 adults in January 1987, with a 4-point margin of error.

8. Figures are based on 1,607 in-person interviews conducted in July 1987, with a 3-point margin of error.

9. Figures are based on 1,089 interviews conducted in August 1987, with a 4-point margin of error.

10. Figures are based on interviews conducted in July 1987, with 838 Democrats and Democratic leaners, with a 4-point margin of error, and with 515 Republicans and Republican leaners, with a 5-point margin of error.

11. Figures on Republicans, Democrats and leaners are based on 1,562 interviews conducted in January 1987, and 1,569 interviews conducted in October 1987, with a 4-point margin of error.

12. Findings are based on 2,109 interviews conducted in January 1988, with a 2-point margin of error.

13. Figures are based on 1,011 telephone interviews conducted in May 1988, with a 4-point margin of error.

14. Figures for trial heat surveys from July through October 1988 are based on samples of at least 1,000 interviews, each with a 4-point margin of error.

15. Figures for the pre-election poll are based on 4,089 interviews conducted November 4–6, 1988, with a 2-point margin of error. The postelection survey was based on 2,022 interviews conducted November 9–11, with a 3-point margin of error.

16. Figures are based on 4,089 interviews conducted November 4–6, 1988. For findings based on samples of this size, one can say with 95 percent confidence that the error attributable to sampling and other random effects could be 2 percentage points in either direction.

CHAPTER 8

1. Figures for questions in this chapter are based on 1,051 interviews conducted in December 1988, with a 4-point margin of error.

INDEX